Design BB2947

Empty-Nester
HOMES

206 Exciting Plans for Empty Nesters, Retirees and Couples Without Children

HOME PLANNERS, INC.
TUCSON, ARIZONA

TABLE OF CONTENTS

Published by Home Planners, Inc.
Editorial and Corporate Offices:
3275 West Ina Road, Suite 110
Tucson, Arizona 85741

Distribution Center:
29333 Lorie Lane
Wixom, Michigan 48393

Rickard D. Bailey, *President and Publisher*
Cindy J. Coatsworth, *Publications Manager*
Paulette Mulvin, *Editor*
Paul D. Fitzgerald, *Book Designer*

Photo Credits
Front and Back Covers: ©1993 Andrew D. Lautman

First Printing, January 1994

10   9   8   7   6   5   4   3   2   1

Printed in the United States of America.

ISBN softcover: 1-881955-13-3
ISBN hardback: 1-881955-12-5

On the front and back covers: This comfortable ranch design (BB2947)—shown
in reverse on the front cover—is the choice of Diane and Julius Perillo of
Frankfort, New York. Its small square footage and convenient one-level plan
work well for their lifestyle. For additional information about this design, see
page 52.

1½-STORY HOMES

Perhaps more than any other type, 1½-story homes lend themselves well to the empty-nester lifestyle. Because they usually contain a master bedroom on the first floor and secondary bedrooms on the second floor, they create convenience for the empty-nester homeowner and provide privacy when family members or guests are visiting. The designs profiled in this section bring a new sense of style to this classic configuration. The homes are long on open floor planning—an important enhancement in a medium-sized home—and contain all the features you may have discovered you now require in a home. Look for amenity-filled gathering areas, studios, well-appointed master suites, thoughtful outdoor living areas, and even space for a home office. Both two- and three-bedroom versions in contemporary and traditional styles can be found. Note the special livability on the second floors of some plans. Designs BB3438 and BB3315 are especially good examples.

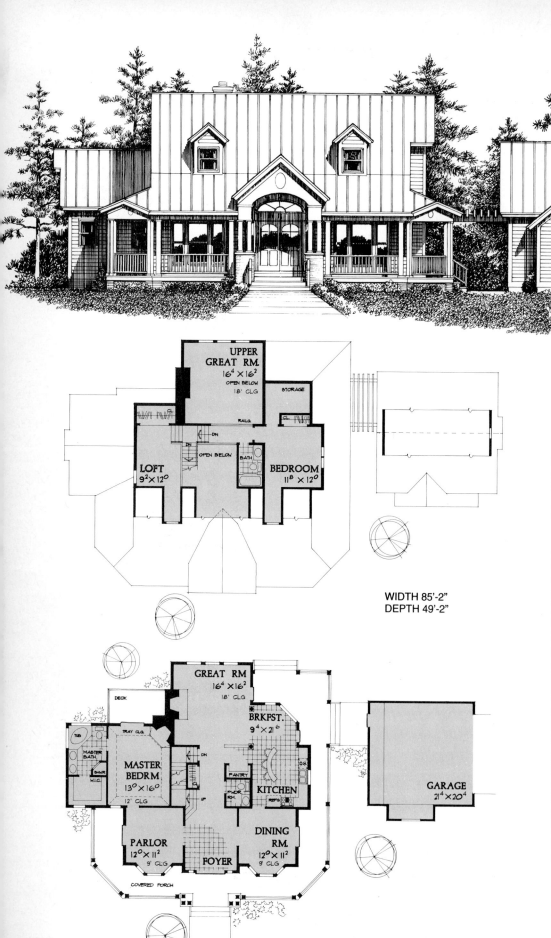

**UPPER
GREAT RM.**
16⁴×16²
OPEN BELOW
18' CLG

STORAGE

RAILG.

CL.

LOFT
9²×12⁰

DN

DN

OPEN BELOW

BATH

BEDROOM
11⁸×12⁰

WIDTH 85'-2"
DEPTH 49'-2"

GREAT RM
16⁴×16²
18' CLG

BRKFST.
9⁴×21⁶

TRAY CLG.

DECK

TUB

MASTER
BATH.

SHWR

W.I.C.

**MASTER
BEDRM**
13⁰×16⁰
12' CLG

DN

PANTRY

PDR.
RM.

KITCHEN

REF.

DW

UP

GARAGE
21⁴×20⁴

PARLOR
12⁰×11²
9' CLG.

FOYER

**DINING
RM.**
12⁰×11²
9' CLG.

COVERED PORCH

Design BB3468

First Floor: 1,618 square feet
Second Floor: 510 square feet
Total: 2,128 square feet

L

● There's nothing lacking
in this contemporary farmhouse. A wraparound porch
ensures a favorite spot for
enjoying good weather. A
large great room sports a
fireplace and lots of natural
light. Grab a snack at the
kitchen island/snack bar or
in the bright breakfast room.
The vaulted foyer grandly
introduces the dining room
and parlor—the master bedroom is just off this room.
Inside it: tray ceiling, fireplace, luxury bath and walk-
in closet. Stairs lead up to a
quaint loft/bedroom—per-
fect for study or snoozing—a
full bath and an additional
bedroom. Designated storage
space also makes this one a
winner.

Design BB3438

First Floor: 1,489 square feet
Second Floor: 741 square feet
Total: 2,230 square feet

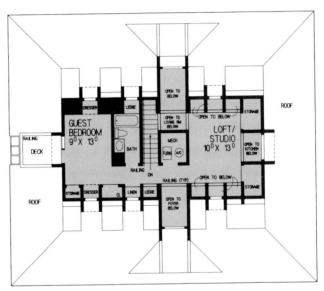

● A unique farmhouse plan which provides a grand floor plan, this home is comfortable in country or suburban settings. Formal entertaining areas share first-floor space with family gathering rooms and work and service areas. The master suite is also on this floor for convenience and privacy. Upstairs is a guest bedroom, private bath and loft area that makes a perfect studio. Special features make this a great place to come home to.

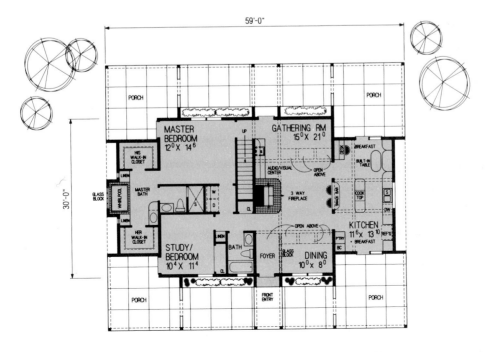

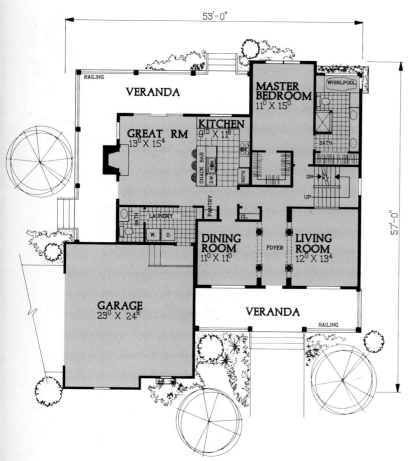

Design BB3462

First Floor: 1,398 square feet
Second Floor: 792 square feet
Total: 2,190 square feet

L

● Get off to a great start with this handsome family farmhouse. Covered porches front and rear assure comfortable outdoor living while varied roof planes add visual interest. Inside, distinct formal and informal living zones provide the best accommodations for any occasion. The columned foyer opens to both the dining and living rooms. The central kitchen services the large family room with an island work counter and snack bar. For everyday chores, a laundry room is conveniently located and also provides access to the garage. On the first floor you'll find the master bedroom suite. It enjoys complete privacy and luxury with its double closets and master bath with double-bowl vanity, whirlpool tub and separate shower. Upstairs, three family bedrooms extend fabulous livability.

Design BB3444

First Floor: 1,453 square feet
Second Floor: 520 square feet
Total: 1,973 square feet

● This compact plan offers full-scale livability on two floors. The first floor begins with an elegant living room—a bay window here allows for an infiltration of natural light. The dining room remains open to this room and will delight with its spaciousness. The kitchen is just beyond and extends room enough for a dinette set. A rear patio is accessible from here. Comfortable gatherings are the name of the game in the family room which enjoys shared space with the kitchen area. A warming fireplace gains attention here as does a pair of graceful windows that flank it. Also on the first floor, the master bedroom expands into a spacious and luxurious bathroom. A garden tub set below a window is sure to satisfy as is a large walk-in closet. For family and guests, two upstairs bedrooms are situated around a Hollywood bath.

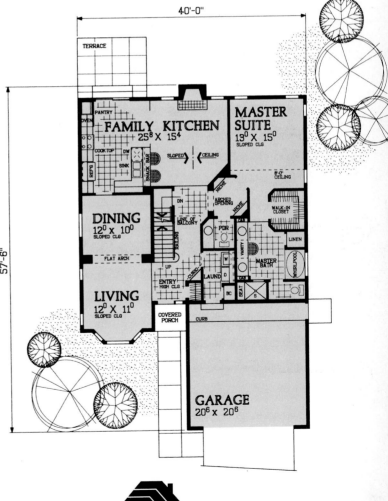

CUSTOMIZABLE

Custom Alterations? See page 221 for customizing this plan to your specifications.

7

Design BB3461

First Floor: 1,391 square feet
Second Floor: 611 square feet
Total: 2,002 square feet

● A Palladian window set in a dormer provides a nice introduction to this 1½-story country home. The two-story foyer draws on natural light and a pair of columns to set a comfortable, yet elegant mood. The living room, to the left, presents a grand space for entertaining. From full-course dinners to family suppers, the dining room will serve its purpose well. The kitchen delights with an island work station and openness to the keeping room. Here, a raised-hearth fireplace provides added comfort. Sleeping accommodations are comprised of four bedrooms, one a first-floor master suite. With a luxurious private bath, including dual lavatories, this room will surely be a favorite retreat. Upstairs, three secondary bedrooms meet the needs of the growing family.

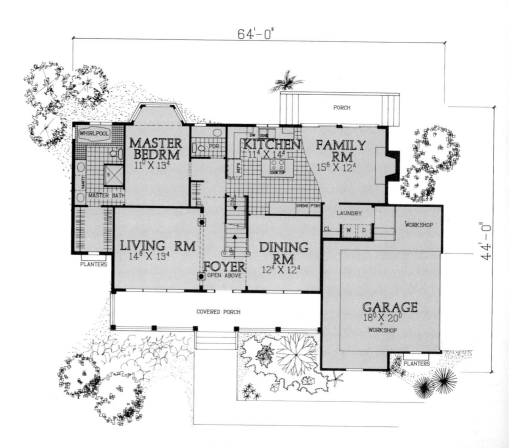

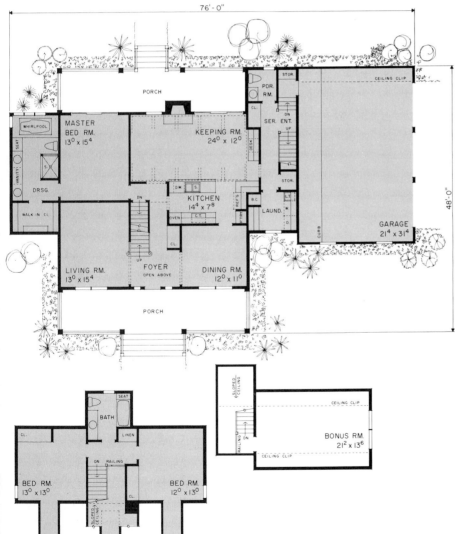

76'-0"

48'-0"

PORCH

MASTER BED RM.
13⁰ x 15⁴

WHIRLPOOL

SEAT

VANITY

DRSG.

WALK-IN CL.

KEEPING RM.
24⁰ x 12⁰

PDR. RM.

STOR.

CL.

SER. ENT.

DN
UP

DESK

STOR.

CEILING CLIP

KITCHEN
14⁴ x 7⁸

D.W. S.

REF'S.

OVEN

C.F.

CL.

B.C.

LAUND.

GARAGE
21⁴ x 31⁴

DN

FOYER
OPEN ABOVE

LIVING RM.
13⁰ x 15⁴

UP

DINING RM.
12⁰ x 11⁰

PORCH

BATH

SEAT

LINEN

CL.

BED RM.
13⁰ x 13⁰

DN RAILING

CL.

BED RM.
12⁰ x 13⁰

SLOPED CEILING

SLOPED CEILING

CEILING CLIP

RAILING

DN

BONUS RM.
21² x 13⁶

CEILING CLIP

Design BB3566

First Floor: 1,635 square feet
Second Floor: 586 square feet
Total: 2,221 square feet
Bonus Room: 321 square feet

● Don't be fooled by the humble appearance of this farmhouse. All the amenities abound. Covered porches are located to both the front and rear of the home. A grand front entrance opens into living and dining rooms. The family will surely enjoy the ambience of the keeping room with its fireplace and beamed ceiling. A service entry, with laundry nearby, separates the garage from the main house. An over-the-garage bonus room allows for room to grow or a nice study. Two quaint bedrooms and full bath make up the second floor. Each bedroom features a lovely dormer window.

Design BB2510

First Floor: 1,191 square feet
Second Floor: 533 square feet
Total: 1,724 square feet

L **D**

● Hometown comfort abounds in this darling 1½-story home. Vertical siding and stone lend interest to the facade. Inside, a family room with a bay window interacts easily with the in-line kitchen. Notice the large, walk-in pantry nearby. The rear dining area opens to the living room—a fireplace here will keep all warm and snug. The master bedroom is situated on the first floor and enjoys direct access to a private rear terrace. A full bath and washer/dryer space complete the amenities on this floor. Upstairs, two secondary bedrooms provide accommodations for the small family or guests. One of the bedrooms enjoys a walk-in closet.

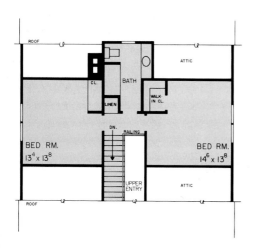

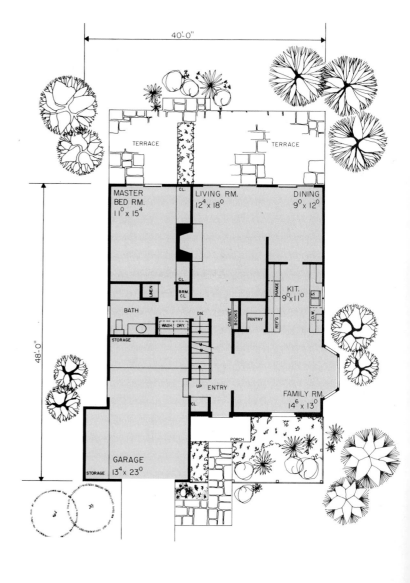

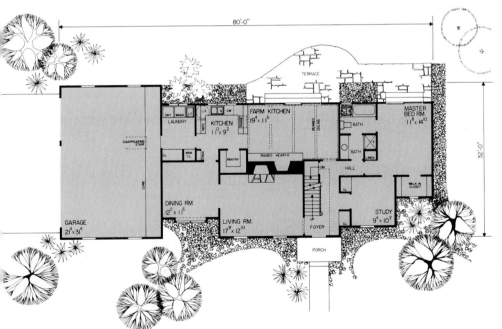

Design BB2563

First Floor: 1,500 square feet
Second Floor: 690 square feet
Total: 2,190 square feet

L **D**

● This charming Cape Cod definitely will capture your heart with its warm appeal. This home offers you and your family a lot of livability. Upon entering this home, to your left, is a nice-sized living room with fireplace. Adjacent is a dining room. An efficient kitchen and a large, farm kitchen eating area with fireplace will be enjoyed by all. A unique feature on this floor is the master bedroom with a full bath and walk-in closet. Also take notice of the first-floor laundry, the pantry and a study for all of your favorite books. Note the sliding glass doors in the farm kitchen and master bedroom. Upstairs you'll find two bedrooms, one with a walk-in closet. Also here, a sitting room and a full bath are available. Lastly, this design accommodates a three-car garage.

CUSTOMIZABLE

Custom Alterations? See page 221 for customizing this plan to your specifications.

11

Design BB3343

First Floor: 1,953 square feet
Second Floor: 895 square feet
Total: 2,848 square feet

● Beyond the simple traditional styling of this home's exterior are many of the amenities required by today's lifestyles. Among them: a huge country kitchen with fireplace, an attached greenhouse/dining area, a media room off the two-story foyer, split-bedroom planning, and a second-floor lounge. There are three bedrooms upstairs, which share a full bath.

Design BB2883
First Floor: 1,919 square feet
Second Floor: 895 square feet
Total: 2,814 square feet

● A country-style home is part of America's fascination with the rural past. This home's emphasis of the traditional home is in its gambrel roof, dormers and fanlight windows. Having a traditional exterior from the street view, this home has window walls and a greenhouse, which opens the house to the outdoors in a thoroughly contemporary manner. The interior meets the requirements of today's active family. Like the country houses of the past, it has a gathering room for family get-togethers or entertaining. The adjacent two-story greenhouse doubles as the dining room. There is a pass-through snack bar to the country kitchen here. This country kitchen just might be the heart of the house with its two areas — work zone and sitting room. There are four bedrooms on the two floors — the master bedroom suite on the first floor; three more on the second floor. A lounge, overlooking the gathering room and front foyer, is also on the second floor.

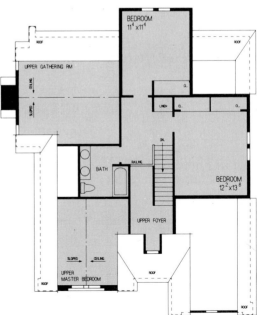

CUSTOMIZABLE

Custom Alterations? See page 221 for customizing this plan to your specifications.

Design BB3302

First Floor: 1,326 square feet
Second Floor: 542 square feet
Total: 1,868 square feet

● A cottage fit for a king! Appreciate the highlights: a two-story foyer, a rear living zone (gathering room, terrace, and dining room), pass-through snack bar in kitchen, a two-story master bedroom. Two upstairs bedrooms share a full bath.

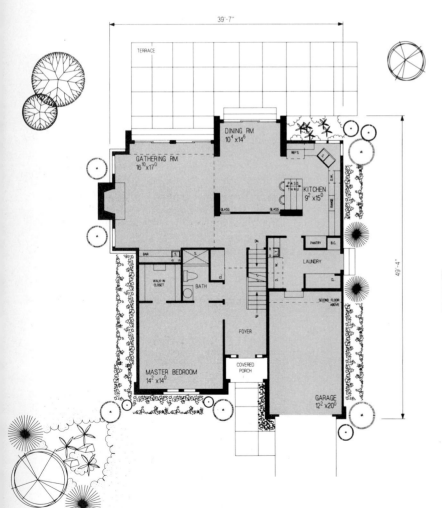

Design BB3331

First Floor: 1,115 square feet
Second Floor: 690 square feet
Total: 1,805 square feet

● Who could guess that this compact design contains three bedrooms and two full baths? The kitchen has indoor eating space in the dining room and outdoor eating space in an attached deck. A fireplace in the two-story gathering room welcomes company.

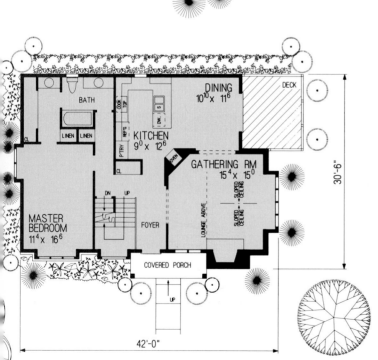

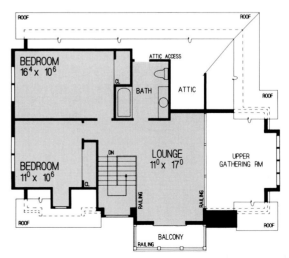

Design BB2967

First Floor: 1,877 square feet
Second Floor: 467 square feet
Total: 2,344 square feet

● Special interior amenities
abound in this unique
1½-story Tudor. Living
areas include an open
gathering room/dining room
area with fireplace and
pass-through to the breakfast room. Quiet time can be
spent in a sloped-ceiling
study. Look for plenty of
workspace in the island
kitchen and workshop/
storage area. Sleeping areas
are separated for utmost
privacy: an elegant master
suite on the first floor, two
bedrooms and a full bath on
the second. Note the un-
usual curved balcony seat
in the stairwell and the
second floor ledge—a per-
fect spot for displaying
plants or collectibles.

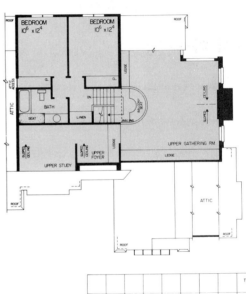

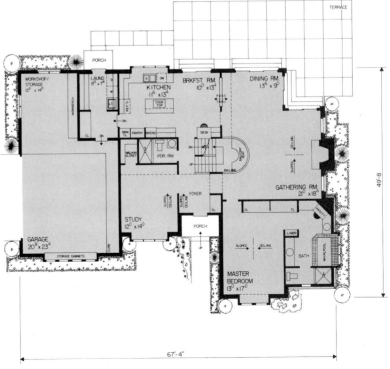

Design BB2964

First Floor: 1,441 square feet
Second Floor: 621 square feet
Total: 2,062 square feet

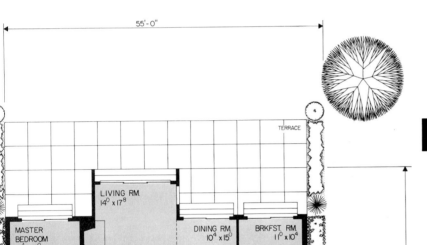

55'-0"

TERRACE

LIVING RM.
14⁰ x 17⁸

DINING RM.
10⁴ x 15⁰

BRKFST. RM.
11⁰ x 10⁴

MASTER BEDROOM
14⁴ x 16⁰

BALCONY OVER

SNACK BAR

KITCHEN
11⁰ x 13⁰

VANITY

WALK-IN CLOSET

DN   UP

OPEN ABOVE

CL.

FOYER

PDR. RM.

LAUND.
6⁰ x 10⁰

OVENS

PTRY.

BC.

REF'G

COOK TOP

DW

WHIRLPOOL

BATH

COVERED PORCH

59'-8"

GARAGE
21⁸ x 22⁸

CURB

STORAGE

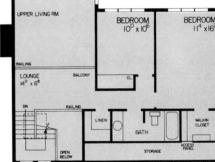

UPPER LIVING RM.

BEDROOM
10⁰ x 10⁶

BEDROOM
11⁴ x 16²

RAILING

LOUNGE
14⁰ x 6⁸

BALCONY

CL.

DN

RAILING

LINEN

BATH

WALK-IN CLOSET

OPEN BELOW

STORAGE

ACCESS PANEL

● Tudor houses have their own unique exterior design features. They include: gable roofs, simulated beam work, stucco and brick surfaces, diamond-lite windows, muntins, panelled doors, varying roof planes and hefty cornices. This outstanding two-story features a first-floor master bedroom, plus two more with lounge upstairs. The living room is dramatically spacious. It has a two-story sloping ceiling which permits it to look upward to the lounge. Large glass areas across the rear further enhance the bright, cheerful atmosphere of this area as well as the bedroom, dining and breakfast rooms. The open staircase to the upstairs has plenty of natural light as does the stairway to the basement recreation area.

For spacious living, this good-looking house will make a fine home-building candidate. The entry gives way to double closets—more than just a coat closet for your storage needs. This area also dons an open staircase. Directly in back of the foyer is the gathering room with its through-fireplace to a quaint seating area—perfect for intimate conversations. The dining room remains open to these living spaces and enjoys direct terrace access through a set of sliding glass doors. The large, gourmet kitchen features a wall of cooking amenities and also makes use of a snack-bar pass-through to the breakfast nook. Three bedrooms grace this plan and include a first-floor master suite and two secondary bedrooms off a second-floor lounge.

Design BB2718

First Floor: 1,941 square feet
Second Floor: 791 square feet
Total: 2,732 square feet

D

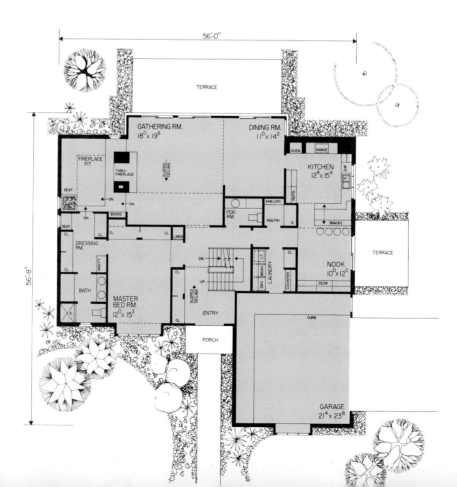

BEDROOM
10⁴ x 14⁰
+ DORMER

DESK   BOOKS   DESK

HALL

BEDROOM
11⁸ x 14⁰
+ DORMER

LINEN

DN
RAILING

BATH

OPEN TO
FOYER BELOW

LEDGE   LEDGE

Design BB3467

First Floor: 1,276 square feet
Second Floor: 658 square feet
Total: 1,934 square feet

L

● Bold and beautiful, this Neo-classic farmhouse will delight family and friends alike. Lap wood siding combined with a standing seam metal roof provides a wealth of visual appeal. Inside, living takes off with a great kitchen and family room combination. Or take in brunch on the wood deck located just off this area. For more formal occasions, a split dining room and living room—with a fireplace—will serve well. A covered wraparound porch is accessible from both rooms and makes outdoor living a pleasure. Located at the rear of the first floor, the master bedroom extends the finest accommodations including a private bath and a walk-in closet. Upstairs, two bedrooms with dormers will comfortably lodge family and guests.

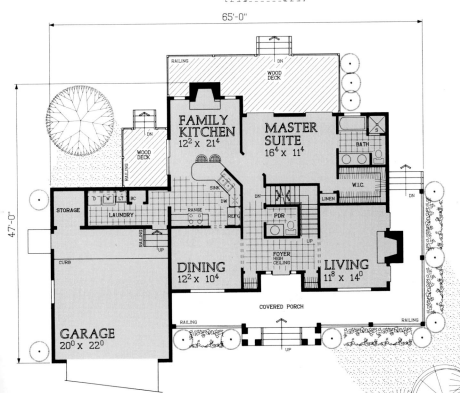

65'-0"

RAILING   DN
                    WOOD
                    DECK

47'-0"

WOOD
DECK

DN
RAILING

FAMILY
KITCHEN
12² x 21⁴

SINK

DW

MASTER
SUITE
16⁴ x 11⁴

BATH

S

W.I.C.

STORAGE

D W LT BC

LAUNDRY

RANGE

REFG

DN

PDR

LINEN

DN

RAILING

UP

FOYER
HIGH
CEILING

UP

CURB

DINING
12² x 10⁴

LIVING
11⁸ x 14⁰

COVERED PORCH

GARAGE
20⁰ x 22⁰

RAILING   RAILING

UP

Design BB2500

First Floor: 1,851 square feet
Second Floor: 762 square feet
Total: 2,613 square feet

L **D**

● The large family will enjoy the wonderful living patterns of this charming home. Don't miss the covered rear porch and the many features of the family room. The master suite, conveniently separated from the family bedrooms on the second floor, has its own bath and a huge walk-in closet. Two more giant-sized storage areas—one a linen closet—are found upstairs.

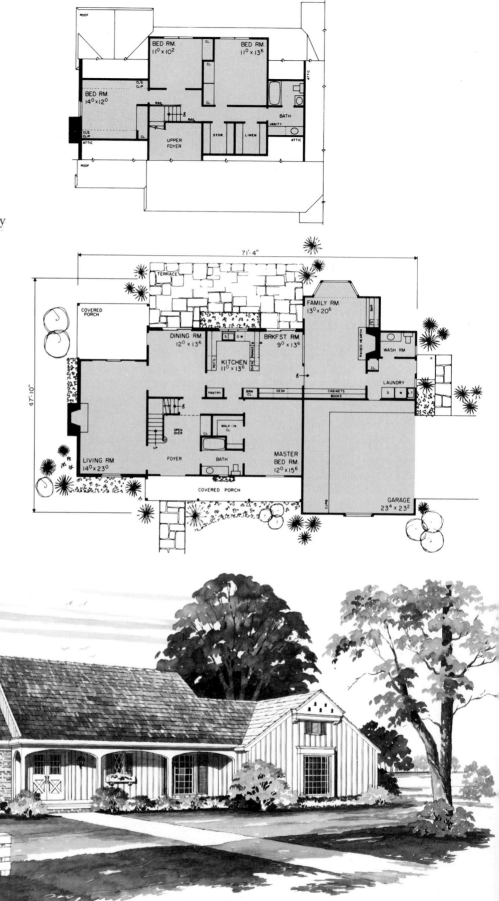

Design BB3351

First Floor: 1,794 square feet
Second Floor: 887 square feet
Total: 2,681 square feet

L **D**

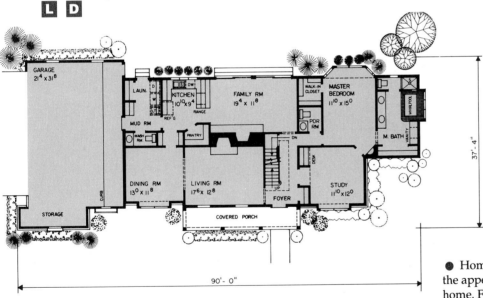

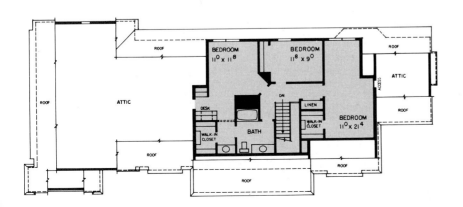

● Home-grown comfort is the key to the appeal of this traditionally styled home. From the kitchen with attached family room to the living room with fireplace and attached formal dining room, this plan has it all. Notice the first-floor master bedroom with whirlpool tub and adjacent study. A nearby powder room turns the study into a convenient guest room. On the second floor are three more bedrooms with ample closet space and a full bath. The two-car garage has a large storage area.

Design BB3315
Square Footage: 3,248

● Besides the covered front veranda, look for another full-width veranda to the rear of this charming home. The master bedroom, breakfast room, and gathering room all have French doors to this outdoor space. A handy wet bar/tavern enhances entertainment options. The upper lounge could be a welcome haven.

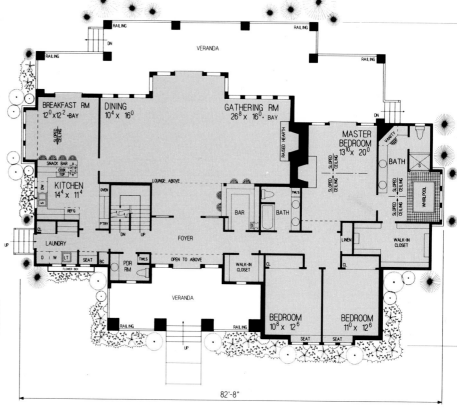

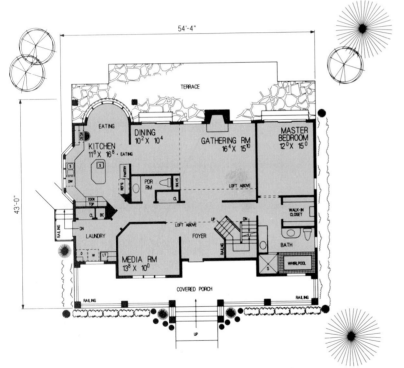

Design BB3321

First Floor: 1,636 square feet
Second Floor: 572 square feet
Total: 2,208 square feet

L **D**

● Cozy and completely functional, this 1½-story bungalow has many amenities not often found in homes its size. The covered porch at the front opens at the entry to a foyer with angled staircase. To the left is a media room, to the rear the gathering room with fireplace. Attached to the gathering room is a formal dining room with rear terrace access. The kitchen features a curved casual eating area and island work station. The right side of the first floor is dominated by the master suite. It has access to the rear terrace and a luxurious bath. Upstairs are two family bedrooms connected by a loft area overlooking the gathering room and foyer.

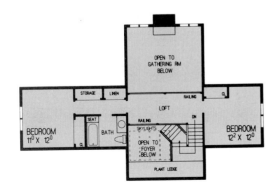

CUSTOMIZABLE

Custom Alterations? See page 221 for customizing this plan to your specifications.

23

Design BB3330

First Floor: 1,394 square feet
Second Floor: 320 square feet
Total: 1,714 square feet

● Outdoor living and open floor planning are highlights of this moderately sized plan. Amenities include a private hot tub on a wooden deck that is accessible via sliding glass doors in both bedrooms, and a two-story gathering room. An optional second-floor plan allows for a full 503 square feet of space with a balcony.

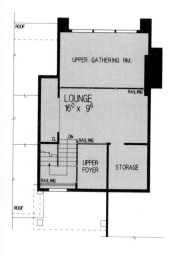

ROOF

UPPER GATHERING RM.

LOUNGE
16⁰ x 9⁶

RAILING

DN RAILING

UPPER FOYER

STORAGE

RAILING

ROOF

RAILING

BALCONY

ROOF

MASTER BEDROOM
16⁰ x 19⁰

CL DN RAILING

UPPER FOYER

BATH

RAILING

ROOF

OPTIONAL FLOOR PLAN

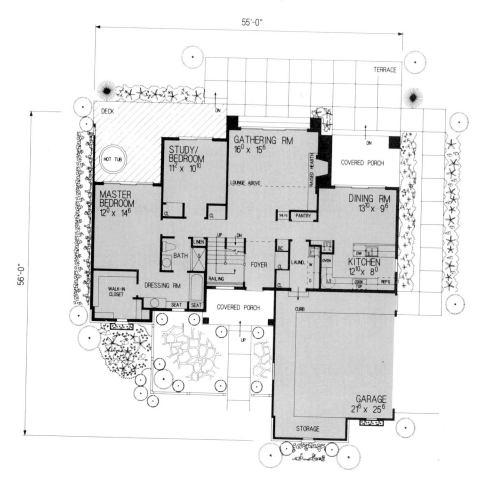

55'-0"

TERRACE

DECK

DN

HOT TUB

STUDY/ BEDROOM
11² x 10¹⁰

GATHERING RM
16⁰ x 15⁶

DN

COVERED PORCH

LOUNGE ABOVE

RAISED HEARTH

56'-0"

MASTER BEDROOM
12⁰ x 14⁶

CL

CL

DINING RM
13¹⁰ x 9⁶

PANTRY

BATH

LINEN

UP DN

BC

LAUND.

OVEN

DW

KITCHEN
12¹⁰ x 8⁰

WALK-IN CLOSET

DRESSING RM

FOYER

CL

RAILING

SEAT SEAT

COVERED PORCH

CURB

COOK TOP

REF'S

UP

GARAGE
21⁶ x 25⁶

STORAGE

Design BB2853

First Floor: 1,161 square feet
Second Floor: 475 square feet
Total: 1,636 square feet

● Natural stone, board-and-batten, multi-pane windows, overhanging eaves and a covered front porch highlight the exterior of this two-story home. Inside, a sunken gathering room gains attention with its raised-hearth fireplace and interplay with the elegant dining room. Here, a skylight and window bay brighten family banquets as well as formal entertainments. A snack-bar pass-through to the kitchen furthers the functionality of this area. The first-floor master suite enjoys a private bath and a walk-in closet. Upstairs, two bedrooms share a Hollywood bath. A cozy lounge area looks out on the downstairs living areas. Built-in bookshelves further enhance the livability present here.

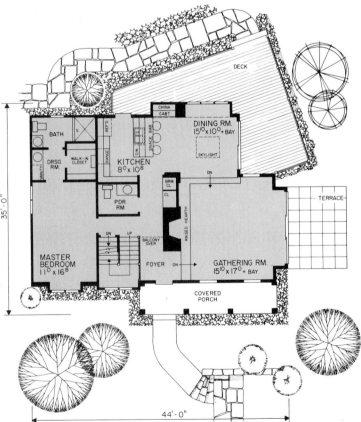

Design BB2892
Square Footage: 1,623

● What a striking contemporary! It houses an efficient floor plan with many outstanding features. The foyer has a sloped ceiling and an open staircase to the basement. To the right of the foyer is the work center. Note the snack bar, laundry and covered dining porch, along with the step-saving kitchen. Both the gathering and dining rooms overlook the backyard. Each of three bedrooms has access to an outdoor area. The second-floor loft could be used as a sewing room, den or lounge.

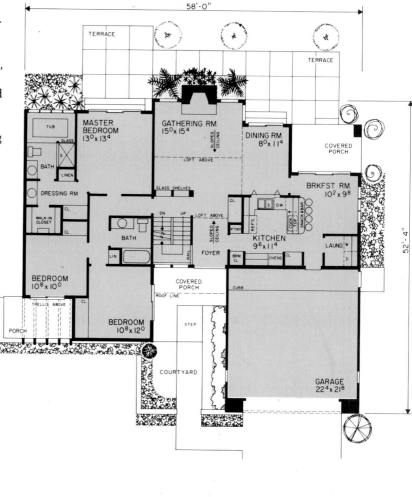

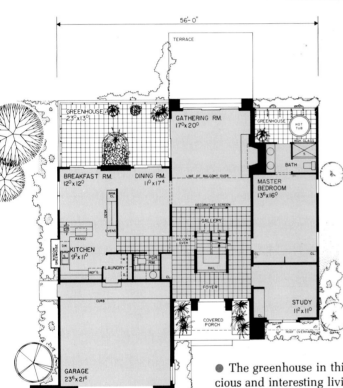

Design BB2884 First Floor: 1,855 square feet
Second Floor: 837 square feet; Total: 2,692 square feet

● The greenhouse in this design enhances its energy-efficiency and allows for spacious and interesting living patterns. Being a one-and-a-half story design, the second floor could be developed at a later date when the space is needed. The greenhouses add an additional 418 sq. ft. to the above quoted figures.

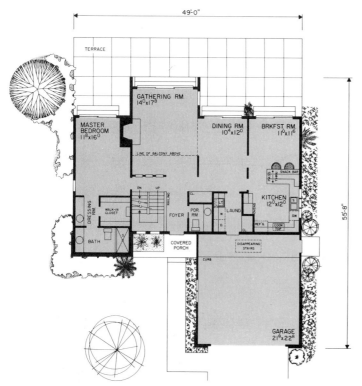

Design BB2905

First Floor: 1,342 square feet
Second Floor: 619 square feet
Total: 1,961 square feet

L **D**

● All of the livability in this plan is in the back! Each first floor room, except the kitchen, has access to the rear terrace via sliding glass doors. A great way to capture an excellent view. This plan is also ideal for a narrow lot seeing that its width is less than 50 feet. Two bedrooms and a lounge, overlooking the gathering room, are on the second floor.

Design BB2708

First Floor: 2,108 square feet
Second Floor: 824 square feet
Total: 2,932 square feet

D

● If you like your contemporary design with a touch of traditional styling, this plan, with its exact proportions and fine features, may be the one you're looking for. Inside is a plan with lots of extras. Notables include a master suite with dressing room, twin vanities, huge walk-in closet and access to a private terrace out back. It also features a roomy study that leads to a small patio in front, combo dining room and gathering room with a raised-hearth fireplace, and loads of pantry storage. On the second floor is a spacious lounge that's open to the gathering room below.

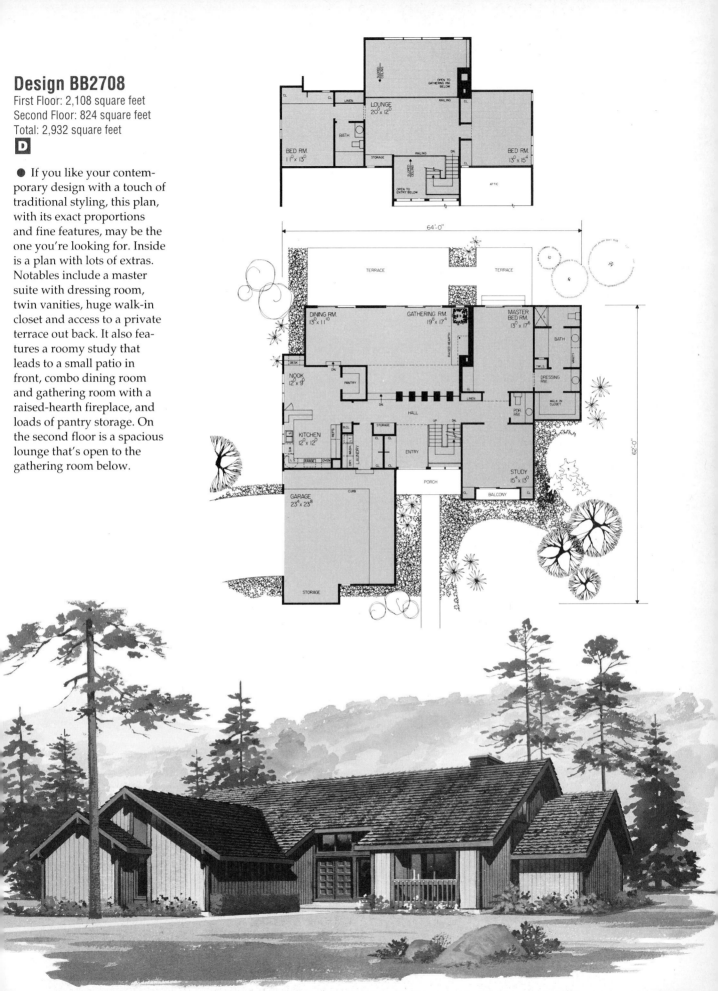

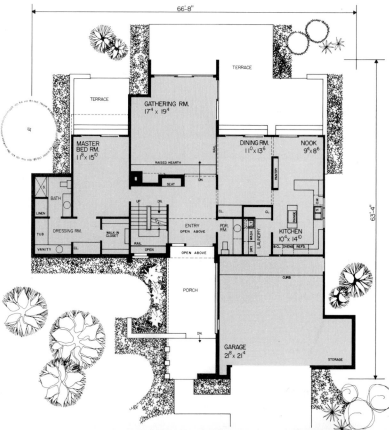

Design BB2729

First Floor: 1,590 square feet
Second Floor: 756 square feet
Total: 2,346 square feet

L

● A sheltered walkway and double front doors make a welcome entrance to this remarkable contemporary home. The two-story entry and sunken gathering room (with a raised-hearth fireplace) add dimension. Indoor/outdoor living relationships are incorporated into the design; each of the first-floor living areas opens to a terrace. The first-floor master suite, which includes a large walk-in closet, dressing room, and separate shower and tub, offers much privacy. Two additional second-floor bedrooms feature private baths and dressing rooms.

Design BB4334

First Floor: 1,838 square feet
Second Floor: 640 square feet
Total: 2,478 square feet

● Grand sloping rooflines and a design created for southern orientation are the unique features of this contemporary home. Outdoor living is enhanced by a solar greenhouse off the breakfast room, a sun space off the master bedroom, a greenhouse window in the dining room, a casual breakfast deck, and full-width deck to the rear. The split-bedroom plan allows for the master suite (with fireplace, and huge walk-in closet) to be situated on the first floor and two family bedrooms and a full bath to find space on the second floor. Be sure to notice the balcony overlook to the sloped-ceiling living room below.

LIFESTYLE HOME PLANS

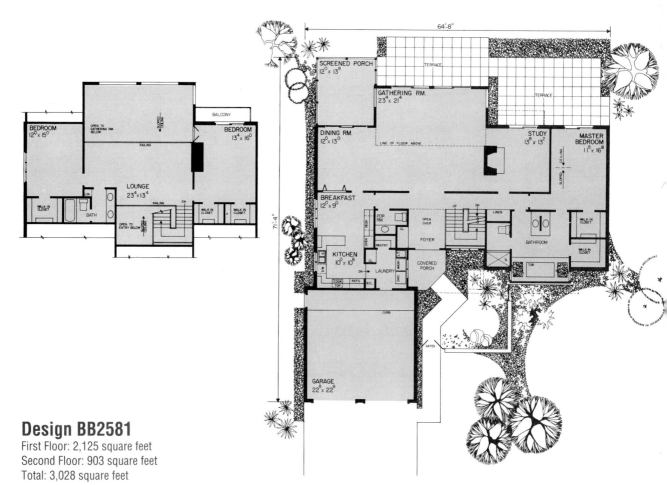

Design BB2581

First Floor: 2,125 square feet
Second Floor: 903 square feet
Total: 3,028 square feet

● A study with a fireplace! What a fine attraction to find in this lovely three-bedroom home. And the fine features certainly do not stop there. The gathering room has a sloped ceiling and two sliding glass doors to the rear terrace. The study and master bedroom (which has first floor privacy and convenience) also have glass doors to the wrap-around terrace. Adjacent to the gathering room is a formal dining room and screened-in porch. The efficient kitchen with its many built-ins has easy access to the first floor laundry. The separate breakfast nook has a built-in desk. The second floor has two bedrooms each having at least one walk-in closet. Also, a lounge overlooking the gathering room below and a balcony. Note the oversized two-car garage for storing bikes and lawn mowers. The front courtyard adds a measure of privacy to the covered porch entrance.

Design BB2771

First Floor: 2,087 square feet
Second Floor: 816 square feet
Total: 2,903 square feet

● This design will provide an abundance of livability for your family. The second floor is highlighted by an open lounge which overlooks both the entry and the gathering room below.

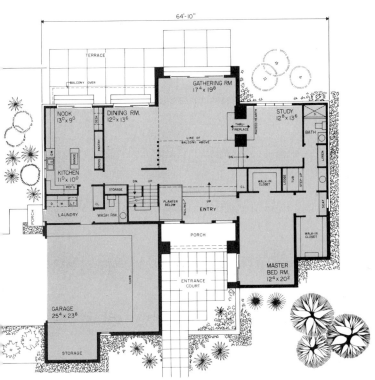

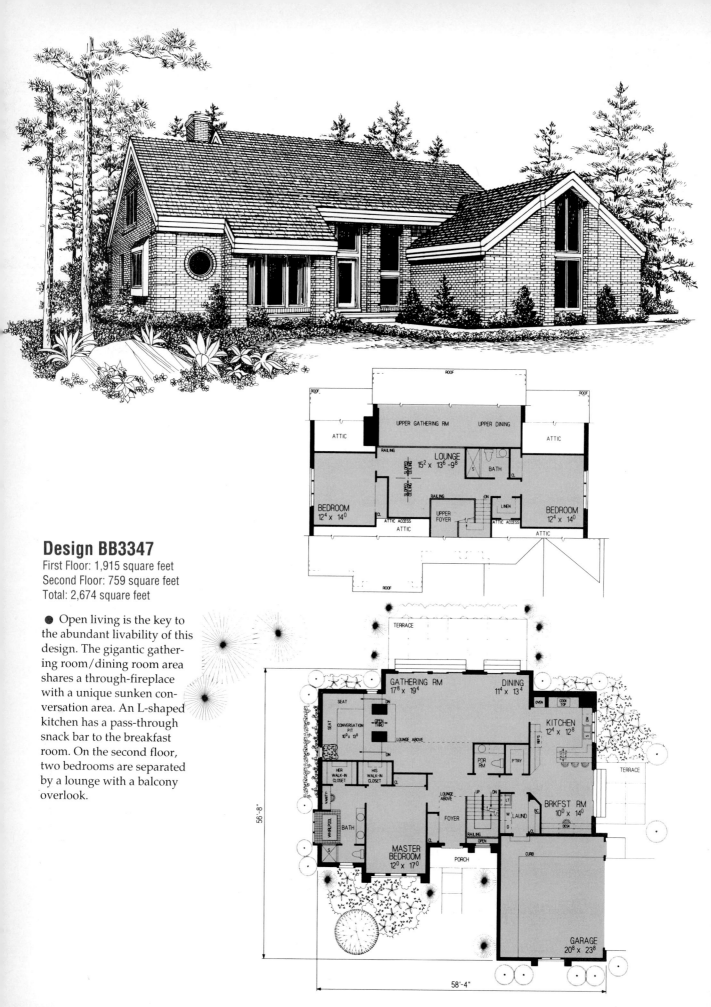

Design BB3347

First Floor: 1,915 square feet
Second Floor: 759 square feet
Total: 2,674 square feet

● Open living is the key to the abundant livability of this design. The gigantic gathering room/dining room area shares a through-fireplace with a unique sunken conversation area. An L-shaped kitchen has a pass-through snack bar to the breakfast room. On the second floor, two bedrooms are separated by a lounge with a balcony overlook.

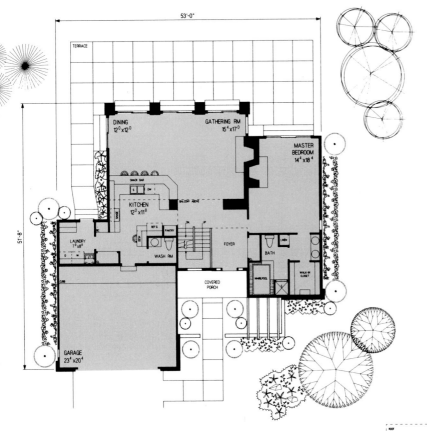

Design BB2490

First Floor: 1,414 square feet
Second Floor: 620 square feet
Total: 2,034 square feet

● Split-bedroom planning makes the most of this contemporary plan. The master suite pampers with a lavish bath and a fireplace. The living areas are open and have easy access to the rear terrace.

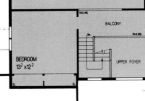

CUSTOMIZABLE

Custom Alterations? See page 221 for customizing this plan to your specifications.

Design BB3455

First Floor: 1,408 square feet
Second Floor: 667 square feet
Total: 2,075 square feet

● Whether you're just starting out or looking to retire, this 1½-story, sun-country design will make an excellent home. The focal point of the first floor, the two-story living room utilizes a central fireplace and columns for comfort and elegance. Open to the living room, the dining room complements this space with its influx of natural light. The kitchen services this room easily and also enjoys a cozy breakfast nook. An island work counter in the kitchen guarantees ease in food preparation. Note the service entry to the garage; a full washer/dryer set-up adds convenience to laundry chores. On the second floor you'll find a skylit balcony—a dramatic yet purposeful design feature—leading to two bedrooms.

48'-0"

SITTING RM. 7¹⁰ X 9⁰

MASTER BEDROOM 12⁰ X 15⁸

LIVING ROOM 14⁰ X 15⁴

DINING RM. 12⁰ X 10⁰

DESK

BRKFST. 12⁴ X 9⁰

KITCHEN 12⁴ X 9⁶

DRESSING ROOM

VANITY

DN UP

WORK ISLAND

SHOWER

WHIRLPOOL

CL CL

PWDR RM.

OVEN

D W

FOYER

REF'G

D.W.

PORCH

GARAGE 20⁴ X 22⁸

BEDROOM 7¹⁰ X 9⁰

BEDROOM 12⁸ X 10⁰

OPEN BELOW

LINEN

RAILING

BATH

BALCONY

RAILING

STORAGE

STORAGE

UPPER FOYER

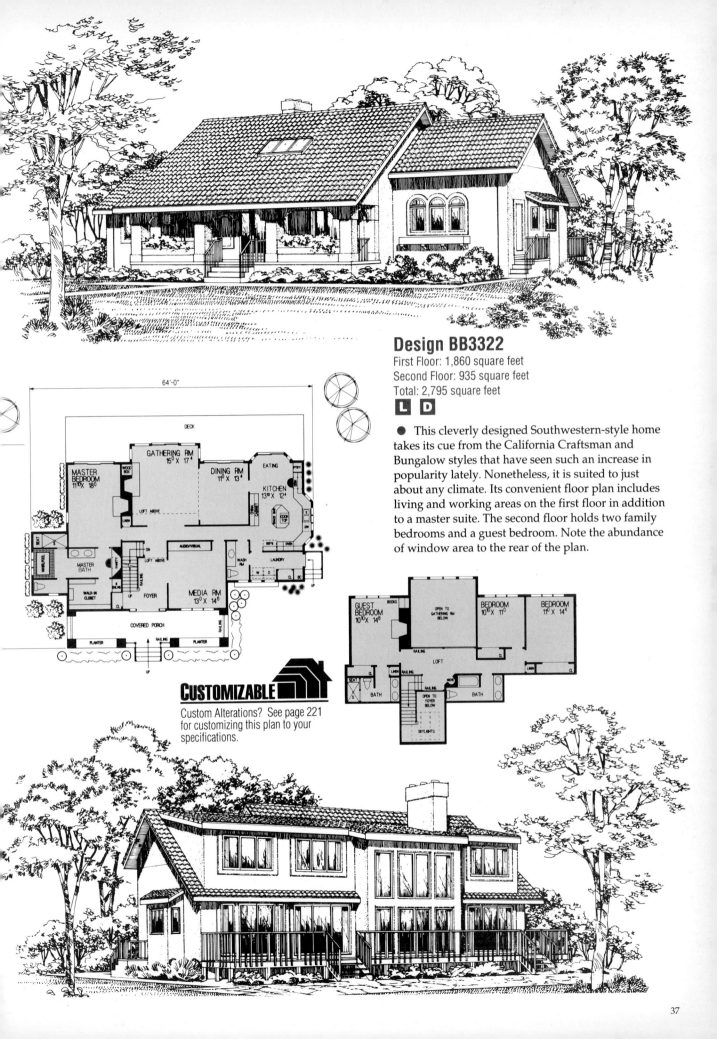

Design BB3322

First Floor: 1,860 square feet
Second Floor: 935 square feet
Total: 2,795 square feet

L **D**

● This cleverly designed Southwestern-style home takes its cue from the California Craftsman and Bungalow styles that have seen such an increase in popularity lately. Nonetheless, it is suited to just about any climate. Its convenient floor plan includes living and working areas on the first floor in addition to a master suite. The second floor holds two family bedrooms and a guest bedroom. Note the abundance of window area to the rear of the plan.

CUSTOMIZABLE

Custom Alterations? See page 221 for customizing this plan to your specifications.

64'-0"

DECK

GATHERING RM
15⁰ X 17⁴

DINING RM
11⁰ X 13⁴

EATING

MASTER BEDROOM
11¹⁰ X 18⁰

WOOD BOX

KITCHEN
13¹⁰ X 12⁴

LOFT ABOVE

LINEN

COOK TOP

DW

REF'S   OVEN

MASTER BATH

AUDIO/VISUAL

LOFT ABOVE

WASH RM

LAUNDRY

W D

WALK-IN CLOSET

UP   RAILING

FOYER

MEDIA RM
13⁰ X 14⁶

UP

SEAT

WHIRLPOOL

COVERED PORCH

PLANTER   RAILING   PLANTER

RAILING

UP

GUEST BEDROOM
10¹⁰ X 14⁶

BOOKS

OPEN TO GATHERING RM BELOW

BEDROOM
10¹⁰ X 11⁰

BEDROOM
11⁰ X 14⁴

RAILING

CL

LOFT

SEAT   CL

LINEN   RAILING

BATH

RAILING

BATH

OPEN TO FOYER BELOW

SKYLIGHTS

Design BB3558

First Floor: 2,328 square feet
Second Floor: 603 square feet
Total: 2,931 square feet

L **D**

● This home will keep even the most active family from feeling cramped. A broad foyer opens to a living room that measures 24 feet across and features sliding glass doors to a rear terrace and a covered porch. Adjacent to the kitchen is a conversation area with additional access to the covered porch, a snack bar, fireplace and a window bay. A butler's pantry leads to the formal dining room. Placed conveniently on the first floor, the master suite features a roomy bath with a huge walk-in closet and dual vanities. Two large bedrooms are found on the second floor.

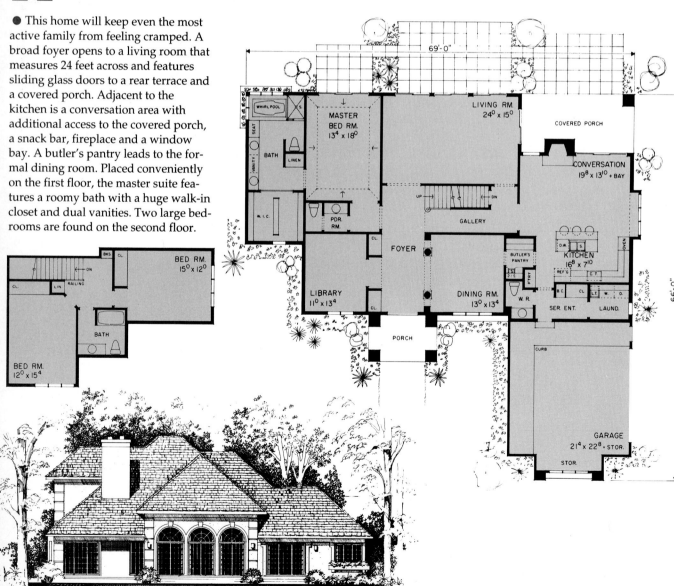

BEDRM
11⁰ X 11⁴

BEDRM
11⁰ X 15⁰

OPEN BELOW
RAILING

BEDRM
11² X 13⁴

LINEN

DN

RAILING

BATH

MASTER
BEDRM
12⁰ X 17⁸

FAMILY RM
15⁰ X 14⁰

BRKFST
11⁴ X 9⁰

COVERED PORCH

BOOKS

WORKBENCH

LAUNDRY

WORKSHOP

BOOKS

SNACK BAR

OPEN ABOVE

DN

KITCHEN
11⁰ X 11⁸

CURB

PANTRY

REF'G

LINEN

VANITY

MASTER BATH

PDR RM

CL

DN

RAILING

LIVING RM
13⁰ X 15⁰

FOYER

UP

DINING
11⁰ X 12⁰

GARAGE
19⁴ X 20⁴

COVERED
PORCH

STORAGE

PLANTERS

PLANTERS

62'-0"

41'-0"

Design BB3458

First Floor: 1,617 square feet
Second Floor: 725 square feet
Total: 2,342 square feet

● Palladian windows adorn the facade of this excellent, fully functional plan. The foyer introduces the formal zones of the house with a volume living room to the left and a dining room to the right. The kitchen easily services this area and also enjoys a large breakfast room on the other side. A step away, the service entry presents a washer and dryer as well as passage to the two-car, side-load garage. A curb in the garage expands to storage space or becomes a perfect spot for a workbench. For sleeping, four bedrooms each exhibit uniqueness. The master suite—on the ground level—has terrace access, a generous, private bath and a walk-in closet. Upstairs, a balcony over-looking the two-story family room leads to the secondary bedrooms. A compart-mented bath with dual lavs adds to con-venience.

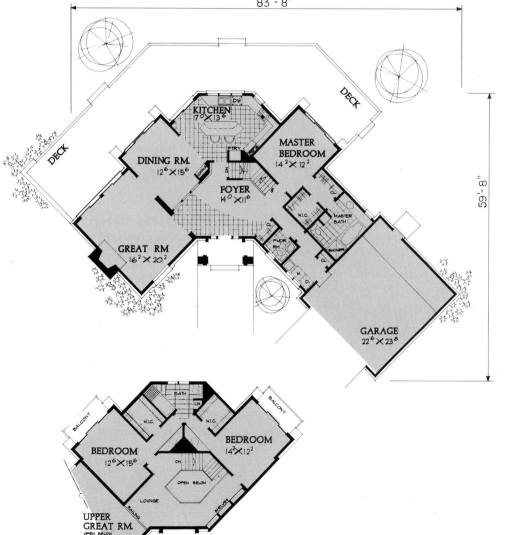

83' - 8"

59' - 8"

DECK

DECK

DECK

KITCHEN
17⁰×13⁶

DINING RM.
12⁶×15⁶

MASTER
BEDROOM
14²×12²

FOYER
14⁰×11⁶

CHINA

W.I.C.

MASTER
BATH

GREAT RM
16²×20²

PDR.
RM.

SHOWER

W.D.

GARAGE
22⁶×23⁸

BALCONY

BATH

LIN

BALCONY

W.I.C.

W.I.C.

BEDROOM
12⁶×15⁶

BEDROOM
14²×12²

DN

OPEN BELOW

LOUNGE

RAILING

SHELVES

UPPER
GREAT RM.
OPEN BELOW

Design BB3310

First Floor: 1,668 square feet
Second Floor: 905 square feet
Total: 2,573 square feet

● If you're looking for a different angle on a new home, try this enchanting transitional house. The open foyer creates a rich atmosphere. To the left you'll find a great room with raised-brick hearth and sliding glass doors that lead out onto a wraparound deck. The kitchen enhances the first floor with a snack bar and deck access. The master bedroom, with balcony and bath with whirlpool, is located on the first floor for privacy. Upstairs, two family bedrooms, both with balconies and walk-in closets, share a full bath. Don't overlook the lounge and elliptical window that give the second floor added charisma.

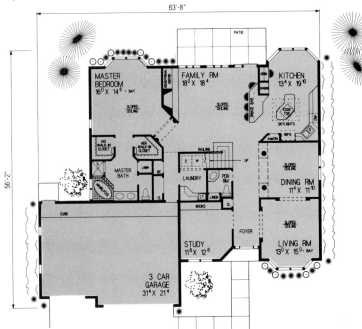

Design BB3441

First Floor: 2,022 square feet
Second Floor: 845 square feet
Total: 2,867 square feet

L

● Special details make the difference between a house and a home. A snack bar, audio/visual center and a fireplace make the family room livable. A desk, island cook top, bay, and skylights enhance the kitchen area. The dining room features two columns and a plant ledge. The first-floor master suite includes His and Hers walk-in closets, a spacious bath, and a bay window. On the second floor, one bedroom features a walk-in closet and private bath, while two additional bedrooms share a full bath.

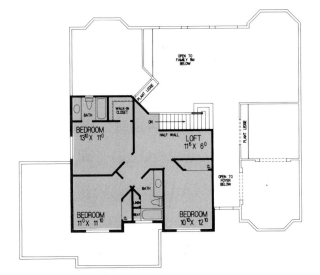

CUSTOMIZABLE

Custom Alterations? See page 221 for customizing this plan to your specifications.

Design BB3403

First Floor: 2,240 square feet
Second Floor: 660 square feet
Total: 2,900 square feet

L D

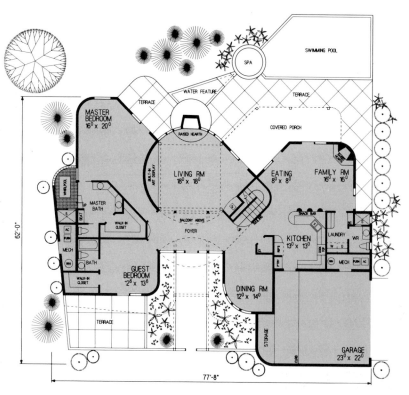

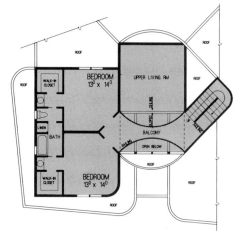

● There is no end to the distinctive features in this Southwestern contemporary. Formal living areas are concentrated in the center of the plan, perfect for entertaining. To the right of the plan, the kitchen and family room function well together as a working and living area. Also note the separate laundry room. The optional guest bedroom or den and the master bedroom are located to the left of the plan. Upstairs, the remaining two bedrooms are reached by a balcony overlooking the living room and share a bath with twin vanities.

ONE-STORY HOMES
Under 2,000 Square Feet

A natural for empty-nesters, the smaller one-story home may be the first consideration for many. However, those looking to down-size in terms of space and number of rooms do not necessarily want to lose anything in the way of features. The homes in this section will not disappoint! They range in size from just over 1,200 square feet to just under 2,000 square feet and offer all the livability of homes that are much larger. Some contain formal living and dining spaces for elegant entertaining. Others have open, casual gathering areas for more relaxed living. A few even offer both formal and informal living areas to suit both needs. All feature convenient floor plans with extra-special master suites and integrated outdoor livability. These will be especially good choices for empty-nesters who are looking for a plan that can be converted to universal design in the future, should physical limitations become a consideration. Of special interest are the one-story Tudors (see pages 60-65) and the volume-look traditionals (see pages 90-92).

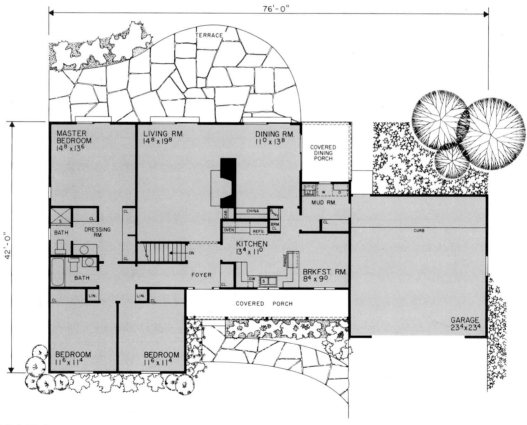

Design BB2672

Square Footage: 1,717

L **D**

● The traditional appearance of this one-story is emphasized by its covered porch, multi-paned windows, narrow clapboard and vertical wood siding. Not only is the exterior eye-appealing but the interior has an efficient plan and is very livable. The front U-shaped kitchen will work with the breakfast room and mud room, which houses the laundry facilities. An access to the garage is here. Outdoor dining can be enjoyed on the covered porch adjacent to the dining room. Both of these areas, the porch and dining room, are convenient to the kitchen. Sleeping facilities consist of three bedrooms and two full baths. Note the three sets of sliding glass doors leading to the terrace.

Design BB3466
Square Footage: 1,800

L **D**

● Small but inviting, this one-story ranch-style farm-house is the perfect choice for a small family or empty-nesters. It's loaded with amenities even the most particular homeowner can appreciate. For example, the living room and dining room each have plant shelves, sloped ceilings and built-ins to enhance livability. The living room also sports a warming hearth. The master bedroom contains a well-appointed bath with dual vanity and walk-in closet. The additional bedroom has its own bath with linen storage. The kitchen is separated from the breakfast nook by a clever bar area. Access to the two-car garage is through a laundry area with washer/dryer hookup space.

CUSTOMIZABLE

Custom Alterations? See page 221 for customizing this plan to your specifications.

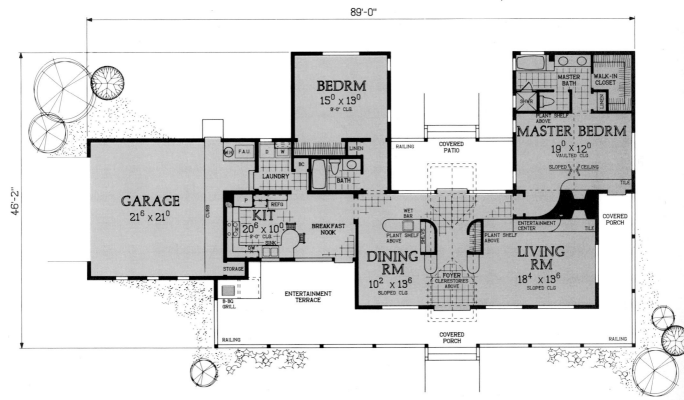

Design BB3314
Square Footage: 1,951

● Formal living areas in this plan are joined by a sleeping wing that holds three bedrooms. Two verandas and a screened porch enlarge the plan and enhance indoor/outdoor livability. Notice the abundant storage space.

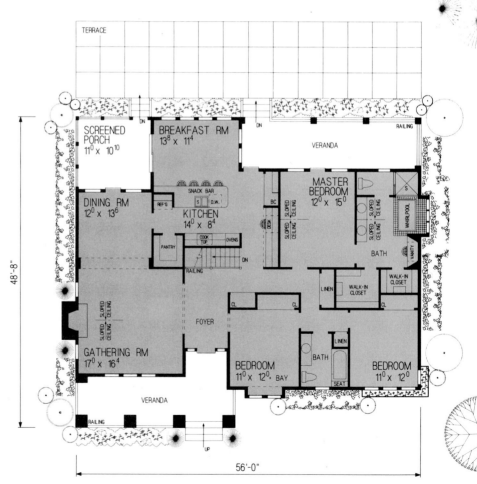

Design BB3465
Square Footage: 1,410

L

● An L-shaped veranda employs tapered columns to support a standing-seam metal roof. Horizontal siding with brick accents and multi-pane windows enhance the exterior of this home. Most notable, however, is the metal roof with its various planes. Complementing this is a massive stucco chimney that captures the ambi-

ence of the West. A hardworking interior will delight those building within a modest budget. A 36' front room provides plenty of space for both living and family dining activities. A fireplace makes a delightful focal point. The kitchen, set aside, will be free of annoying cross-room traffic. Adjacent to the kitchen is the passage-

way to the garage. To one side is the laundry area, to the other, the stairs to the basement. The centrally located main bath has twin lavatories and a nearby linen closet. One of the two secondary bedrooms has direct access to the veranda. The master bedroom is flanked by the master bath and its own private covered porch.

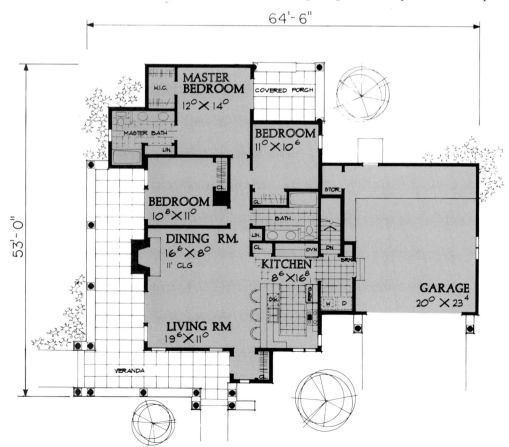

Design BB3460

Square Footage: 1,389

● A double dose of charm, this special farmhouse plan offers two elevations in its blueprint package. With this one, a delightful wraparound porch provides excellent outdoor livability. Inside, a formal living/dining room combination has a warming fireplace and a cheery bay window. The kitchen separates this area from the more casual family room. In the kitchen, you'll find an efficient snack bar that services the family room, as well as a pantry for additional storage space. Three bedrooms include two family bedrooms served by a full bath, and a lovely master suite with its own private bath with separate lavatories. Notice the location of the washer and dryer—convenient to all of the bedrooms.

CUSTOMIZABLE

Custom Alterations? See page 221 for customizing this plan to your specifications.

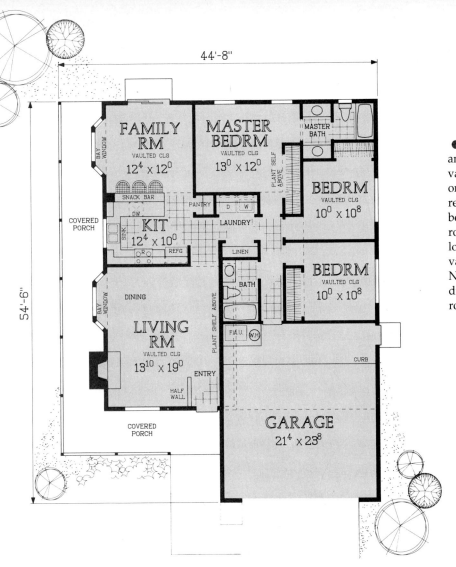

44'-8"

54'-6"

FAMILY RM
VAULTED CLG
12⁴ x 12⁰

MASTER BEDRM
VAULTED CLG
13⁰ x 12⁰

MASTER BATH

BEDRM
VAULTED CLG
10⁰ x 10⁸

BAY WINDOW

COVERED PORCH

SNACK BAR

PANTRY

DW

D   W

KIT
12⁴ x 10⁰

SINK

REFG

R

LAUNDRY

PLANT SELF ABOVE

LINEN

BATH

BEDRM
VAULTED CLG
10⁰ x 10⁸

BAY WINDOW

DINING

LIVING RM
VAULTED CLG
13¹⁰ x 19⁰

PLANT SHELF ABOVE

F.A.U.   W.H

ENTRY

CURB

HALF WALL

COVERED PORCH

GARAGE
21⁴ x 23⁸

● A front porch, decorative dormer and interesting roof planes set this elevation apart from its sister elevation on the previous page. The floor plan remains the same and very livable bedrooms include two family bedrooms served by a full bath, and a lovely master suite with its own private bath with separate lavatories. Notice the location of the washer and dryer—convenient to all of the bedrooms.

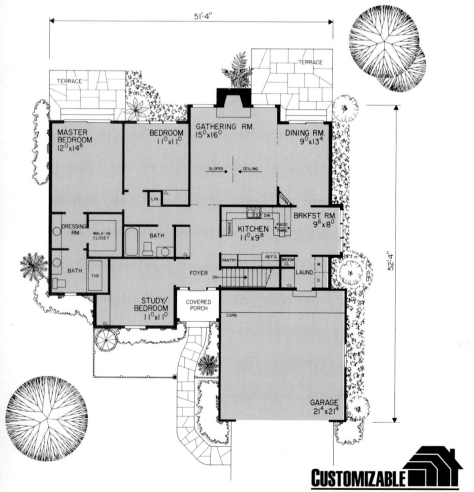

51'-4"

TERRACE

TERRACE

MASTER
BEDROOM
12⁰x14⁸

BEDROOM
11⁰x11⁰

GATHERING RM.
15⁰x16⁰

DINING RM.
9⁰x13⁴

SLOPED ← → CEILING

CL.

LIN.

DRESSING
RM.

WALK-IN
CLOSET

BATH

KITCHEN
11⁰x9⁸

RANGE   S.F. DW.

PASS THRU

BRKFST RM.
9⁶x8⁰

CL.

BATH

TUB

PANTRY

FOYER

DN.

REF'G.   BROOM CL.

LAUND.

W.

D.

CL.

STUDY/
BEDROOM
11⁰x11⁰

COVERED
PORCH

CURB

52'-4"

GARAGE
21⁴x21⁴

Design BB2878

Square Footage: 1,521

L **D**

● This charming one-story Traditional design offers plenty of livability in a compact size. Thoughtful zoning puts all bedroom sleeping areas to one side of the house apart from household activity in the living and service areas. The home includes a spacious gathering room with sloped ceiling, in addition to formal dining room and separate breakfast room. There's also a handy pass-thru between the breakfast room and an efficient, large kitchen. The laundry is strategically located adjacent to garage and breakfast/kitchen areas for handy access. A master bedroom enjoys its own suite with private bath and walk-in closet. A third bedroom can double as a sizable study just off the central foyer. This design offers the elegance of Traditional styling with the comforts of modern lifestyle.

CUSTOMIZABLE

Custom Alterations? See page 221 for customizing this plan to your specifications.

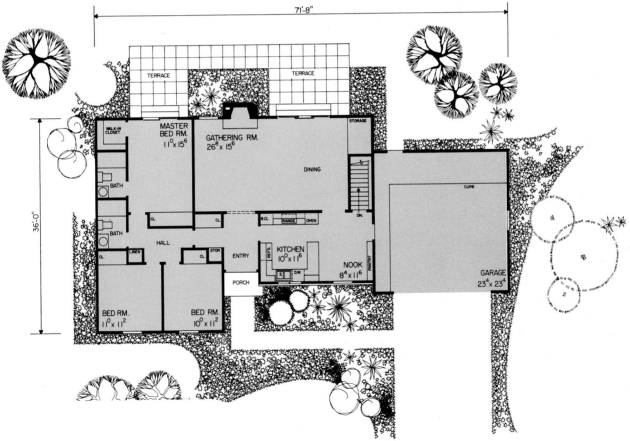

Within the floor plan:

- 71'-8"
- 36'-0"
- TERRACE
- TERRACE
- WALK-IN CLOSET
- MASTER BED RM. 11⁰ x 15⁶
- GATHERING RM. 26⁸ x 15⁶
- STORAGE
- BATH
- DINING
- CURB
- BATH
- CL.
- CL.
- B.CL.
- RANGE
- OVEN
- DN.
- HALL
- LINEN
- STOR.
- CL.
- ENTRY
- REFG.
- KITCHEN 10⁰ x 11⁶
- NOOK 8⁴ x 11⁶
- PANTRY
- GARAGE 23⁴ x 23³
- PORCH
- D.W.
- BED RM. 11⁰ x 11²
- BED RM. 10⁰ x 11²

Design BB2597

Square Footage: 1,515

L D

● Whether it be a starter house you are after, or one in which to spend your retirement years, this pleasing frame home will provide a full measure of pride in ownership. The contrast of vertical and horizontal lines, the double front doors and the coach lamp post at the garage create an inviting exterior. Efficiently planned, the floor plan functions in an orderly manner. The 26-foot gathering room has a delightful view of the rear yard and will take care of those formal dining occasions. There are two full baths serving the three bedrooms. Additional features include: plenty of storage facilities, two sets of glass doors to the terraces, a fireplace in the gathering room, a basement and an attached two-car garage to act as a buffer against the wind.

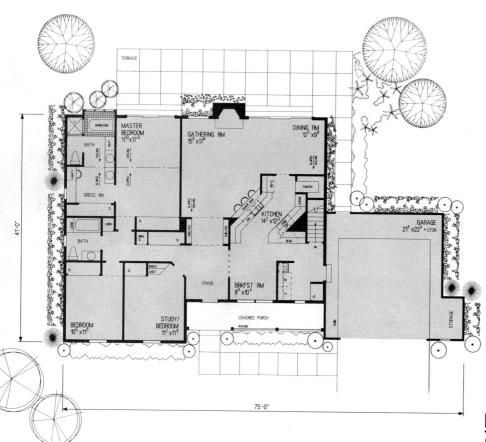

Design BB2947

Square Footage: 1,830

● This charming one-story Traditional home greets visitors with a covered porch. A galley-style kitchen shares a snack bar with the spacious gathering room where a fireplace is the focal point. An ample master suite includes a luxury bath with whirlpool tub and separate dressing room. Two additional bedrooms, one that could double as a study, are located at the front of the home.

CUSTOMIZABLE

Custom Alterations? See page 221 for customizing this plan to your specifications.

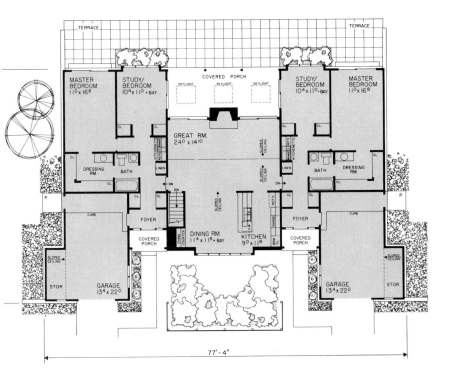

Design BB2869

Square Footage: 1,986

● This traditional one-story design offers the economical benefits of shared living space without sacrificing privacy. The common area of this design is centrally located between the two private, sleeping wings. The common area, 680 square feet, is made up of the great room, dining room and kitchen. Sloping the ceiling in this area creates an open feeling as will the sliding glass doors on each side of the fireplace. These doors lead to a large covered porch with skylights above. Separate outdoor entrances lead to each of the sleeping wings. Two bedrooms, dressing area, full bath and space for an optional kitchenette occupy 653 square feet in each wing. Additional space will be found in the basement which is the full size of the common area. Don't miss the covered porch and garage with additional storage space.

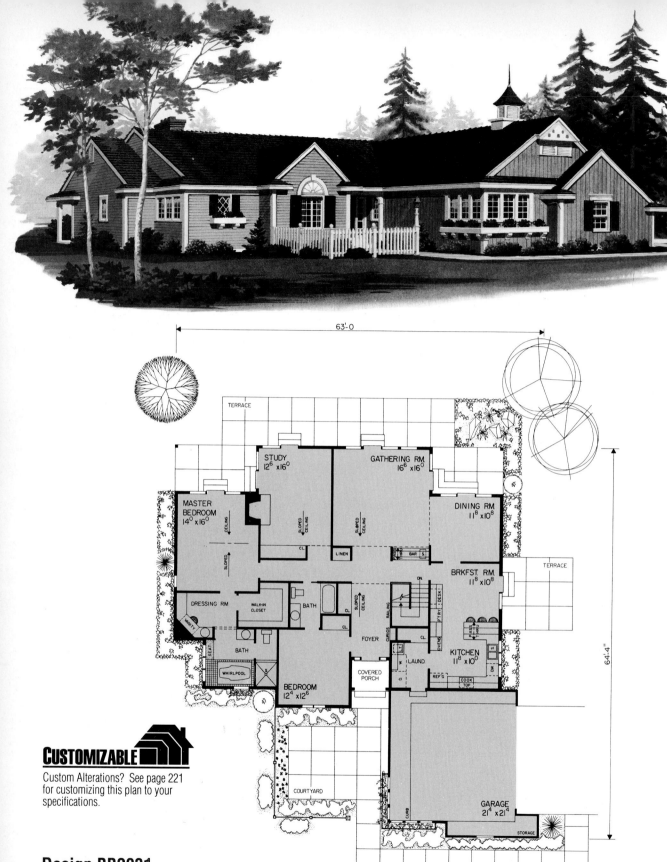

TERRACE

STUDY
12⁶ x16⁰

GATHERING RM
16⁶ x16⁰

MASTER
BEDROOM
14⁰ x16⁰

DINING RM
11⁸ x10⁸

SLOPED CEILING

SLOPED CEILING

SLOPED

CL

LINEN

BAR

S.

TERRACE

BRKFST. RM
11⁸ x10⁸

DRESSING RM

WALK-IN
CLOSET

BATH

CL

SLOPED
CEILING

RAILING

ON

P'NTRY

DESK

PASS
THRU

OVENS

SEAT

VANITY

BATH

CL

FOYER

CURIOS

CL

LIN

KITCHEN
11⁶ x10⁰

W

LAUND

WHIRLPOOL

S

DN

CL

REF'G

COOK
TOP

DW

BEDROOM
12⁴ x12⁶

COVERED
PORCH

63'-0

64'4"

COURTYARD

CURB

GARAGE
21⁴ x21⁴

STORAGE

CUSTOMIZABLE

Custom Alterations? See page 221
for customizing this plan to your
specifications.

Design BB2931
Square Footage: 1,998

● Little details make the difference.
Consider these that make this such a
charming showplace: Picket-fenced
courtyard, carriage lamp, window
boxes, shutters, muntined windows,
multi-gabled roof, cornice returns, vertical and horizontal siding with corner

boards, front door with glass side lites,
etc. Inside this appealing exterior there
is a truly outstanding floor plan for the
small family or empty-nesters. The
master bedroom suite is long on luxury, with a separate dressing room, private vanities, and whirlpool bath. An

adjacent study is just the right retreat.
There's room to move and — what a
warm touch! — it has its own fireplace.
Other attractions: roomy kitchen and
breakfast area, spacious gathering
room, rear and side terraces, and an
attached two-car garage with storage.

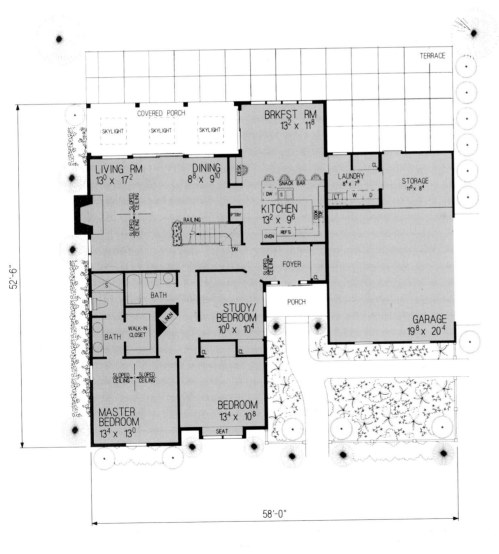

Design BB3340

Square Footage: 1,611

● You may not decide to build this design simply because of its delightful covered porch. But it certainly will provide its share of enjoyment if this plan is your choice. Notice also how effectively the bedrooms are arranged out of the traffic flow of the house. One bedroom could double nicely as a TV room or study. The living room/dining area is highlighted by a fireplace, sliding glass doors to the porch, and an open staircase with built-in planter to the basement.

Design BB2565
Square Footage: 1,540

L **D**

● This modest-sized floor plan has much to offer in the way of livability. With three elevations to choose from—Tudor, Colonial or contemporary—and a flexible floor plan, you're sure to find a pleasing combination. The expansive living room features a fine raised-hearth fireplace and a beamed ceiling. The kitchen will delight with its island range and adjacent breakfast nook. A laundry room and service entrance to the garage are a step away. The open stairwell to the basement is handy and leads to what may be developed into a recreation area. Three bedrooms—or have two and a study—include a private master bedroom with its own bath. For convenience in deciding what is right for you, all elevations are included in the blueprint package.

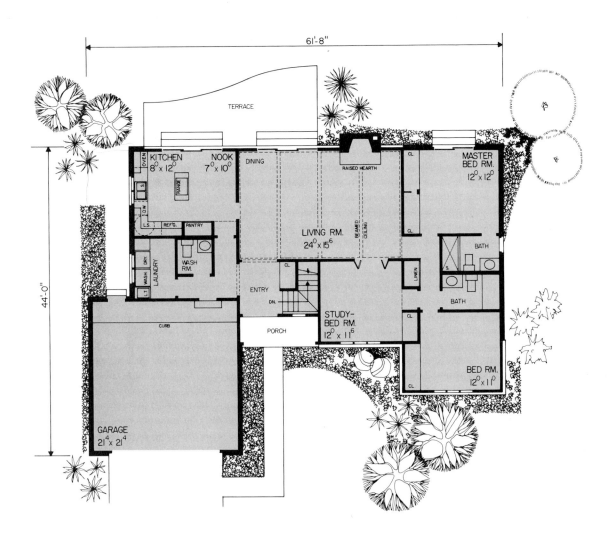

61'-8"

TERRACE

44'-0"

KITCHEN
8⁰ x 12⁰

NOOK
7⁰ x 10⁰

DINING

RAISED HEARTH

CL.

MASTER
BED RM.
12⁰ x 12⁰

OVEN

RANGE

LIVING RM.
24⁰ x 15⁶

BEAMED
CEILING

CL.

BATH

S.

REF'G.

PANTRY

L.S.

DW

WASH
RM.

LAUNDRY

DRY

WASH

L.T.

CL.

LINEN

BATH

ENTRY

DN.

STUDY-
BED RM.
12⁰ x 11⁶

CL.

CURB

PORCH

CL.

GARAGE
21⁴ x 21⁴

BED RM.
12⁰ x 11⁰

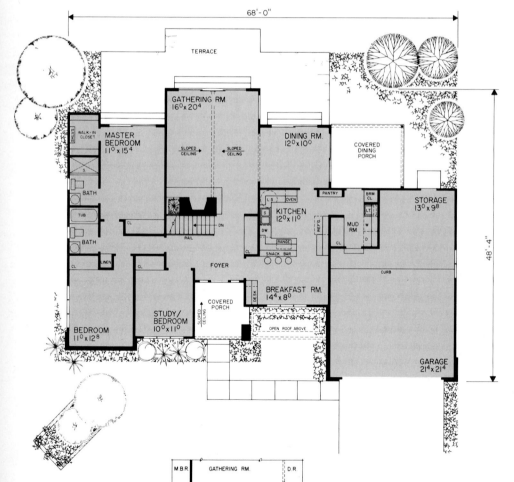

TERRACE

GATHERING RM.
16⁰ x 20⁴

SLOPED CEILING — SLOPED CEILING

DINING RM.
12⁰ x 10⁰

COVERED DINING PORCH

WALK-IN CLOSET

MASTER BEDROOM
11⁰ x 15⁴

BATH

TUB

BATH

LINEN

CL

CL

PANTRY

BRM CL

STORAGE
13⁰ x 9⁸

L S   OVEN

KITCHEN
12⁰ x 11⁰

S

DW

RANGE

SNACK BAR

REFG.

MUD RM.

CL

CURB

FOYER

DN

RAIL

CL

BEDROOM
11⁰ x 12⁸

STUDY/
BEDROOM
10⁰ x 11⁰

COVERED PORCH

SLOPED CEILING

DESK

BREAKFAST RM.
14⁴ x 8⁰

OPEN ROOF ABOVE

GARAGE
21⁴ x 21⁴

68'-0"

48'-4"

M.B.R.   GATHERING RM.   D.R.

CL

AIR COND

CL   K.

CL

FOYER

STUDY   PORCH   B.R.

OPTIONAL NON-BASEMENT

Design BB2803

Square Footage: 1,679

L **D**

● With a stone facade, this house extends great rustic charm. Its sister elevations (shown on pages 59 and 60) share the same livable floor plan—note the basement option that makes this plan that much more accommodating to varying tastes and regions. Inside, the front foyer leads to a large gathering room with a beamed ceiling and a fireplace. An adjacent dining room further extends lifestyle potential with access to a covered dining porch. The kitchen also services a breakfast room while leading to a nearby mud room. Three bedrooms include one that will easily convert to a study. The master suite enjoys a private bath and two closets—one a walk-in.

CUSTOMIZABLE

Custom Alterations? See page 221 for customizing this plan to your specifications.

Design BB2804

Square Footage: 1,674

L **D**

● Stuccoed arches, multi-pane windows and a gracefully sloped roof accent the exterior of this Spanish-inspired design. With the same floor plan as BB2803, and sporting the non-basement option, this design will find itself in accord with sun-country building practices. If you're building in a rather different environment, the Tudor featured on the next page offers a gracious look while maintaining the same great layout.

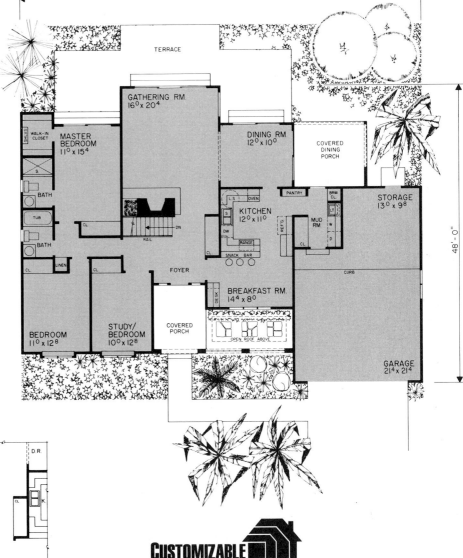

67'-4"

48'-0"

TERRACE

GATHERING RM.
16⁰ x 20⁴

DINING RM.
12⁰ x 10⁰

COVERED DINING PORCH

WALK-IN CLOSET

MASTER BEDROOM
11⁰ x 15⁴

BATH

TUB

BATH

KITCHEN
12⁰ x 11⁰

PANTRY

MUD RM.

STORAGE
13⁰ x 9⁸

LINEN

FOYER

CURB

BREAKFAST RM.
14⁴ x 8⁰

BEDROOM
11⁰ x 12⁸

STUDY/ BEDROOM
10⁰ x 12⁸

COVERED PORCH

DESK

OPEN ROOF ABOVE

GARAGE
21⁴ x 21⁴

OPTIONAL NON-BASEMENT

M.B.R.   GATHERING RM.   D.R.

AIR COND.

K

CL

FOYER

STUDY   PORCH   B.R.

CUSTOMIZABLE

Custom Alterations? See page 221 for customizing this plan to your specifications.

59

Design BB2802

Square Footage: 1,729

L **D**

● Here's yet another exterior
elevation choice for the plan
featured on the preceding two
pages. This elegant Tudor
shows off the same great livability. It does so through the effec-
tive use of half-timbered stucco
and brick as well as with an
authentic bay window in front.
The covered porch serves as a
fitting introduction to all the
inside amenities. The gathering
room gains a lot of the attention
with its rustic appeal and outside access. The house gourmet
can't miss with the full-sized
kitchen to work in. Also noteworthy is the expanse of storage
space present in the two-car
garage and the huge amount of
room available for a workbench.

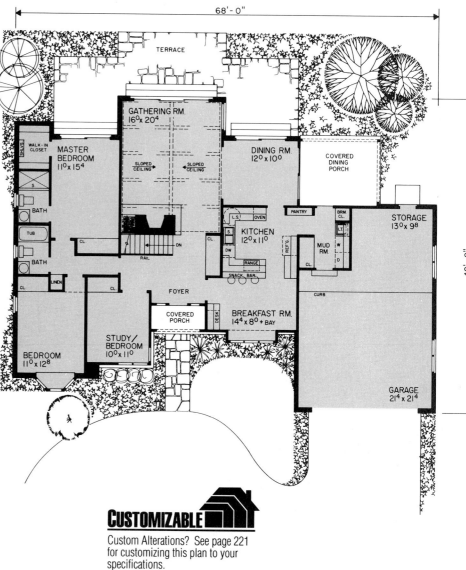

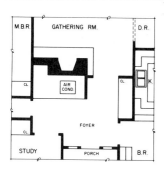

OPTIONAL NON - BASEMENT

CUSTOMIZABLE

Custom Alterations? See page 221
for customizing this plan to your
specifications.

60

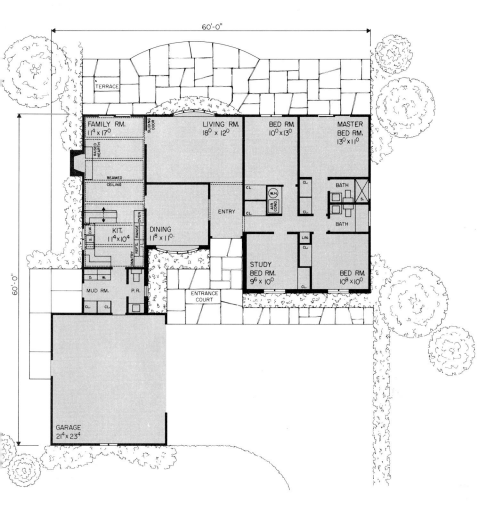

TERRACE

60'-0"

FAMILY RM.
11⁴ x 17⁰

RAISED HEARTH

BEAMED CEILING

SLIDING DOOR

LIVING RM.
18⁰ x 12⁰

BED RM.
10⁰ x13⁰

MASTER BED RM.
13⁰ x 11⁰

CL.

W.H.

CL.

BATH

AIR COND.

CL.

CL.

ENTRY

BATH

KIT.
11⁴ x10⁴

PANTRY

REFG.

RANGE

OVEN

DINING
11⁸ x 11⁰

S.

LIN.

CL.

60'-0"

D.

W.

MUD RM.

P.R.

STUDY BED RM.
9⁶ x 10⁰

BED RM.
10⁸ x 10⁰

CL.

CL.

CL.

CL.

ENTRANCE COURT

GARAGE
21⁴ x 23⁴

Design BB2170

Square Footage: 1,646

L **D**

● An L-shaped home with an enchanting Olde English styling. The wavy-edged siding, the simulated beams, the diamond lite windows, the unusual brick pattern and the interesting roof lines all are elements which set the character of authenticity. The center entry routes traffic directly to the formal living and sleeping zones of the house. Between the kitchen-family room area and the attached two-car garage is the mud room. Here is the washer and dryer with the extra powder room nearby. The family room is highlighted by the beamed ceilings, the raised hearth fireplace and sliding glass doors to the rear terrace. The work center with its abundance of cupboard space will be fun in which to function. Four bedrooms, two full baths and good closet space are features of the sleeping area.

Design BB3373

Square Footage: 1,376

● This charmingly compact plan has three facades from which to choose: Greek Revival (BB3373), Tudor (BB3374) or Southwestern (BB3375). The interior plan contains a large living room/dining room combination, a media room, a U-shaped kitchen with breakfast room and two bedrooms. If the extra space is needed, the media room could serve as a third bedroom. Note the terrace to the rear of the plan off the dining room and the sloped ceilings throughout.

Design BB3374

Square Footage: 1,376

Design BB3375

Square Footage: 1,376

L **D**

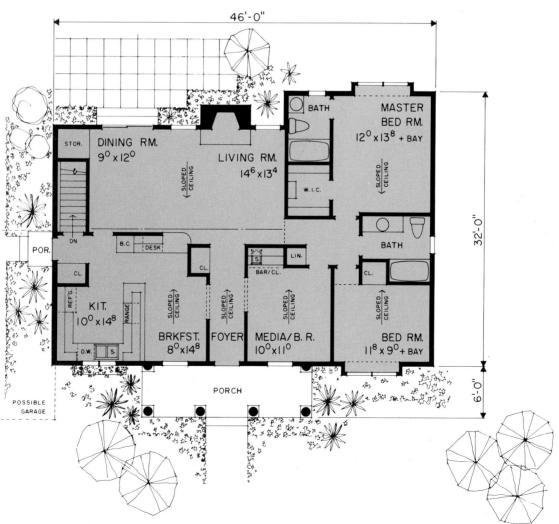

46'-0"

STOR.

DINING RM.
9⁰ x 12⁰

LIVING RM.
14⁶ x 13⁴

SLOPED CEILING

BATH

MASTER
BED RM.
12⁰ x 13⁸ + BAY

SLOPED CEILING

W. I. C.

DN

B.C. DESK

CL.

BAR/CL.

LIN.

S.

BATH

POR.

CL.

REF'G.

KIT.
10⁰ x 14⁸

RANGE

SLOPED CEILING

SLOPED CEILING

SLOPED CEILING

CL.

SLOPED CEILING

D.W.   S.

BRKFST.
8⁰ x 14⁸

FOYER

MEDIA/B. R.
10⁰ x 11⁰

BED RM.
11⁸ x 9⁰ + BAY

32'-0"

POSSIBLE
GARAGE

PORCH

6'-0"

63

Design BB2607

Square Footage: 1,208

L **D**

● This English Tudor cottage will delight young and old with its warm, open interior. The front porch gives way to the main living area of the house. With a fireplace and windows that overlook both front and rear yards, this space becomes a most pleasant one to inhabit. The dining room features a built-in china cabinet—built-in bookshelves are just around the corner. The U-shaped kitchen is wonderfully efficient with its double sink, dishwasher, pantry and adjacent eating bay. A laundry area and half bath also occupy this end of the house. At the other end, two bedrooms share a full bath.

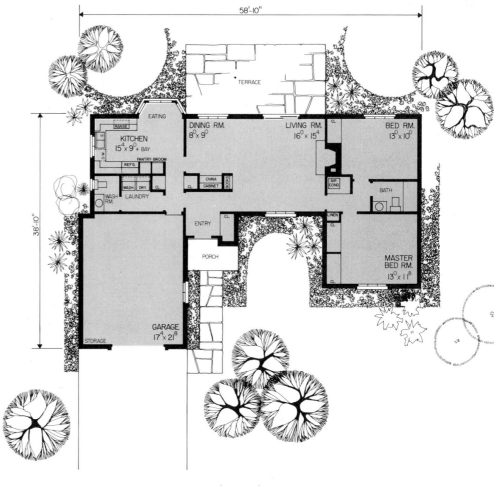

OPTIONAL BASEMENT

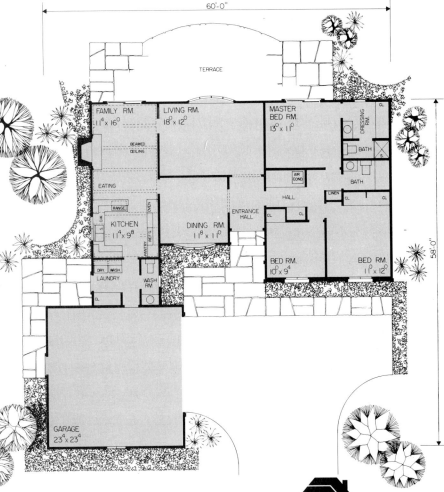

TERRACE

FAMILY RM.
11⁴ x 16⁰

LIVING RM.
18⁰ x 12⁰

MASTER BED RM.
13⁰ x 11⁰

DRESSING RM.

CL.

BATH

S.

BEAMED CEILING

AIR COND.

BATH

EATING

HALL

LINEN

CL.

CL.

RANGE

OVEN

ENTRANCE HALL

CL.

CL.

KITCHEN
11⁴ x 9⁸

DW

REF. G.

PANTRY

DINING RM.
11⁸ x 11⁰

BED RM.
10⁰ x 9⁴

BED RM.
11⁵ x 12⁰

DRY.

WASH.

LAUNDRY

WASH RM.

CL.

GARAGE
23⁵ x 23⁴

60'-0"

58'-0"

Design BB2606

Square Footage: 1,499

MASTER BED RM.

LINEN

BATH

DN

ENT. HALL

HALL

CL.

BED RM.

CL.

CL.

BED RM.

OPTIONAL BASEMENT

● This modest sized house with its 1,499 square feet could hardly offer more in the way of exterior charm and interior livability. Measuring only 60 feet in width means it will not require a huge, expensive piece of property. The orientation of the garage and the front drive court are features which promote an economical use of property. In addition to the formal, separate living and dining rooms, there is the informal kitchen/family room area. Note the beamed ceiling, the fireplace, the sliding glass doors and the eating area of the family room.

CUSTOMIZABLE

Custom Alterations? See page 221 for customizing this plan to your specifications.

Design BB3355

Square Footage: 1,387

L D

● Though it's only just under 1,400 total square feet, this plan offers three bedrooms (or two with study) and a sizable gathering room with fireplace and sloped ceiling. The galley kitchen provides a pass-through snack bar and has a planning desk and attached breakfast room. Besides two smaller bedrooms with a full bath, there's an extravagant master suite with large dressing area, double vanity and raised whirlpool tub. The full-length terrace to the rear of the house extends the living potential to the outdoors.

CUSTOMIZABLE

Custom Alterations? See page 221 for customizing this plan to your specifications.

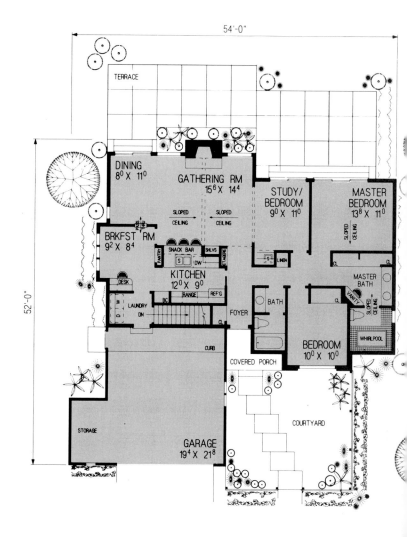

Design BB3442

Square Footage: 1,273

● For those just starting out or the empty-nester, this unique one-story plan is sure to delight. A covered-porch introduces a dining room with a coffered ceiling and views out two sides of the house. The kitchen is just off this room and is most efficient with a double sink, dishwasher and pantry. The living room gains attention with a volume ceiling, fireplace and access to a covered patio. The master bedroom also features a volume ceiling while enjoying the luxury of a private bath. In it, a walk-in closet, washer/dryer, double-bowl vanity, garden tub, separate shower and compartmented toilet comprise the amenities. Not to be overlooked, a second bedroom may easily convert to a media room or study—the choice is yours.

CUSTOMIZABLE
Custom Alterations? See page 221 for customizing this plan to your specifications.

Design BB3345
Square Footage: 1,738

Custom Alterations? See page 221
for customizing this plan to your
specifications.

● This quaint shingled cottage offers an unexpected amount of living space in just over 1,700 square feet. The large gathering room with fireplace, dining room with covered porch, and kitchen with breakfast room handle formal parties as easily as they do the casual family get-together. Three bedrooms, one that could also serve as a study, are found in a separate wing of the house. Give special attention to the storage space in this home and the extra touches that set it apart from many homes of equal size.

Design BB3481A
Square Footage: 1,901

L

In just under 2,000 square feet, this pleasing one-story home bears all the livability of houses twice its size. A combined living and dining room offers elegance for entertaining; with two elevations to choose from, the living room can either support an octagonal bay or a bumped-out nook. The U-shaped kitchen finds easy access to the breakfast nook and rear family room; sliding glass doors lead from the family room to a back stoop. The master bedroom has a quaint potshelf and a private bath with a spa tub, a double-bowl vanity, a walk-in closet and a compartmented toilet. With two additional family bedrooms—one may serve as a den if desired—and a hall bath with dual lavatories, this plan offers the best in accommodations. Both elevations come with the blueprint package.

Design BB3481B
Square Footage: 1,908

L

Width 42'-4"
Depth 63'-10"

CUSTOMIZABLE
Custom Alterations? See page 221 for customizing this plan to your specifications.

Design BB2505
Square Footage: 1,366

● This plan offers you a choice of three distinctively different exteriors—each is detailed in the set of blueprints you receive. One, with traditional flair, sets the pace with its use of vertical siding. The two remaining exteriors both exhibit contemporary styling—one makes use of raised and varying roof planes. Whichever you choose, the floor plan stays the same. In less than 1,400 square feet, the amenities abound. A large, central gathering room enjoys the warmth of a raised-hearth fireplace and the companionship of a formal dining room. The galley-style kitchen also services a bayed breakfast nook. Three bedrooms comprise the sleeping wing of the house. The master bedroom enjoys a walk-in closet and a private bath.

CUSTOMIZABLE

Custom Alterations? See page 221 for customizing this plan to your specifications.

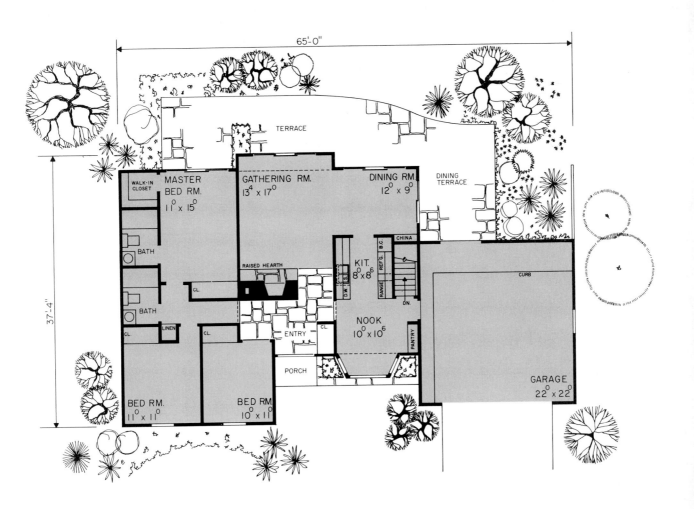

65'-0"

37'-4"

WALK-IN
CLOSET

MASTER
BED RM.
11⁰ x 15⁰

GATHERING RM.
13⁴ x 17⁰

DINING RM.
12⁰ x 9⁰

DINING
TERRACE

TERRACE

BATH

RAISED HEARTH

CL.

KIT.
8⁰ x 8⁶

CHINA

REFG. B.C.

RANGE

DN.

CURB

BATH

CL.

LINEN

CL.

ENTRY

CL.

D.W. S.

NOOK
10⁰ x 10⁶

PANTRY

PORCH

GARAGE
22⁰ x 22⁰

BED RM.
11⁰ x 11⁰

BED RM.
10⁰ x 11⁰

Design BB3350

Square Footage: 1,777

L **D**

● Though smaller in size, this traditional one-story provides a family-oriented floor plan that leaves nothing out. Besides the formal living room (or study if you prefer) and dining room, there's a gathering room with fireplace, snack bar, and sliding glass doors to the rear terrace. The U-shaped kitchen is in close proximity to the handy utility area just off the garage. Of particular note is the grand master bedroom with garden whirlpool tub, walk-in closet and private terrace. The sleeping area is completed with two family bedrooms to the front.

OPTIONAL NON-BASEMENT

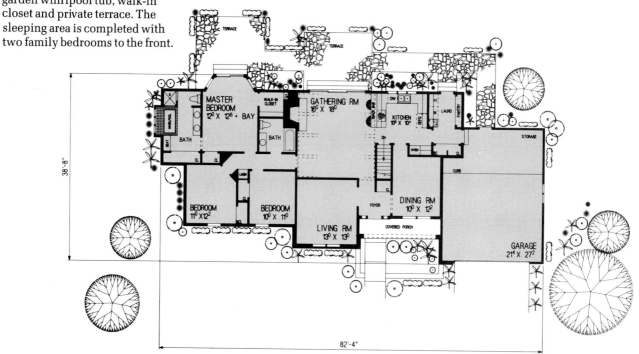

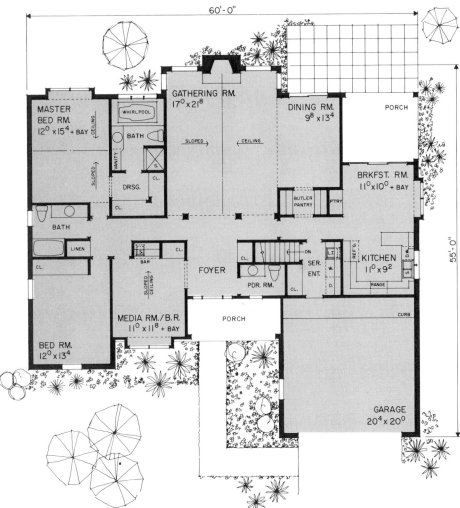

Design BB3376
Square Footage: 1,999

L **D**

● Small families or empty nesters will appreciate the layout of this traditional ranch. The foyer opens to the gathering room with fireplace and sloped ceiling. The dining room is open to the gathering room for entertaining ease and contains sliding doors to a rear terrace. The breakfast room also provides access to a covered porch for dining outdoors. The media room to the left of the home offers a bay window and a wet bar, or it can double as a third bedroom.

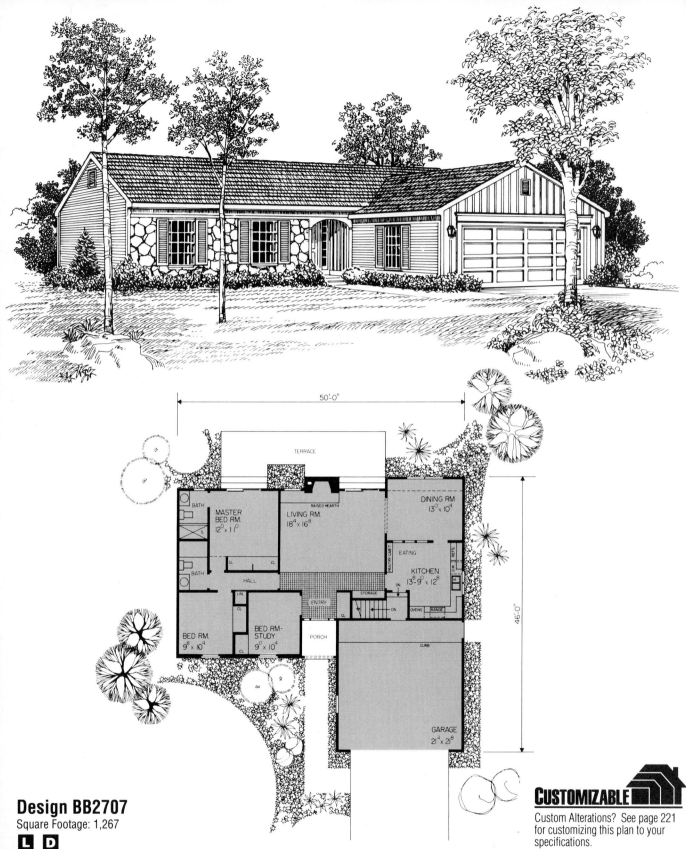

Design BB2707

Square Footage: 1,267

[L] [D]

● Here is a charming Early American adaptation that will serve as a picturesque and practical retirement home. Also, it will serve admirably those with a small family in search of an efficient, economically built home. The living area, highlighted by the raised hearth fireplace, is spacious. The kitchen features eating space and easy access to the garage and basement. The dining room is adjacent to the kitchen and views the rear yard. Then, there is the basement for recreation and hobby pursuits. The bedroom wing offers three bedrooms and two full baths. Don't miss the sliding doors to the terrace from the living room and the master bedroom. Storage units are plentiful including a pantry cabinet in the eating area of the kitchen. This plan will be efficient and livable.

CUSTOMIZABLE

Custom Alterations? See page 221 for customizing this plan to your specifications.

Design BB2805

Square Footage: 1,547

L **D**

● Choices abound with the introduction of three exteriors for one fabulous floor plan. On this page, a traditional exterior delights with its employment of various exterior building materials. The next two pages display a Tudor exterior as well as a contemporary one. Inside each, you'll find yourself at home. A grand living room connects to a dining room. A pair of sliding glass doors offers passage to a covered rear porch—skylights here offer an additional degree of livability. The U-shaped kitchen expands into a spacious breakfast room—also with access to the rear porch. Three bedrooms—or two and a TV room or study—comprise the sleeping quarters. Don't miss the large storage area in the garage—perfect for all of your seasonal items. An optional non-basement plan adds to the flexibility of this design.

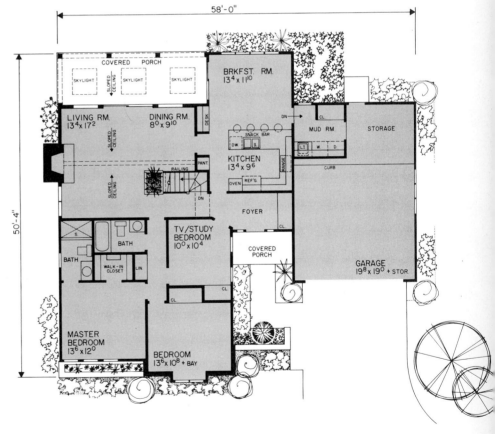

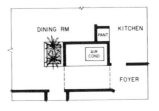

OPTIONAL NON-BASEMENT

Design BB2806

Square Footage: 1,584

● Like the home on the last page, this Tudor provides an excellent facade for this same floor plan. Shown with a side-entry garage, the authenticity in the facade is not lost. The breakfast room presents the perfect atmosphere for high tea or family dinners. Nearby, the combination living/dining room provides an elegant entertaining area. In the master bedroom, a walk-in closet and a private bath will delight.

58'-0"

50'-4"

COVERED PORCH

SKYLIGHT   SLOPED CEILING   SKYLIGHT   SKYLIGHT

BRKFST. RM.
13⁴ x 11¹⁰

LIVING RM.
13⁴ x 17²

DINING RM.
8⁰ x 9¹⁰

DESK

SLOPED CEILING

SNACK BAR

DN

CL.

MUD RM.

STORAGE

DW   S

KITCHEN
13⁴ x 9⁶

RANGE

LT   W   D.

CURB

SLOPED CEILING

RAILING

PANT.

OVEN   REF'G.

DN

FOYER

CL.

BATH

BATH

WALK-IN CLOSET   LIN.

TV/STUDY
BEDROOM
10⁰ x 10⁴

COVERED PORCH

CL.

GARAGE
19⁸ x 19⁰ + STOR.

MASTER BEDROOM
13⁶ x 12⁰

CL.

BEDROOM
13⁶ x 10⁸ + BAY

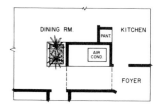

DINING RM.   KITCHEN

PANT.

AIR COND

FOYER

OPTIONAL NON-BASEMENT

Design BB2807

Square Footage: 1,576

L D

● In this contemporary rendition of the plan featured on the preceding two pages, a wonderful exterior emphasizes a most desirable floor plan. Notice the slight redefinition of the front bedrooms—to maintain the sleek stylings of a contemporary, the bumped-out wall and bay window are replaced with a flush wall and vertical siding.

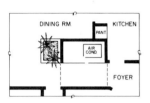

OPTIONAL NON-BASEMENT

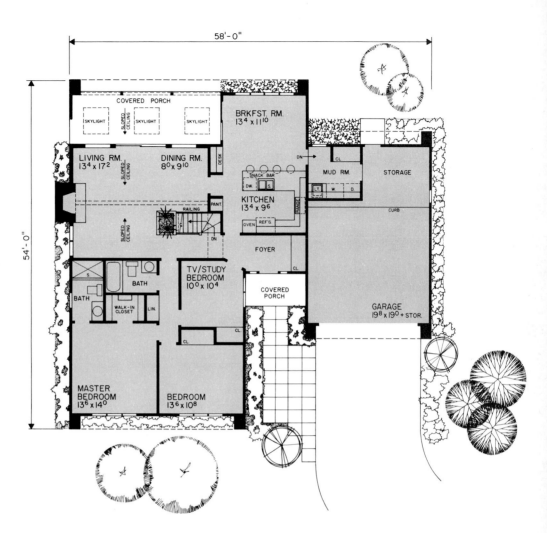

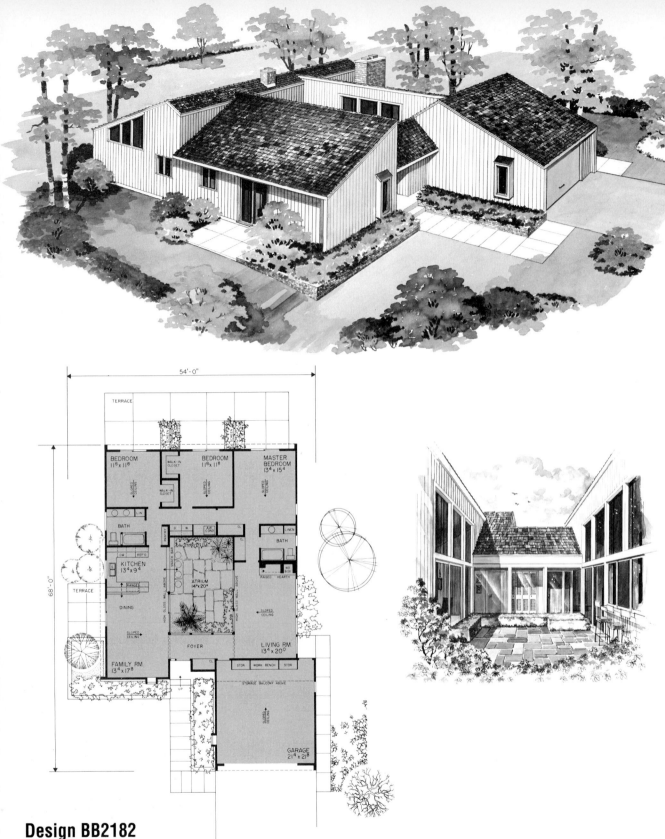

Design BB2182

Square Footage: 1,558
Atrium: 280 square feet

● What a great new dimension in living is represented by this unique contemporary design! Each of the major zones comprise a separate unit which, along with the garage, clusters around the atrium. High sloped ceilings and plenty of glass areas assure a feeling of spaciousness. The quiet living room will enjoy its privacy, while activities in the informal family room will be great fun functioning with the kitchen. A snack bar opens the kitchen to the atrium. The view, above right, shows portions of snack bar and the front entry looking through the glass wall. There are two full baths strategically located to service all areas conveniently. Storage facilities are excellent, indeed. Don't miss the storage potential found in the garage. There is a work bench and storage balcony above.

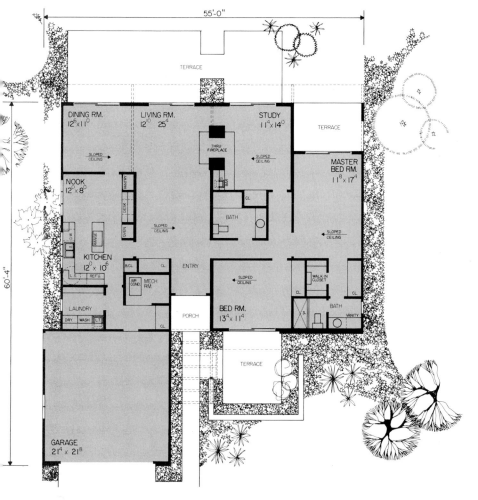

DINING RM.
12⁶ x 11⁰

LIVING RM.
12¹⁰ 25⁴

STUDY
11¹ x 14⁰

TERRACE

SLOPED CEILING

THRU-FIREPLACE

SLOPED CEILING

MASTER BED RM.
11⁸ x 17⁴

NOOK
12⁵ x 8⁰

PANTRY

DESK

BATH

CL

SLOPED CEILING

SLOPED CEILING

OVEN

RANGE

KITCHEN
12⁰ x 10⁶

B.CL

CL

ENTRY

AIR COND.

MECH. RM.

REF'G.

SLOPED CEILING

WALK IN CLOSET

CL

CL

LAUNDRY

PORCH

BED RM.
13⁴ x 11⁴

BATH

VANITY

DRY WASH

CL

GARAGE
21⁴ x 21⁸

TERRACE

TERRACE

55'-0"

60'-4"

Design BB2754

Square Footage: 1,844

● In this contemporary plan, livability extends from the front walkway to the rear terrace. An elongated living room greets you at the entry. On further inspection, the glamour of this living space is apparent. The living room shares a through-fireplace with the study—both rooms enjoy passage to the terrace outside. A dining room opens to the living room and also possesses a set of sliding glass doors for outdoor access. In the kitchen, an island range and prep area make meal time a breeze. A laundry room sits near the garage and will delight with its conveniences. Two bedrooms also pamper as each has its own terrace. The master bedroom fancies its own private bath as well as two closets—one a walk-in.

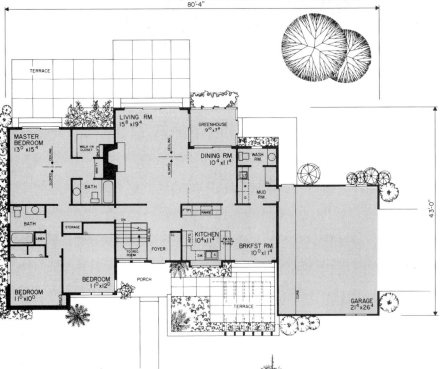

Design BB2871

Square Footage: 1,905

D

● A greenhouse area off the dining room and living room provides a cheerful focal point for this comfortable three-bedroom Trend home. The spacious living room features a cozy fireplace and sloped ceiling. In addition to the dining room, there's a less formal breakfast room just off the modern kitchen. Both kitchen and breakfast areas look out into a front terrace. Stairs just off the foyer lead down to a recreation room. Master bedroom suite opens to a terrace. A mud room and washroom off the garage allow rear entry to the house during inclement weather.

Design BB2795
Square Footage: 1,952

● This three-bedroom design
leaves no room for improvement.
Any size family will find it difficult
to surpass the fine qualities that this
home offers. Begin with the exterior.
This fine contemporary design has
open trellis work above the front,
covered private court. This area is
sheltered by a privacy wall extend-
ing from the projecting garage.
Inside, the floor plan will be just as
breathtaking. Begin at the foyer and
choose a direction. To the left is the
sleeping wing equipped with three
bedrooms and two baths. Straight
ahead from the foyer is the gathering room with through-fireplace to
the dining room. To the right is the
work center. This area includes a
breakfast room, a U-shaped kitchen
and laundry.

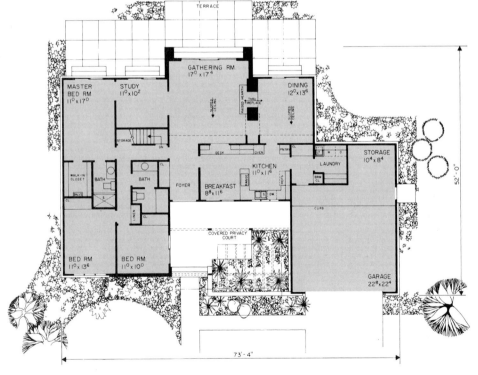

Design BB2753
Square Footage: 1,539

D

● This three-bedroom home makes use of full living patterns—a central living room with a fireplace accommodates formal gatherings while a family room takes care of everyday situations. The kitchen enjoys direct access to both the dining room and the eating area. Or take your meals outside—a porch off the family room presents a pleasing atmosphere for dining and relaxing. The front study may convert to a bedroom if desired. Access to a terrace surrounded by a privacy wall is a prominent feature of this room. Two other bedrooms include a master bedroom. It utilizes a walk-in closet in addition to another set of closets, a private bath and outdoor access.

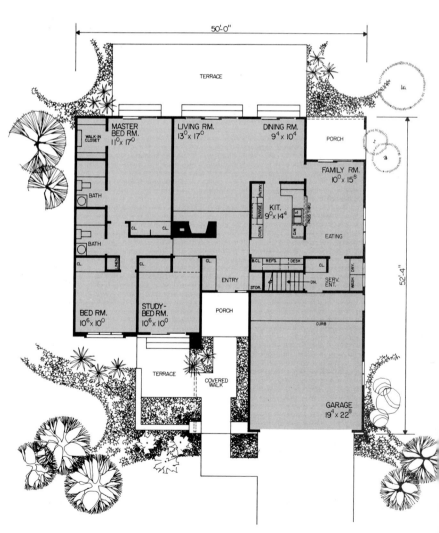

Design BB2528

Square Footage: 1,754

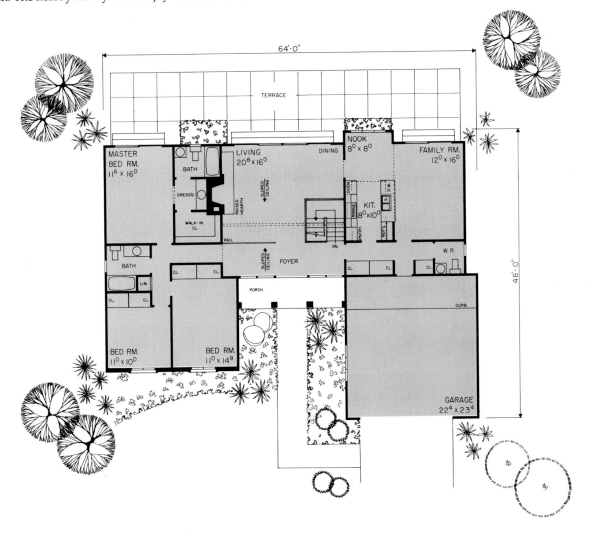

This inviting, U-shaped western ranch adaptation offers outstanding living potential behind its double front doors. A formal living room/dining room combination serves as the focal point and pleases with its raised-hearth fireplace and terrace access. Adjacent is a breakfast nook and galley-style kitchen. The nearby family room enjoys the convenience of a wash room. The family sleeping quarters are comprised of a master bedroom and two secondary bedrooms. In the master, a large walk-in closet, a dressing area with a bowl and vanity and a full bath provide full livability. Don't miss the sliding glass doors here, too, that lead out onto the back terrace.

Design BB2818

Square Footage: 1,566

● This is most certainly an outstanding contemporary design. Study the exterior carefully before your journey to inspect the floor plan. The vertical lines are carried from the siding to the paned windows to the garage door. The front entry is recessed so the overhanging roof creates a covered porch.

Note the planter court with privacy wall. The floor plan is just as outstanding. The rear gathering room has a sloped ceiling, raised hearth fireplace, sliding glass doors to the terrace and a snack bar with pass-thru to the kitchen. In addition to the gathering room, there is the living room/study. This

room could be utilized in a variety of ways depending on your family's choice. The formal dining room is convenient to the U-shaped kitchen. Three bedrooms and two closely located baths are in the sleeping wing. This plan includes details for the construction of an optional basement.

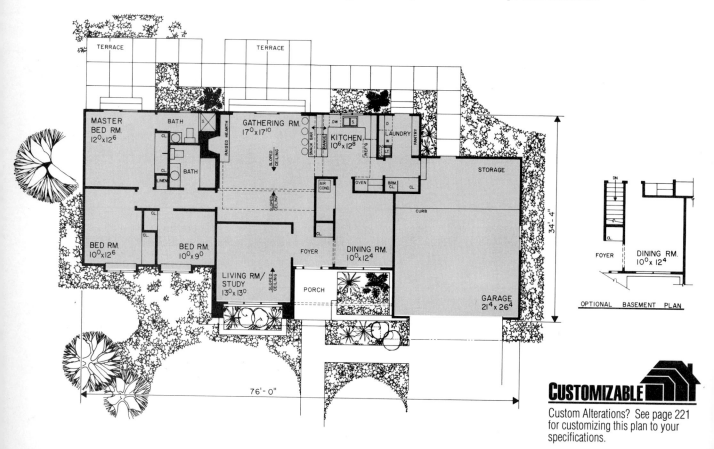

CUSTOMIZABLE

Custom Alterations? See page 221 for customizing this plan to your specifications.

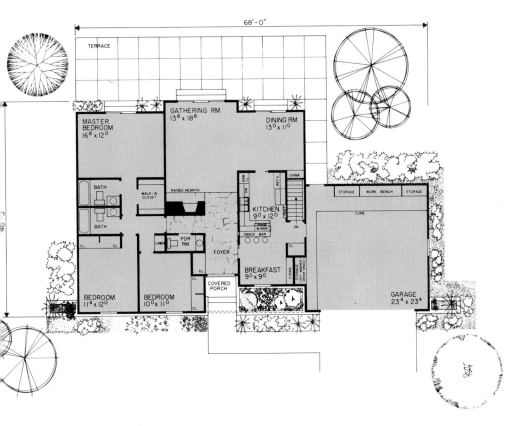

TERRACE

68' - 0"

MASTER BEDROOM
16⁸ x 12⁰

GATHERING RM.
13⁸ x 18⁸

DINING RM.
13⁰ x 11⁰

BATH

WALK-IN CLOSET

RAISED HEARTH

CHINA

KITCHEN
9⁰ x 12⁰

BATH

LINEN

PDR RM.

SNACK BAR

STORAGE   WORK BENCH   STORAGE

CURB

BEDROOM
11⁴ x 12⁰

BEDROOM
10⁰ x 11⁰

FOYER

BREAKFAST
9⁰ x 9⁰

COVERED PORCH

GARAGE
23⁴ x 23⁴

Design BB2671

Square Footage: 1,589

L **D**

● The rustic exterior of
this one-story home fea-
tures vertical wood siding.
The entry foyer is floored
with flagstone and leads to
the three areas of the plan:
sleeping, living, and work
center. The sleeping area
has three bedrooms. The
master bedroom has sliding
glass doors to the rear terrace. The living area, consisting of gathering and
dining rooms, also has
access to the terrace. The
work center is efficiently
planned. It houses the
kitchen with snack bar,
breakfast room with built-
in china cabinet and stairs
to the basement. This is a
very livable plan. Special
amenities include a raised-
hearth fireplace and a
walk-in closet in the master
bedroom.

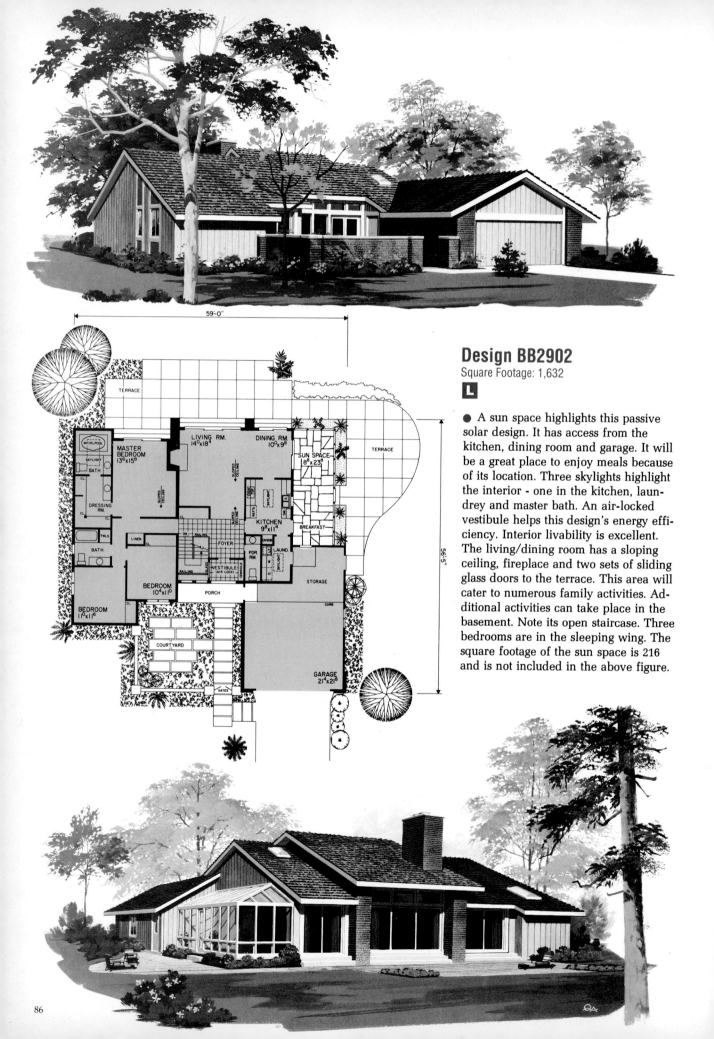

Design BB2902
Square Footage: 1,632

L

● A sun space highlights this passive solar design. It has access from the kitchen, dining room and garage. It will be a great place to enjoy meals because of its location. Three skylights highlight the interior - one in the kitchen, laundrey and master bath. An air-locked vestibule helps this design's energy efficiency. Interior livability is excellent. The living/dining room has a sloping ceiling, fireplace and two sets of sliding glass doors to the terrace. This area will cater to numerous family activities. Additional activities can take place in the basement. Note its open staircase. Three bedrooms are in the sleeping wing. The square footage of the sun space is 216 and is not included in the above figure.

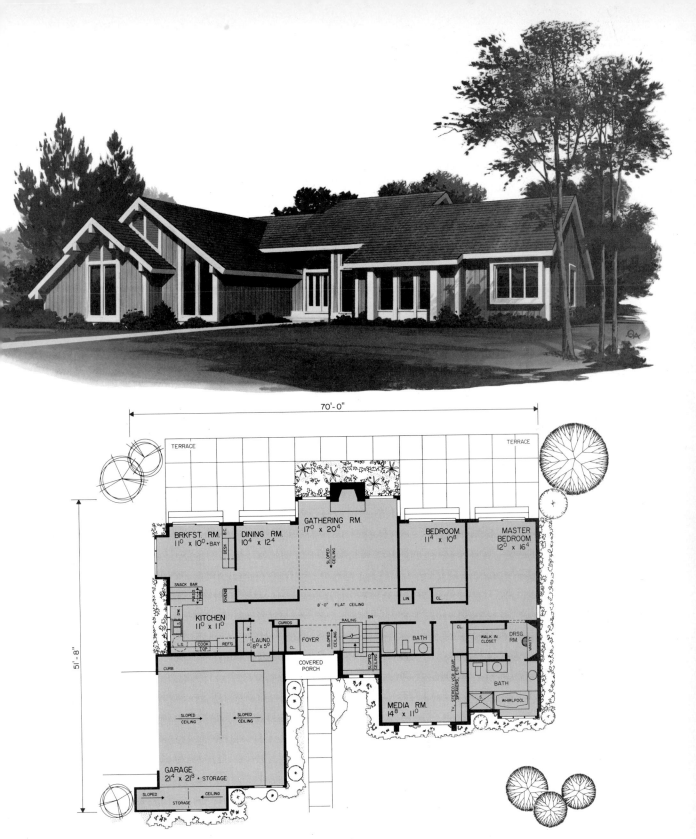

Design BB2913

Square Footage: 1,835

D

● This smart design features multi-gabled ends, varied roof lines, and vertical windows. It also offers efficient zoning by room functions and plenty of modern comforts for Contemporary family lifestyle. A covered porch leads through a foyer to a large central gathering room with fireplace, sloped ceiling, and its own special view of a rear terrace. A modern kitchen with snack bar has a pass-thru to a breakfast room with view of the terrace. There's also an adjacent dining room. A media room isolated along with bedrooms from the rest of the house offers a quiet private area for listening to stereos or VCRs. A master bedroom suite includes its own whirlpool. A large garage includes extra storage.

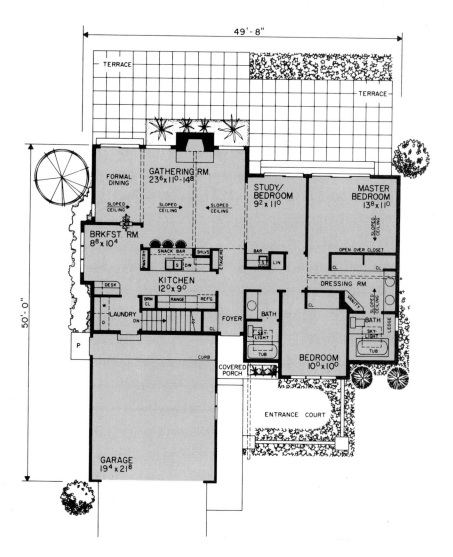

TERRACE

TERRACE

49'-8"

50'-0"

FORMAL DINING

SLOPED CEILING

GATHERING RM. 23⁶ x 11⁰-14⁸

SLOPED CEILING

SLOPED CEILING

STUDY/ BEDROOM 9² x 11⁰

MASTER BEDROOM 13⁸ x 11⁰

SLOPED CEILING

BRKFST. RM. 8⁸ x 10⁴

PANTRY

SNACK BAR

SHLVS

ETAGERE

BAR

LIN

OPEN OVER CLOSET

CL

CL

DESK

KITCHEN 12⁰ x 9⁰

BRM CL

RANGE

REF'G

DRESSING RM.

VANITY

SLOPED CEILING

W

LAUNDRY

DN

FOYER

BATH

CL

BATH

LEDGE

P

CURB

SKY LIGHT

TUB

BEDROOM 10⁰ x 10⁰

SKY LIGHT

TUB

COVERED PORCH

ENTRANCE COURT

GARAGE 19⁴ x 21⁸

Design BB2864

Square Footage: 1,387

L D

● Projecting the garage to the front of a house is very economical in two ways. One, it reduces the required lot size for building (in this case the overall width is under 50 feet); Two, it will protect the interior from street noise. Many other characteristics about this design deserve mention, too. Upon entering, the foyer will take you to the various areas. The interior kitchen has an adjacent breakfast room and a snack bar on the gathering room side. A study with wet bar is adjacent. Sliding glass doors here and in the master bedroom open to the terrace.

CUSTOMIZABLE

Custom Alterations? See page 221 for customizing this plan to your specifications.

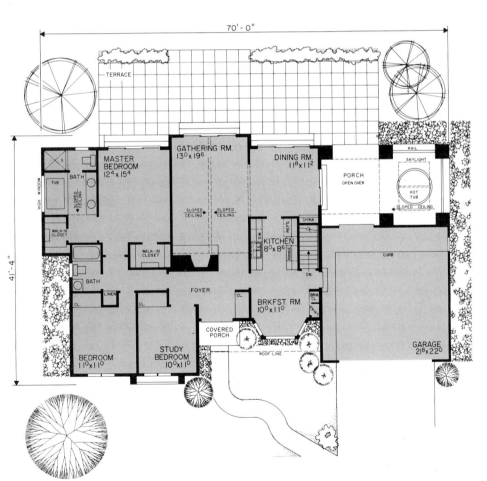

70'- 0"

TERRACE

MASTER BEDROOM 12⁴x15⁴

GATHERING RM. 13⁰x19⁶

DINING RM. 11⁸x11²

PORCH OPEN OVER

RAIL

SKYLIGHT

HOT TUB

SLOPED CEILING

BATH

TUB

SLOPED CEILING

WALK-IN CLOSET

SLOPED CEILING

SLOPED CEILING

HIGH WINDOW

WALK-IN CLOSET

KITCHEN 8⁰x8⁶

CHINA

REF'S

RANGE

DN

CURB

41'- 4"

BATH

LINEN

FOYER

CL.

BRKFST. RM. 10⁰x11⁰

BR'M. CL.

CL.

CL.

COVERED PORCH

ROOF LINE

GARAGE 21⁸x22⁰

BEDROOM 11⁰x11⁰

STUDY BEDROOM 10⁰x11⁰

Design BB2809
Square Footage: 1,551

● This contemporary home will delight all with its great indoor/outdoor livability. A front covered porch provides a nice welcome to the inside where a gathering room draws attention. Here, a sloped ceiling and raised-hearth fireplace along with sliding glass doors to a back terrace lend themselves to the comfort of this room. Attached is a dining room with access to a porch and hot tub. The kitchen, which easily serves the dining room, also enjoys a bayed breakfast room—perfect for quiet conversations and more. Three bedrooms include a master suite with a walk-in closet and bath with dual lavatories, a soaking tub and a compartmented stool and shower. If you like, make one of the secondary bedrooms into a study.

Design BB3453

Square Footage: 1,442

● This volume home impresses with its stately rooflines and stucco exterior. The front porch opens to an eleven-foot ceiling in the foyer. Straight ahead, an elegant living room serves as a prelude to the dramatic circular dining bay. Here, family and guests alike will revel in the fine views out the back of the house. The kitchen, with its advantageous snack bar, offers an abundance of counter and cabinet space. The media room, with its closet space and access to a full hall bath, could easily convert to a bedroom. In the master bedroom you'll find a lengthy closet in addition to a stunning bath. Glass block provides privacy to the toilet and shower while the spa tub delights in its well-illuminated nook. Dual lavatories complete the amenities in this room.

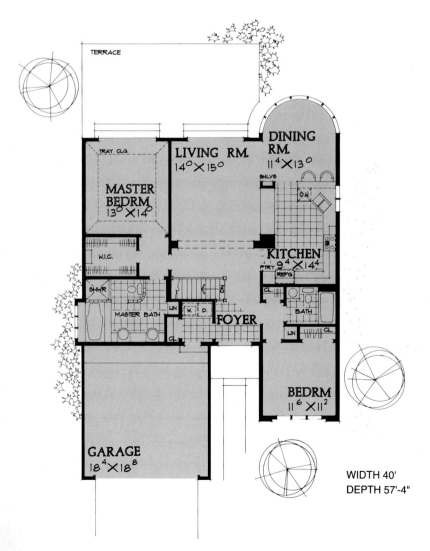

WIDTH 40'
DEPTH 57'-4"

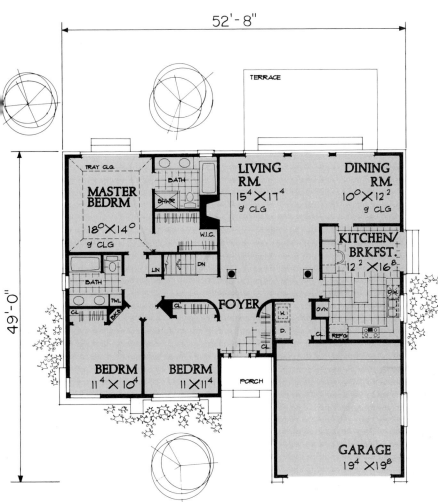

52'-8"

TERRACE

TRAY CLG.

MASTER
BEDRM
18⁰ X 14⁰
9' CLG

BATH

SHWR

W.I.C.

LIVING
RM.
15⁴ X 17⁴
9' CLG

DINING
RM.
10⁰ X 12²
9' CLG

KITCHEN/
BRKFST.
12² X 16⁸

49'-0"

BATH

TWL

CL

DRS

LIN

DN

FOYER

CL

W.

D.

OVN

CL

REFG

BEDRM
11⁴ X 10⁴

BEDRM
11⁰ X 11⁴

PORCH

GARAGE
19⁴ X 19⁸

Design BB3454

Square Footage: 1,699

L **D**

● Volume looks are achieved
through the use of a high-
pitched, hipped roof. The front
gable with lower projecting
brick pillars acts as a pleasing
architectural feature. Another
delightful architectural feature
is the radial window above the
front door; it brings an extra
measure of natural light to the
foyer. An efficient, spacious
interior comes through in this
compact floor plan. Through a
pair of columns, an open living
and dining room area creates a
warm space for all sorts of pursuits. Sliding glass doors guarantee a bright, cheerful interior
while providing easy access to
outdoor living. The L-shaped
kitchen has an island work
surface, a practical planning
desk and an informal eating
space. The breakfast area has
access to an outdoor living
area—perfect for enjoying a
morning cup of coffee. Sleeping
arrangements are defined by the
master suite with its tray ceiling
and sliding glass doors to the
yard as well as two family
bedrooms.

Design BB3569
Square Footage: 1,981

L **D**

● A graceful entry opens
this impressive one-story
design; the foyer introduces
an open gathering room/din-
ing room combination. A
front-facing study could easily convert into a bedroom for
guests—a full bath is directly
accessible from the rear of
the room. In the kitchen,
such features as an island
cooktop and a built-in desk
add to livability. A corner
bedroom takes advantage of
front and side views. The
master bedroom accesses the
rear terrace and also sports a
bath with dual lavatories and
a whirlpool. Other special
features of the house include
multi-pane windows, a
warming fireplace, a cozy
covered dining porch and a
two-car garage. Note the
handy storage closet in the
laundry area.

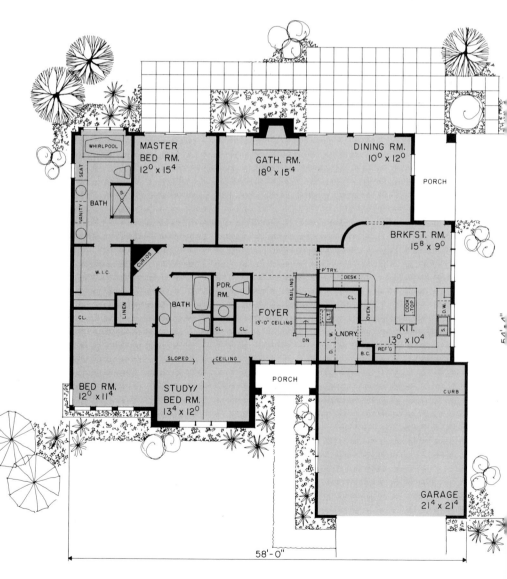

ONE-STORY HOMES
Over 2,000 Square Feet

*I*f you are like most empty-nesters, this is a time when you are really able to enjoy life. Your children are on their own and there's time and energy for doing all the things you never could before. Perhaps you'll want to pursue a new hobby. Maybe you'll investigate the possibility of working out of a home office. You might even make good on your resolutions to get in shape. Whatever pursuits you foresee, you'll want the space to make it happen. Larger one-story homes accommodate these changes in lifestyle easily. While allowing convenient access to every zone of the house, they also contain all of the spaces for an enhanced way of life. Formal living and dining spaces are offset nicely by more casual family and gathering rooms. You'll also find dens and studies, unique gourmet kitchens, plenty of terrace and patio space, and special areas for hobbies and exercise. Many plans include very special features, such as a greenhouse (see Design BB3357 on page 111) or His and Hers walk-in closets (see Design BB2880 on page 120).

Design BB3440
Square Footage: 2,300

L **D**

● Pack 'em in! There's plenty of room for everyone in this three-, or optional four-bedroom home. The expansive gathering room welcomes family and guests with a through-fireplace to the dining room, an audio/visual center, and a door to the outside. The kitchen includes a wide pantry, a snack bar, and a separate eating area. Included in the master suite: two walk-in closets, shower, whirlpool tub and seat, dual vanities, and linen storage.

CUSTOMIZABLE

Custom Alterations? See page 221 for customizing this plan to your specifications.

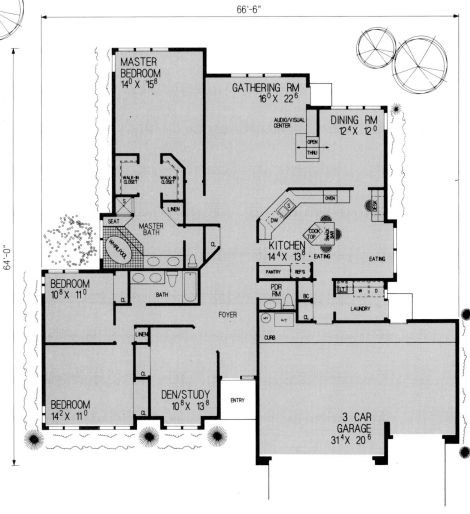

Design BB3408

Square Footage: 2,406

L

● Interesting angles make for interesting rooms. The sleeping zone features two large bedrooms with unique shapes and a master suite with spectacular bath. A laundry placed nearby is both convenient and economical, located adjacent to a full bath. The central kitchen offers a desk and built-in breakfast table. Meals can also be enjoyed in the adjacent eating area, formal dining room with stepped ceiling, or outside on the rear patio. A planter and glass block wall separate the living room and family room, which is warmed by a fireplace.

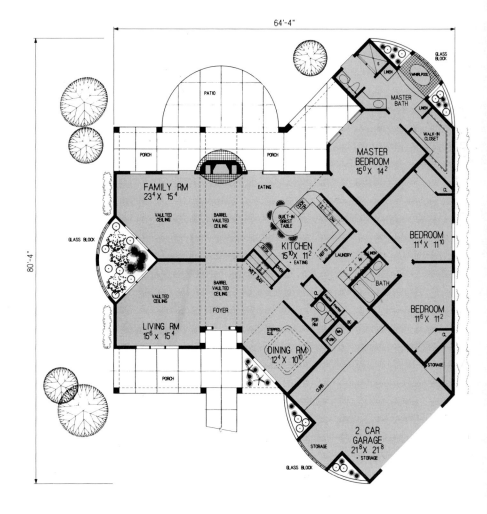

Design BB3319

Square Footage: 2,274

L **D**

● This attractive bungalow design separates the master suite from family bedrooms and puts casual living to the back in a family room. The formal living and dining areas are centrally located and have access to a rear terrace, as does the master suite. The kitchen sits between formal and informal living areas. The two family bedrooms are found to the front of the plan. A home office or study opens off the front foyer and the master suite.

Custom Alterations? See page 221 for customizing this plan to your specifications.

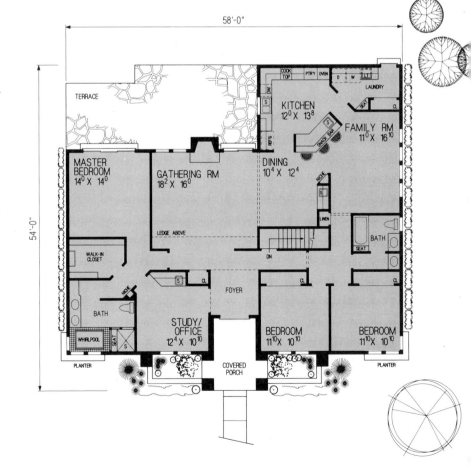

Design BB3559

Square Footage: 2,916

L D

● Intricate details make the most of
this lovely one-story: high, varied
rooflines, circle and half-circle window
detailing, multi-pane windows and a
solid chimney stack. The floor plan
caters to comfortable living. Besides
the living room/dining room area to
the rear, there is a large conversation
area with fireplace and plenty of windows. The kitchen is separated from
living areas by an angled snack-bar
counter. A media room to the front of
the plan provides space for more private activities. Three bedrooms grace
the right side of the plan. The master
suite features a tray vaulted ceiling
and sliding glass doors to the rear terrace. The dressing area is graced by
His and Hers walk-in closets, a double-
bowl lavatory and a compartmented
commode. The shower area is highlighted with glass block and is sunken
down one step. A garden whirlpool
finishes off the area.

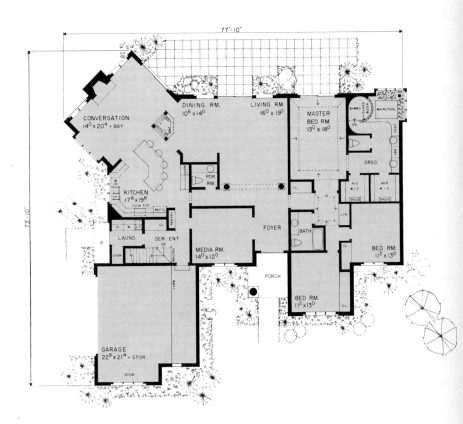

Custom Alterations? See page 221
for customizing this plan to your
specifications.

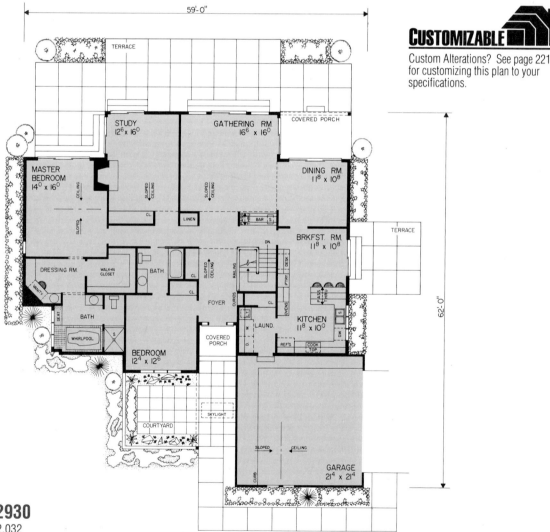

Design BB2930

Square Footage: 2,032

● The clean lines of this L-shaped contemporary are enhanced by the interesting, wide overhanging roof planes. Horizontal and vertical siding compliment one another. The low privacy fence adds interest as it forms a delightful front courtyard adjacent to the covered walkway to the front door.

Here's a floor plan made to order for the active small family or empty-nesters. Sloping ceilings and fine glass areas foster a spacious interior. The master bedroom has an outstanding dressing room and bath layout. The guest room has its own full bath. Note how this bath can function as a handy

powder room. A favorite room will be the study with its fireplace and two sets of sliding glass doors. Don't miss the open-planned gathering and dining rooms, or the kitchen/laundry area. The breakfast room has its own terrace. Notice the rear covered porch. Fine indoor-outdoor relationships.

Design BB3560
Square Footage: 2,189

Simplicity is the key to the stylish good looks of this home's facade. A walled garden entry and large window areas appeal to outdoor enthusiasts. Inside, the kitchen forms the hub of the plan. It opens directly off the foyer and contains an island counter and work counter with eating space on the living area side. A sloped ceiling, fireplace, and sliding glass doors to a rear terrace are highlights in living area. The master bedroom also sports sliding glass doors to the terrace. Its dressing area is enhanced with double walk-in closets and lavatories. A whirlpool tub and seated shower are additional amenities. Two family bedrooms are found on the opposite side of the house. They share a full bath with twin lavatories.

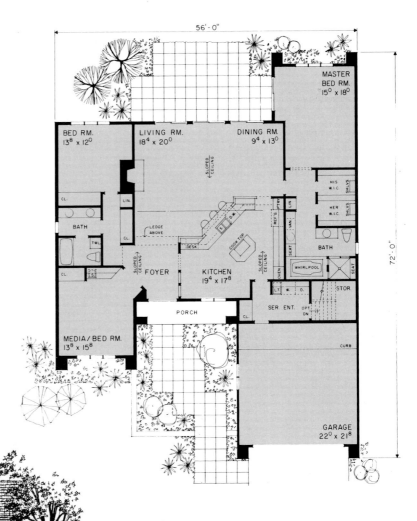

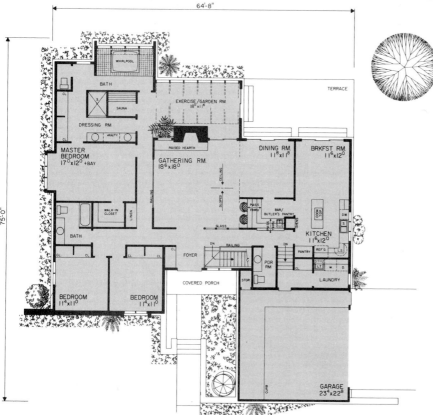

Design BB2873
Square Footage: 2,838

● This modern three-bedroom home incorporates many of the Contemporary features so popular today. A large gathering room with cozy raised-hearth fireplace and sloped ceiling is central focus and centrally located. Adjacent to the gathering room is a dining room that adjoins a bar or butler's pantry. This handy service area also has pass-thru entry to the central gathering room. Just off the pantry is a large modern kitchen with central cook-top island and adjoining breakfast room. The master bedroom suite is especially luxurious with its own sauna, whirlpool, dressing room, bay window, and adjoining exercise room. This adjacent exercise room could double as a lovely garden room. It's located just off the back terrace. There's even a powder room for guests in front, and a covered porch to keep visitors dry. A laundry is conveniently located off the spacious two-car garage. Note the large view glass off the rear exercise/garden room. This is a comfortable and modern home, indeed.

Design BB2858
Square Footage: 2,231

● This sun oriented design was created to face the south. By doing so, it has minimal northern exposure. It has been designed primarily for the more temperate U.S. latitudes using 2 x 6 wall construction. The morning sun will brighten the living and dining rooms along with the adjacent terrace. Sun enters the garden room by way of the glass roof and walls. In the winter, the solar heat gain from the garden room should provide relief from high energy bills. Solar shades allow you to adjust the amount of light that you want to enter in the warmer months. Interior planning deserves mention, too. The work center is efficient. The kitchen has a snack bar on the garden room side and a serving counter to the dining room. The breakfast room with laundry area is also convenient to the kitchen. Three bedrooms are on the northern wall. The master bedroom has a large tub and a separate shower with a four foot square skylight above. When this design is oriented toward the sun, it should prove to be energy efficient and a joy to live in.

Design BB3368
Square Footage: 2,722

L **D**

● Roof lines are the key to the interesting exterior of this design. Their configuration allows for sloped ceilings in the gathering room and large foyer. The master bedroom suite has a huge walk-in closet, garden whirlpool and separate shower. Two family bedrooms share a full bath. One of these bedrooms could be used as a media room with pass-through wet bar. Note the large kitchen with conversation bay and the wide terrace to the rear.

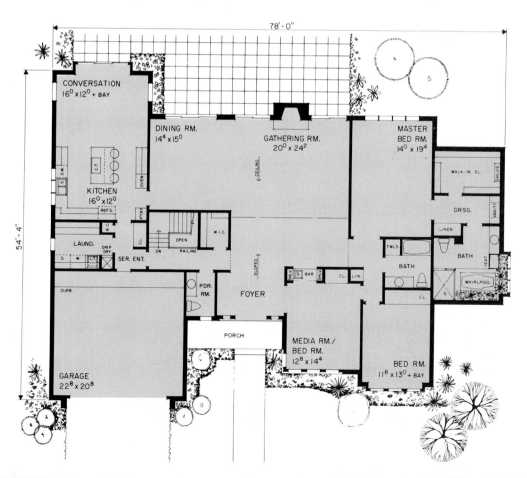

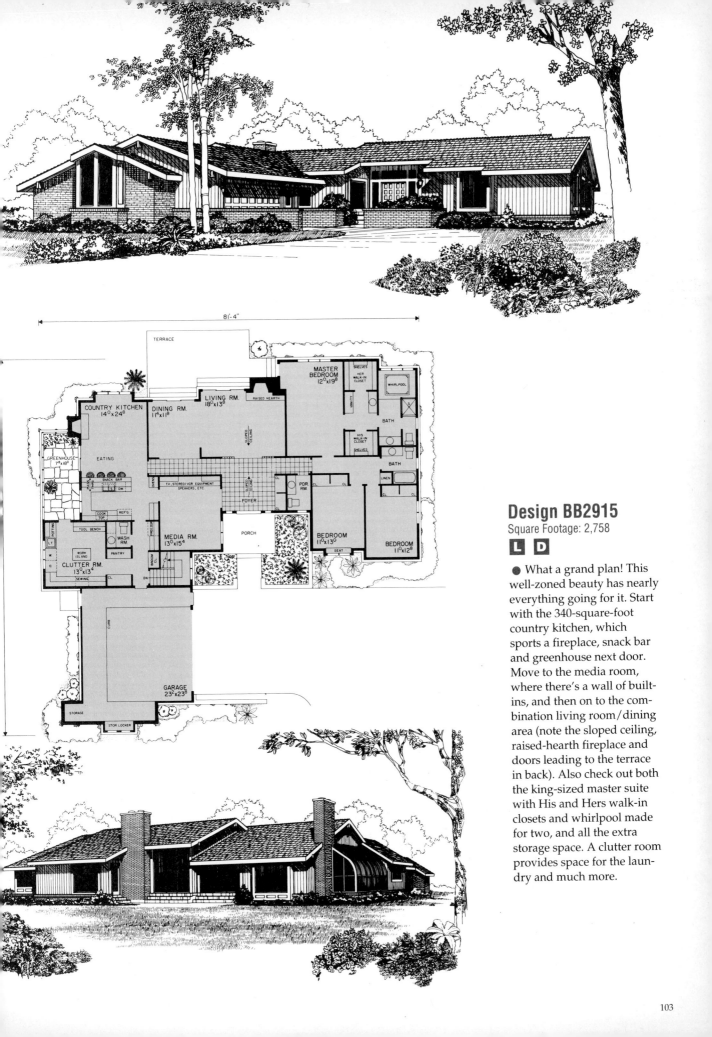

TERRACE

81'-4"

COUNTRY KITCHEN
14⁰x24⁸

DINING RM.
11⁴x11⁸

LIVING RM.
18⁰x13⁸

RAISED HEARTH

MASTER BEDROOM
12⁰x19⁸

SHELVES

HER WALK-IN CLOSET

WHIRLPOOL

BATH

GREENHOUSE
7⁸x18⁰

EATING

SNACK BAR

SLOPED CEILING

HIS WALK-IN CLOSET

SHELVES

BATH

OVEN

T.V. STEREO/VCR EQUIPMENT
SPEAKERS, ETC.

CL

PDR RM.

CL

CL

LINEN

COOK TOP

REF'G

DW

FOYER

CL

TOOL BENCH

PANTRY

MEDIA RM.
13⁰x15⁴

PORCH

BEDROOM
11⁰x13⁰

WASH RM.

WORK ISLAND

PREEZER

BROOM CL.

BEDROOM
11⁰x12⁸

POTTING

CLUTTER RM.
13⁰x13⁴

SEWING

CL

DN

SEAT

CURB

GARAGE
23²x23⁸

STORAGE

STOR LOCKER

Design BB2915

Square Footage: 2,758

L D

● What a grand plan! This well-zoned beauty has nearly everything going for it. Start with the 340-square-foot country kitchen, which sports a fireplace, snack bar and greenhouse next door. Move to the media room, where there's a wall of built-ins, and then on to the combination living room/dining area (note the sloped ceiling, raised-hearth fireplace and doors leading to the terrace in back). Also check out both the king-sized master suite with His and Hers walk-in closets and whirlpool made for two, and all the extra storage space. A clutter room provides space for the laundry and much more.

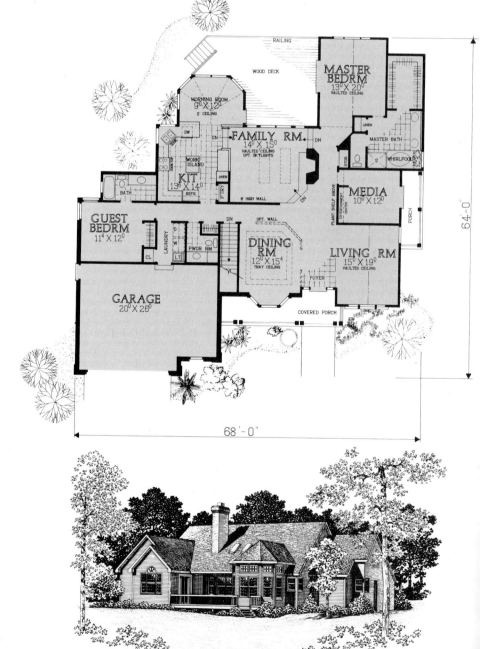

Design BB3600
Square Footage: 2,195

● This unique one-story plan seems tailor-made for a small family or for empty-nesters. Formal areas are situated well for entertaining—living room to the right and formal dining room to the left. A large family room is found to the rear. It has access to a rear wood deck and is warmed in the cold months by a welcome hearth. The U-shaped kitchen features an attached morning room for casual meals. It is near the laundry and a washroom. Bedrooms are split. The master suite sits to the right of the plan and has a walk-in closet and fine bath. A nearby study has a private porch. One family bedroom is on the other side of the home and also has a private bath. If needed, the plan can also be built with a third bedroom sharing the bath.

Design BB1754
Square Footage: 2,080

D

● Boasting a traditional Western flavor, this rugged U-shaped ranch home has the features to assure grand living. The front flower court, inside the high brick wall, creates a delightfully dramatic atmosphere which carries inside. The floor plan is positively unique and exceptionally livable. Wonderfully zoned, the three bedrooms enjoy their full measure of privacy. The formal living and dining rooms function together in a most pleasing fashion. The laundry, kitchen, informal eating and family room fit together to guarantee efficient living patterns.

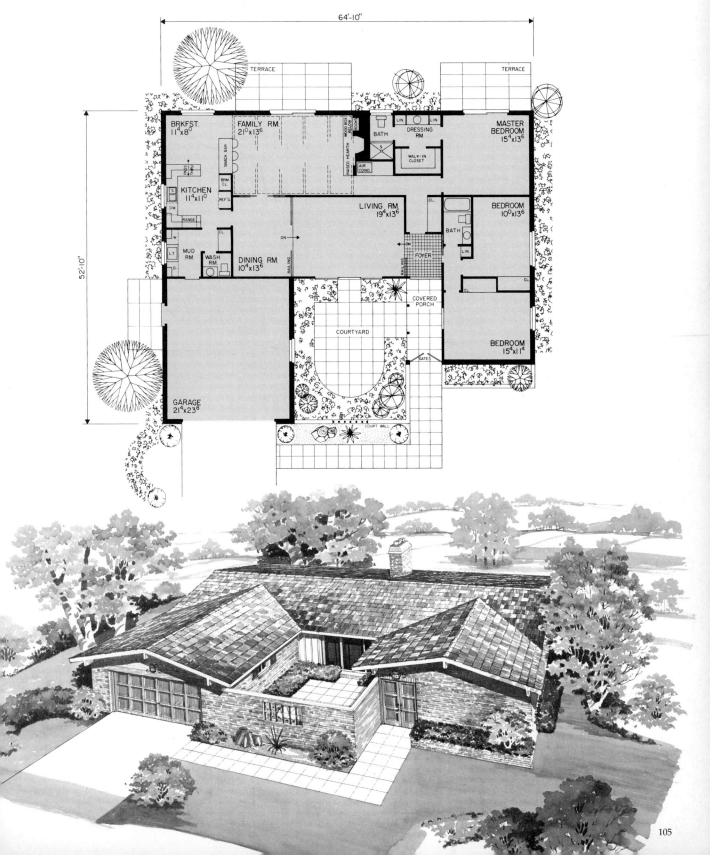

Design BB2789
Square Footage: 2,732

L **D**

● An attached three car garage! What a fantastic feature of this three bedroom contemporary design. And there's more. As one walks up the steps to the covered porch and through the double front doors the charm of this design will be overwhelming. Inside, a large foyer greets all visitors and leads them to each of the three areas, each down a few steps. The living area has a large gathering room with fireplace and a study adjacent on one side and the formal dining room on the other. The work center has an efficient kitchen with island range, breakfast room, laundry and built-in desk and bar. Then there is the sleeping area. Note the raised tub with sloped ceiling.

Design BB2778
Square Footage: 2,761

D

● No matter what the occasion, family and friends alike will enjoy the sizable gathering room which is featured in this plan. A spacious 20' x 23', this room has a thru-fireplace to the study and two sets of sliding glass doors to the large rear terrace. Indoor-outdoor living can also be enjoyed from the dining room, study and master bedroom; all located to face the rear yard. There is a covered dining porch, too, accessible through sliding glass doors in the dining and breakfast rooms. A total of three bedrooms are planned for this design. Each has plenty of closet space. Notice the high lights of the master suite: large walk-in closet, tub plus stall shower and exercise area.

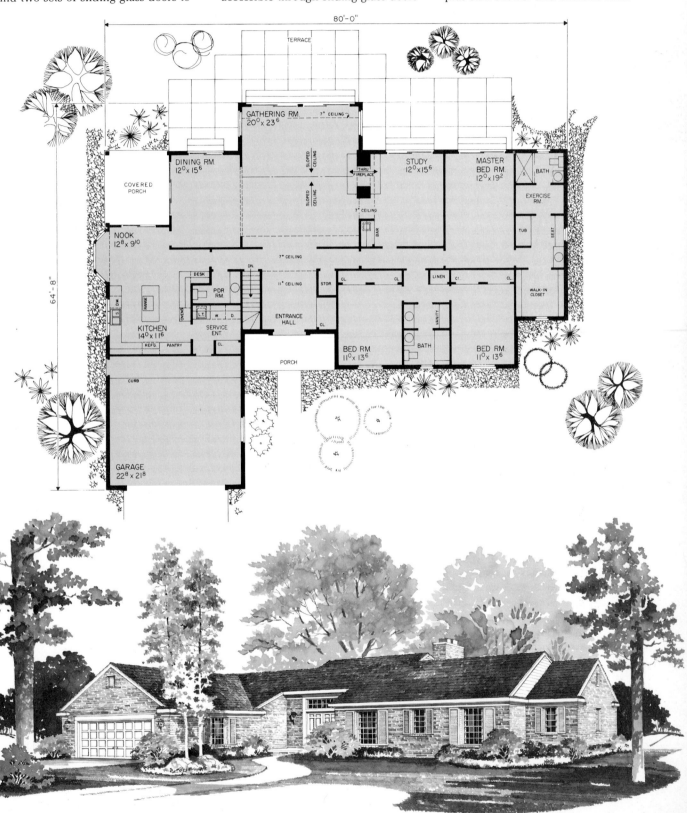

TERRACE

TERRACE

BED RM.
16⁸ x 13⁸

LIVING RM.
21⁴ x 14⁰

NOOK
11⁶ x 9⁸

FAMILY RM.
15¹⁰ x 21⁸

BATH

BED RM.
13⁰ x 12⁰

RANGE OVENS

KITCHEN
11⁶ x 12⁰

SNACK BAR

RAISED HEARTH

LIN.

AIR COND.

DINING RM.
14⁰ x 13⁰

CHINA BOOKS

PANTRY

REF'G

D.W.

S.

LAUNDRY

LIN. CL. CL. CL.

CHINA BOOKS

LINEN CL. CL.

CL.

STUDY
10⁸ x 10⁴

LT W. D.

BATH

GALLERY

SEAT DRESSING RM.

PORCH

TUB VANITY

WALK-IN CLOSET

MASTER BED RM.
13⁰ x 18⁴

GARAGE
21¹⁰ x 23⁸

76'-0"

66'-8"

Design BB2784
Square Footage: 2,980

● The projection of the master bedroom and garage create an inviting U-shaped area leading to the covered porch of this delightful traditionally styled design. After entering through the double front doors, the gallery will lead to each of the three living areas: the sleeping wing of two bedrooms, full bath and study; the informal area of the family room with raised hearth fireplace and sliding glass doors to the terrace and the kitchen/nook area (the kitchen has a pass-thru snack bar to the family room); and the formal area consisting of a separate dining room with built-in china cabinets and the living room. The master bedroom suite, with its lovely bay window, has a large dressing area with a window seat and a walk-in closet. Notice the separate tub and shower in the master bath.

Design BB2594
Square Footage: 2,294

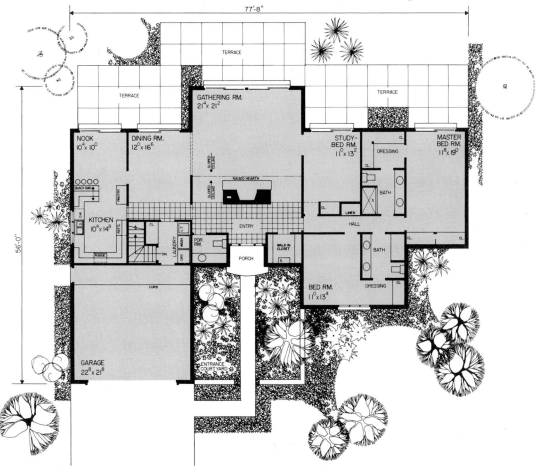

● This handsome home offers a delightful plan for today's home owner. The tiled entry gives way to a spectacular gathering room. In it, a raised-hearth fireplace takes center stage. Two sets of sliding glass doors make up the back wall of the room and lead to an array of terraces out back. The dining room shares in the gathering room's grandness with its roomy interior and outdoor access. The kitchen provides a wealth of storage space and services a breakfast nook with a snack-bar pass-through.

A laundry room adds to everyday conveniences as well as offering passage to the two-car garage. The sleeping quarters are comprised of two secondary bedrooms—one could serve as a study, if desired—and an expansive master bedroom.

Floor plan labels (main level):

TERRACE

GATHERING RM.
17⁴ x 20²

SKYLIGHT

OPEN TO LOWER LEVEL

TERRACE

GARDEN, BOAT, STOR. GARAGE
11⁴ x 21⁰

WALK-IN CLOSET

MASTER BED RM.
12² x 16⁰

DRESSING RM.

BATH

TUB

DINING RM.
12² x 13⁰

KITCHEN
10⁰ x 19⁰

EATING

PANTRY

FAMILY RM.
13⁴ x 19⁰

WALK-IN CLOSET

OPEN

DN.

SHELVES

SHELVES

DESK

COUNTER

LAUNDRY

SERV. ENT.

WASH. DRY.

ENTRY

BATH

BATH

LINEN

LINEN

PORCH

STUDY
11⁸ x 12⁰

CURB

BED RM.
11⁶ x 13⁸

BED RM.
11⁶ x 13⁸

GARAGE
23⁴ x 23⁸

87'-8"

60'-8"

Basement level:

BASEMENT

OPEN TO GATHERING RM. ABOVE

WOOD BOX

FAMILY RM.
27² x 19⁸

CRAWL SPACE

GAMES
19⁰ x 12⁸ – 16⁸

UP

DN.

DN.

UNEX.

UNEX.

Design BB2721
Square Footage: 2,667

● Visually exciting! A sunken gathering room with a sloped ceiling, raised hearth fireplace, corner balcony and skylight . . . the last two features shared by the formal dining room. There's more. Two family rooms . . . one on the lower level (1,153 sq. ft.) with a raised hearth fireplace, another adjacent to the kitchen with a snack bar! Plus a study and game room. A lavish master suite and two large bedrooms. A first floor laundry and reams of storage space, including a special garage for a boat, sports equipment, garden tools etc. There's plenty of space for family activities in this home. From chic dinner parties for friends to birthday gatherings for kids, there's always the right setting . . . and so much room that adults and children can entertain at the same time.

Design BB3357
Square Footage: 2,913

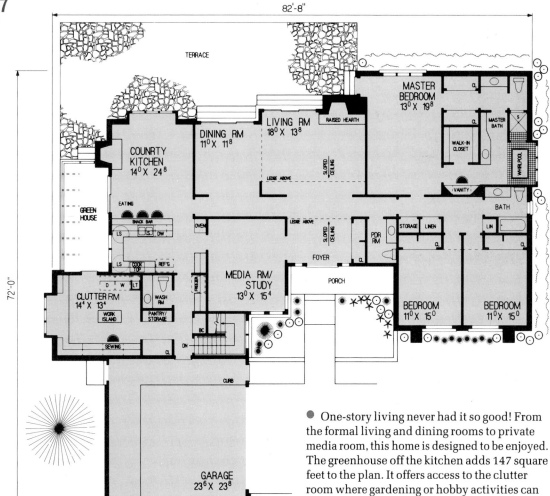

● One-story living never had it so good! From the formal living and dining rooms to private media room, this home is designed to be enjoyed. The greenhouse off the kitchen adds 147 square feet to the plan. It offers access to the clutter room where gardening or hobby activities can take place. A the opposite end of the house are a master bedroom with generous bath and two family bedrooms. Notice the wealth of built-ins throughout the house.

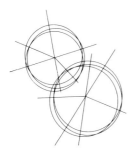

CUSTOMIZABLE

Custom Alterations? See page 221 for customizing this plan to your specifications.

Design BB3346

Square Footage: 2,032

● This home boasts a delightful Tudor exterior with a terrific interior floor plan. Though compact, there's plenty of living space: large study with fireplace, gathering room, dining room, and breakfast room. The master bedroom has an attached bath with whirlpool tub. Note the double walk-in closets.

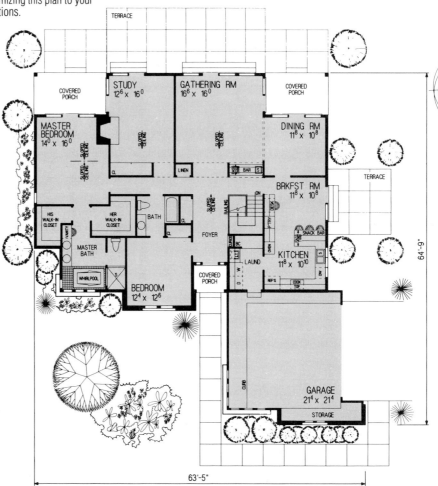

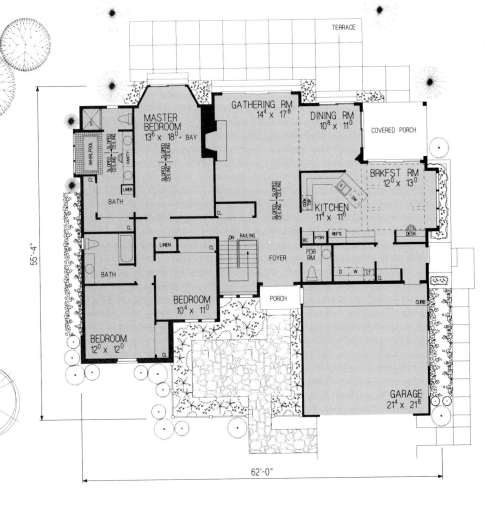

TERRACE

MASTER BEDROOM
13⁶ x 18⁰, BAY

GATHERING RM
14⁴ x 17⁸

DINING RM
10⁸ x 11⁰

COVERED PORCH

WHIRLPOOL

SLOPED CEILING

SLOPED CEILING

VANITY

LINEN

CL

BATH

SLOPED CEILING

SLOPED CEILING

CL

BRKFST RM
12⁰ x 13⁰

KITCHEN
11⁴ x 11⁶

LINEN

CL

DN RAILING

UP

FOYER

PDR RM

BC P'TRY REFG

DESK

D W LT CL

55'-4"

BATH

BEDROOM
10⁴ x 11⁰

PORCH

CURB

BEDROOM
12⁰ x 12⁰

CL

GARAGE
21⁴ x 21⁸

62'-0"

Design BB3336
Square Footage: 2,022

● Compact and comfortable! This three-bedroom home is a good consideration for a small family or empty-nester retirees. Of special note are the covered eating porch and sloped ceilings in the gathering room and master bedroom. The master bath accommodates every need with a whirlpool tub and shower, closet space, vanity and dual sinks. Stairs to the basement and a well-placed powder room are found at the front entry.

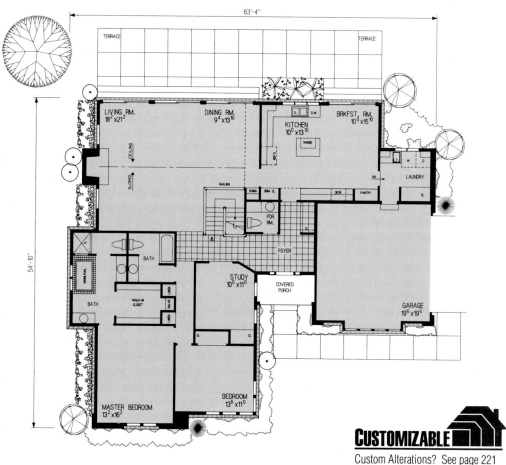

Design BB2962

Square Footage: 2,112

● A Tudor exterior with an efficient floor plan favored by many. Each of the three main living zones — the sleeping zone, living zone, and the working zone — are but a couple steps from the foyer. This spells easy, efficient traffic patterns. Open planning,

sloping ceiling and plenty of glass create a nice environment for the living-dining area. Its appeal is further enhanced by the open staircase to lower level recreation/hobby area. The L-shaped kitchen with its island range and work surface is delightfully opened

to the large breakfast room. Again, plenty of glass area adds to the feeling of spaciousness. Nearby is the step-saving first floor laundry. The sleeping zone has the flexibility of functioning as a two or three bedroom area. Notice the economical back-to-back plumbing.

61'-8"

56'-8"

MASTER BED RM. 12⁴ x 15⁸

WHIRLPOOL

GATHERING RM. 16⁰ x 18⁸

DINING RM. 14⁴ x 10⁰ + BAY

CEILING

BATH

SLOPED

CEILING

RANGE

PTRY

BAR

KITCHEN 11⁰ x 9⁰

DW.

REF'G.

DRSG.

VANITY

SLOPED

RAILING

BED RM. 11⁰ x 10⁴

CL.

CL.

CURIOS

CL.

DN.

BRKFST. RM. 13⁸ x 8⁴

T.V.-V.C.R.-STEREO

FOYER

PDR. RM.

SER. ENT.

LAUND.

LEDGE

LIN.

CL.

L.T. W. D.

BATH

PORCH

CURB

MEDIA RM. 13⁰ x 14⁰

BED RM. 12⁴ x 12⁸

CL.

GARAGE 19⁰ x 21⁸

Design BB3377
Square Footage: 2,217

L **D**

● This Tudor design provides a handsome exterior complemented by a spacious and modern floor plan. The sleeping area is positioned to the left side of the home. The master bedroom features an elegant bath with whirlpool, shower, dual lavs and a separate vanity area. Two family bedrooms share a full bath. A media room exhibits the TV, VCR and stereo. The enormous gathering room is set off by columns and contains a fireplace and sliding doors to the rear terrace. The dining room and breakfast room each feature a bay window.

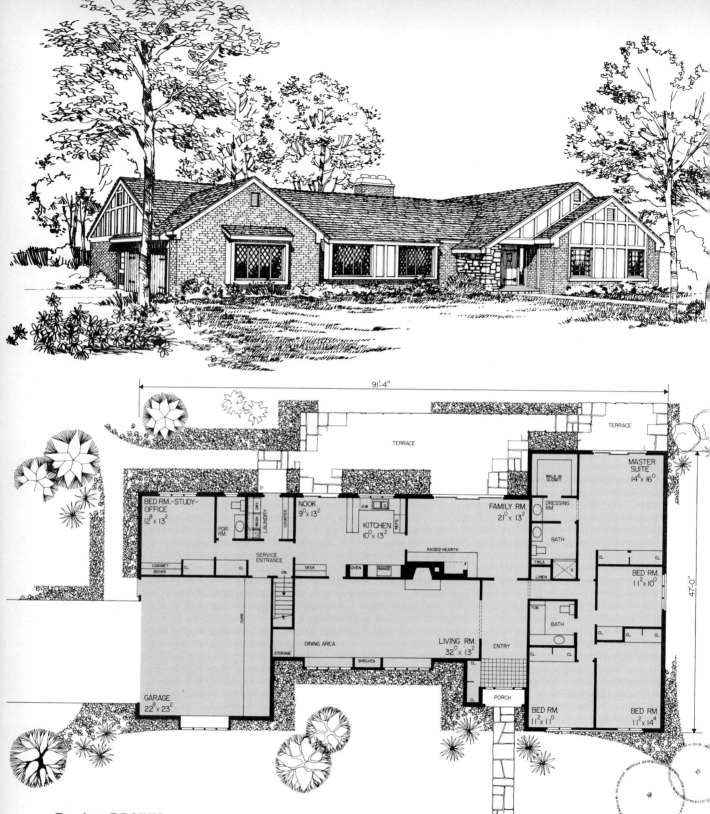

Design BB2573

Square Footage: 2,747

L D

● A Tudor ranch! Combining brick and wood for an elegant look. It has a living/dining room measuring 32' by 13', large indeed. It is fully appointed with a traditional fireplace and built-in shelves, flanked by diagonally paned windows. There's much more! There is a family room with a raised hearth fireplace and sliding glass doors that open onto the terrace. A U-shaped kitchen has lots of built-ins . . . a range, an oven, a desk. Plus a separate breakfast nook. The sleeping facilities consist of three family bedrooms plus an elegant master bedroom suite. A conveniently located laundry with a folding counter is in the service entrance. Adjacent to the laundry is a washroom. The corner of the plan has a study or make it a fifth bedroom if you prefer.

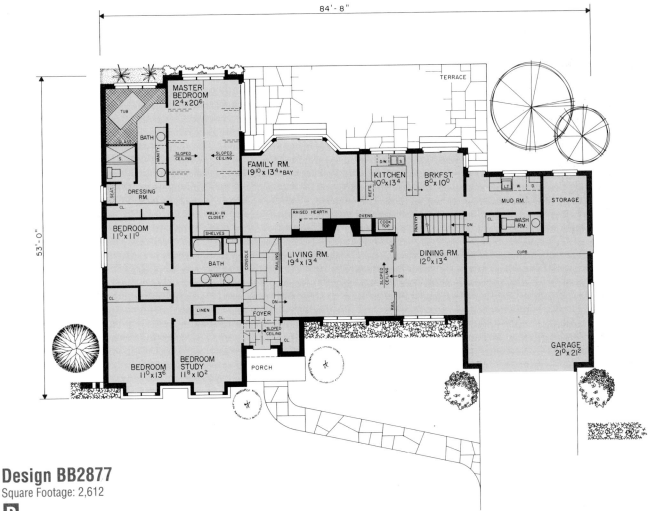

Design BB2877
Square Footage: 2,612

D

● Here's a dramatic, Post-Modern exterior with a popular plan featuring an outstanding master bedroom suite. The bedroom itself is spacious, has a sloped ceiling, a large walk-in closet and sliding glass doors to the terrace. Now ex-amine the bath and dressing area. Two large closets, twin vanities, built-in seat and a dramatically presented corner tub are present. The tub will be a great place to spend the evening hours after a long, hard day. Along with this bed-room, there are three more served by a full bath. The living area of this plan has the formal areas in the front and the informal areas in the rear. Both have a fireplace. The spacious work center is efficiently planned.

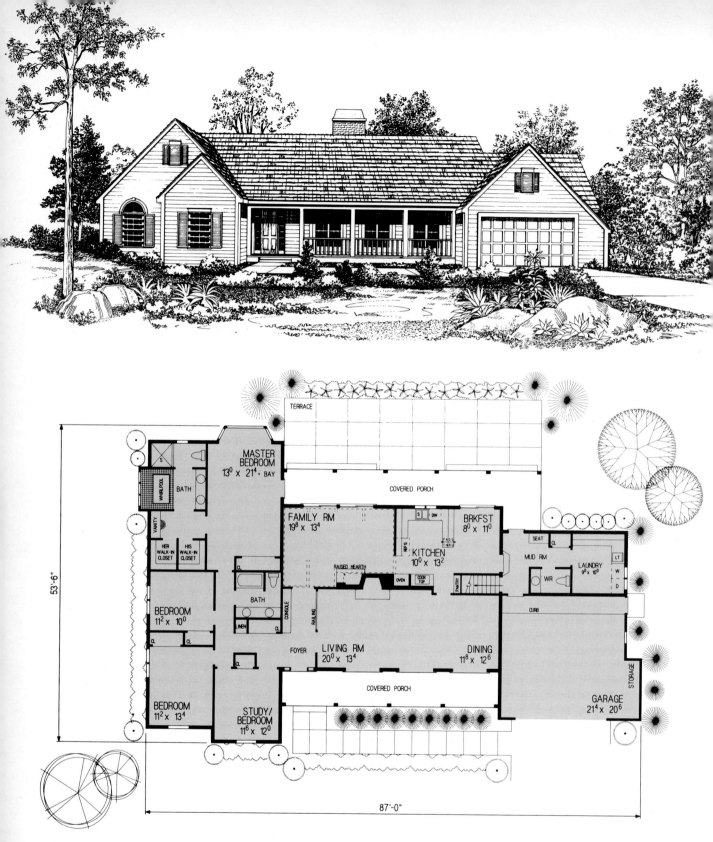

Design BB3348
Square Footage: 2,549

● Covered porches front and rear will be the envy of the neighborhood when this house is built. The interior plan meets family needs perfectly in well-zoned areas: a sleeping wing with four bedrooms and two baths, a living zone with formal and informal gathering space, and a work zone with U-shaped kitchen and laundry with washroom. The master bedroom with deluxe bath, including His and Hers walk-in closets, is noteworthy. Open planning and fireplaces enhance the living areas. Extra storage space is provided in the two-car garage.

Design BB3332

Square Footage: 2,168

● Nothing completes a traditional-style home quite as well as a country kitchen with fireplace. Notice also the sloped-ceiling living room and well-appointed master suite. A handy washroom is near the laundry, just off the garage.

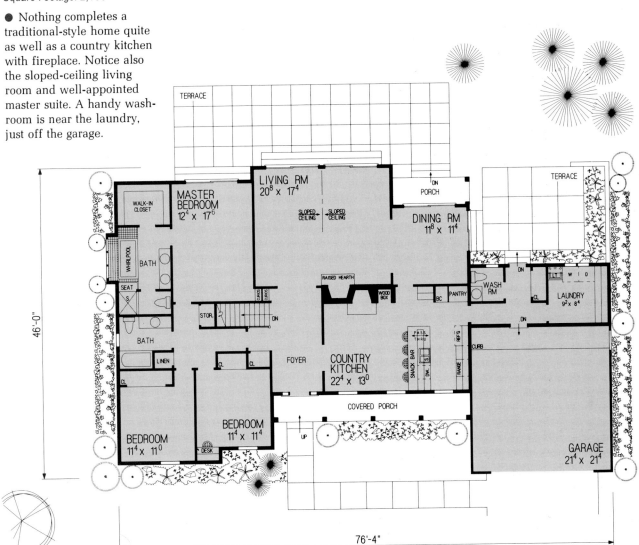

TERRACE

MASTER BEDROOM
12⁴ x 17⁶

WALK-IN CLOSET

WHIRLPOOL

SEAT

BATH

BATH

LINEN

CL

STOR.

CL CL

FOYER

BEDROOM
11⁴ x 11⁰

DESK

BEDROOM
11⁴ x 11⁴

UP

LIVING RM
20⁸ x 17⁴

SLOPED CEILING SLOPED CEILING

RAISED HEARTH

WOOD BOX

DN

COUNTRY KITCHEN
22⁴ x 13⁰

SNACK BAR

PASS THRU

DW

RANGE

COVERED PORCH

PORCH

DN

DINING RM
11⁸ x 11⁴

BC PANTRY

WASH RM

CL

REFG

CURB

TERRACE

DN

W D

LT

LAUNDRY
9² x 8⁴

GARAGE
21⁴ x 21⁴

46'-0"

76'-4"

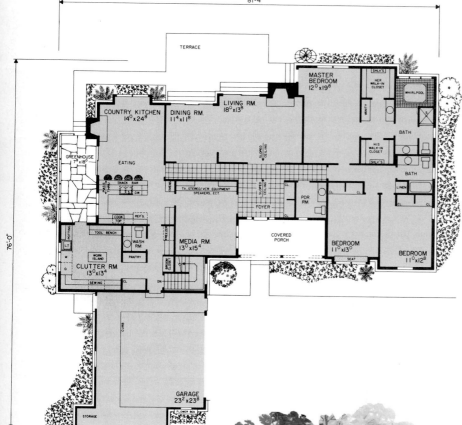

TERRACE

COUNTRY KITCHEN
14⁰x24⁸

DINING RM.
11⁴x11⁸

LIVING RM.
18⁰x13⁸

MASTER BEDROOM
12⁰x19⁸

HER WALK-IN CLOSET

WHIRLPOOL

VANITY

BATH

GREENHOUSE
7⁹x18⁰

EATING

HIS WALK-IN CLOSET

SHLV'S

BATH

LINEN

SNACK BAR

TV, STEREO/VCR EQUIPMENT
SPEAKERS, ECT.

PDR. RM.

CL

CL

SLOPED CEILING

FOYER

TOOL BENCH

WASH RM.

PANTRY

MEDIA RM.
13⁰x15⁴

COVERED PORCH

BEDROOM
11⁰x13⁰

SEAT

BEDROOM
11⁰x12⁸

WORK ISLAND

CLUTTER RM.
13⁰x13⁴

SEWING

DN

GARAGE
23²x23⁸

STORAGE

FLOWER BOX

81'-4"

76'-0"

Design BB2880

Square Footage: 2,907

● This comfortable traditional home offers plenty of modern livability. A clutter room off the two-car garage is the perfect space for workbench, sewing, and hobbies. It includes a work island and bench space. Across the hall one finds a modern media room, the perfect place for stereo speakers, videos, and more. A spacious country kitchen off the greenhouse is a cozy gathering place for family and friends, as well as convenient work area. The 149-foot greenhouse itself easily could be the focal point of this home filled with modern amenities. The house also features a formal dining room, living room with fireplace, covered porch, and three bedrooms including a master bedroom suite.

CUSTOMIZABLE

Custom Alterations? See page 221 for customizing this plan to your specifications.

PLANS WITH TWO OR MORE LEVELS

*S*ometimes a one-story home just isn't enough or doesn't provide the kind of livability you're looking for. Though not specifically designed for the empty-nester lifestyle, many two-story, split-level and hillside homes prove to be the perfect solution to a new way of living. The collection presented in this section allows empty-nesters to live essentially on one floor for most daily situations. On additional floors are secondary bedrooms, play rooms, summer kitchens, lounges, hobby rooms, guest apartments, studios and other optional spaces. Smaller in square footage than most plans with more than one story, these homes will allow empty-nesters who appreciate the space and style of more than one level to enjoy single-level convenience and livability. Represented are styles from ultra-contemporaries to elegant traditionals and farmhouses. Some plans even have unfinished space that can be developed later on as needed. (See Design BB2828 on page 124 and Design BB2887 on page 127.)

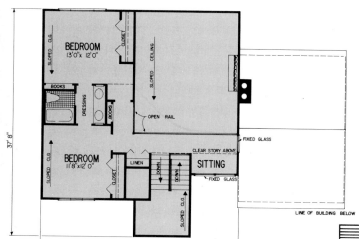

Design BB4115

Entry Level: 1,494 square feet
Upper Level: 597 square feet
Total: 2,091 square feet

● Interior spaces are dramatically proportioned because of the long and varied roof lines of this contemporary. The two-story living area has a sloped ceiling as does the master bedroom and two upper-level bedrooms. Two fireplaces, a huge rear wooden deck, a small upstairs sitting room, and a liberal number of windows make this a most comfortable vacation residence.

LIFESTYLE
HOME PLANS

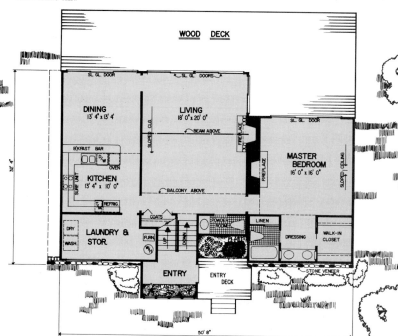

Design BB4308

First Floor: 1,494 square feet
Second Floor: 597 square feet
Basement Level: 1,035 square feet
Total: 3,126 square feet

L

● You can't help but feel spoiled by this design. Behind the handsome facade lies a spacious, amenity-filled plan. Downstairs from the entry is the large living room with sloped ceiling and fireplace. Nearby is the U-shaped kitchen with a pass-through to the din-ing room — a convenient step-saver. Also on this level, the master suite boasts a fireplace and a sliding glass door onto the deck. The living and din-ing rooms also feature deck access. Upstairs are two bedrooms and shared bath. A balcony sitting area overlooks the living room. The enormous lower-level playroom includes a fireplace, a large bar, and sliding glass doors to the patio. Also notice the storage room with built-in workbench.

Design BB2828

First Floor: 1,078 square feet
Second Floor: 1,066 square feet
Total: 2,144 square feet

● The first floor of this contemporary home features an interior kitchen with a snack bar, a living room with raised-hearth fireplace, and a dining room. The first-floor bedroom will make a great guest suite with nearby full bath and terrace access. Upstairs, a large master bedroom is joined by two family bedrooms, one of which could easily serve as a nursery, office or media room. Also notice the two balconies, three skylights and sewing/hobbies room upstairs. Storage space is available everywhere you look—hall closets on second floor, in the first floor laundry room and garage, and in the basement plan.

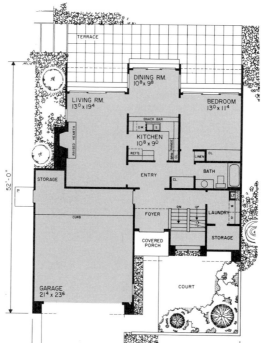

Design BB2827

Upper Level: 1,618 square feet
Lower Level: 1,458 square feet
Total: 3,076 square feet

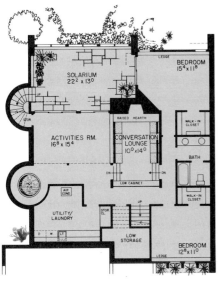

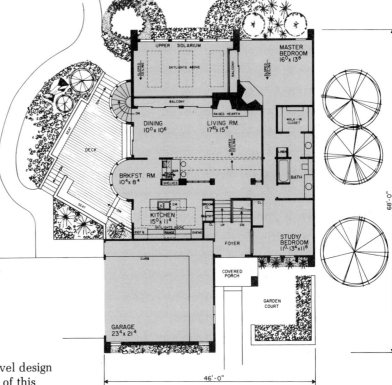

The towering, two-story solarium in this bi-level design is its key to energy savings. Study the efficiency of this floor plan. The conversation lounge on the lower level is a unique focal point.

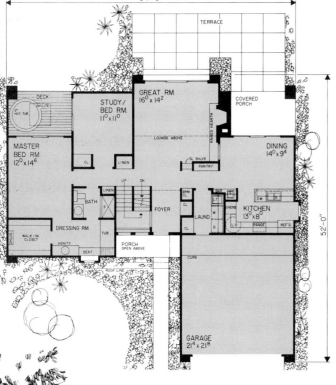

Design BB2822

First Floor: 1,363 square feet
Second Floor: 351 square feet
Total: 1,714 square feet

L

● Here is a truly unique house whose interior was designed with the current decade's economies, lifestyles and demographics in mind. While functioning as a one-story home, the second floor provides an extra measure of livability when required. In addition, this two-story section adds to the dramatic appeal of both the exterior and the interior. Within only 1,363 square feet, this contemporary delivers refreshing and outstanding living patterns for those who are buying their first home, those who have raised their family and are looking for a smaller home and those in search of a retirement home.

ALTERNATE SECOND FLOOR

Design BB2887

First Floor: 1,338 square feet
Second Floor: 661 square feet
Total: 1,999 square feet

● This attractive, contemporary 1½-story will be the envy of many. First, examine the efficient kitchen. Not only does it offer a snack bar for those quick meals but also a large dining room. Notice the adjacent dining porch. The laundry and garage access are also adjacent to the kitchen. An exciting feature is the gathering room with fireplace. The first floor also offers a study with a wet bar and sliding glass doors that open to a private porch. This will make those quiet times cherishable. Adjacent to the study is a full bath followed by a bedroom. Upstairs a large master bedroom suite occupies the entire floor. It features a bath with an oversized tub and shower, a large walk-in closet with built-ins and an open lounge with fireplace. Both the lounge and master bedroom, along with the gathering room, have sloped ceilings. Develop the lower level for additional space.

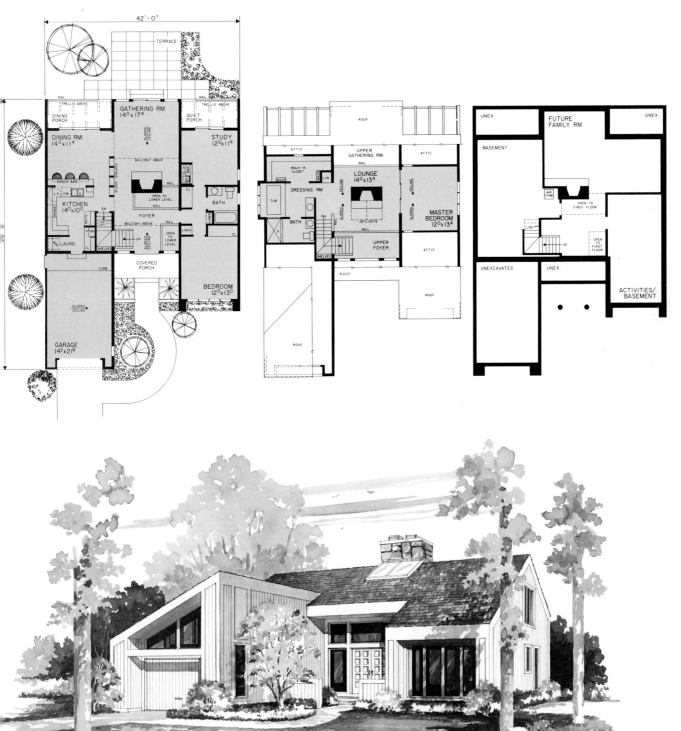

Design BB3450

First Floor: 1,801 square feet
Second Floor: 1,086 square feet
Total: 2,887 square feet

L **D**

● A striking facade includes a covered front porch with four columns. To the left of the foyer is a large gathering room with a fireplace and bay window. The adjoining dining room leads to a covered side porch. The kitchen includes a snack bar, pantry, desk, and eating area. The first-floor master suite provides a spacious bath with walk-in closet, whirlpool and shower. Also on the first floor: a study and a garage workshop. Two bedrooms and a lavish guest suite share the second floor.

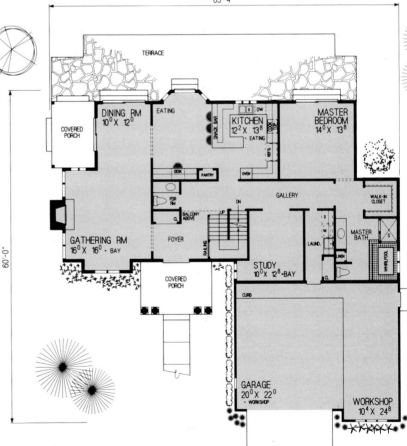

CUSTOMIZABLE
Custom Alterations? See page 221 for customizing this plan to your specifications.

Design BB3323

First Floor: 1,923 square feet
Second Floor: 838 square feet
Total: 2,751 square feet

● This two-story southwestern home was
designed to make living patterns as pleasant
as they can be. Take a step down from the
foyer and go where your mood takes you: a
gathering room with fireplace and an alcove
for reading or quiet conversations, a media
room for enjoying the latest technology, or to
the dining room with sliding glass doors to
the terrace. The kitchen has an island range
and eating space. Also on the first floor is a
large master suite including a sitting area
with terrace access, walk-in closet and
whirlpool. An elegant spiral staircase leads to
two family bedrooms sharing a full bath and
a guest bedroom with private bath.

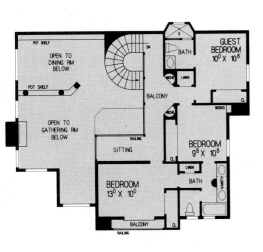

CUSTOMIZABLE

Custom Alterations? See page 221
for customizing this plan to your
specifications.

Design BB3573

First Floor: 1,650 square feet
Second Floor: 1,508 square feet
Total: 3,158 square feet
Bonus Room: 275 square feet
Bedroom Option: 176 square feet

L **D**

● A design for the times, this beautiful transitional home may be built with a fourth bedroom and/or a first-floor bonus room. The entrance court introduces a covered porch. Inside, the tiled foyer offers a dramatic space comprised of a dining room on the left and, separated by a staircase, a living room on the right. Both rooms enjoy their own terrace. Casual living takes off in the family room with its terrace. An expansive kitchen backs up the plan and includes a walk-in pantry and an island countertop. Upstairs, overlooking the dining room, a hallway branches off into three bedrooms, including a delightful master suite. Here, highlights range from two balconies to a bath with a whirlpool tub.

ENTRANCE COURT

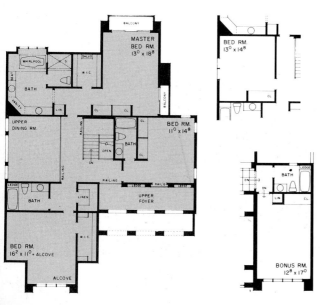

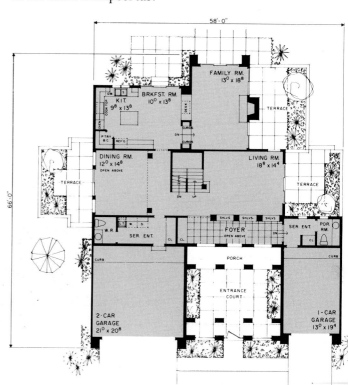

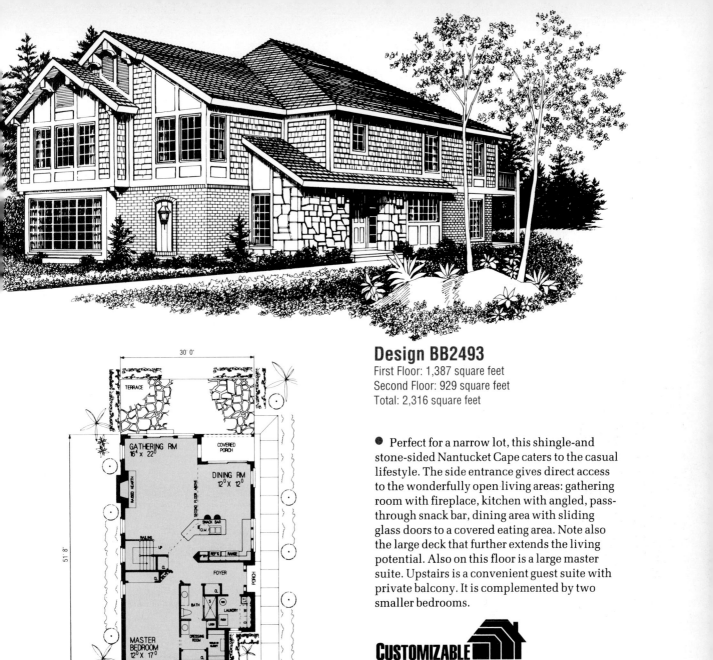

Design BB2493

First Floor: 1,387 square feet
Second Floor: 929 square feet
Total: 2,316 square feet

● Perfect for a narrow lot, this shingle-and-stone-sided Nantucket Cape caters to the casual lifestyle. The side entrance gives direct access to the wonderfully open living areas: gathering room with fireplace, kitchen with angled, pass-through snack bar, dining area with sliding glass doors to a covered eating area. Note also the large deck that further extends the living potential. Also on this floor is a large master suite. Upstairs is a convenient guest suite with private balcony. It is complemented by two smaller bedrooms.

CUSTOMIZABLE

Custom Alterations? See page 221 for customizing this plan to your specifications.

Design BB3393

First Floor: 1,449 square feet
Second Floor: 902 square feet
Total: 2,351 square feet

L **D**

● A turreted facade, dormer window and fish-scale shingle details make this moderately sized Victorian stand out at a glance. Its well-designed floor plan makes it even more attractive. Notice how guests as well as family are accommodated: powder room in the front foyer; gathering room with terrace access, fireplace and attached formal dining room; split-bed-room sleeping arrangements. The master suite contains His and Hers walk-in closets, a separate shower and whirlpool tub and a delightful bay-windowed area. Upstairs there are three more bedrooms (one could serve as a study, one as a media room), a full bath and an open lounge area overlooking the gathering room. Notice the covered porches front and rear and long terrace area.

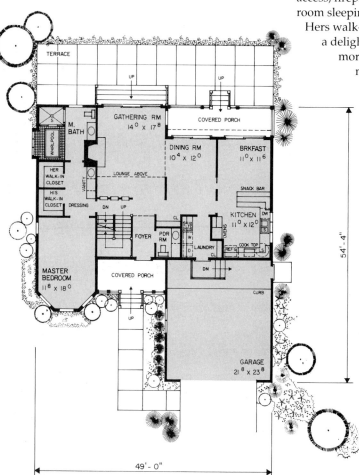

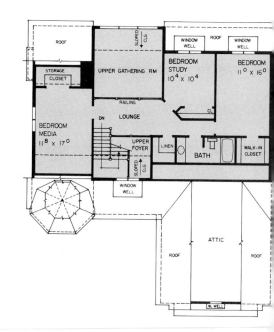

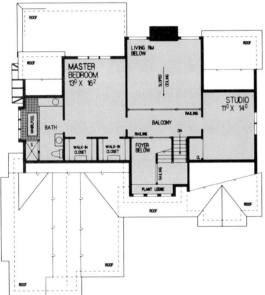

Design BB3390

First Floor: 1,508 square feet
Second Floor: 760 square feet
Total: 2,268 square feet

 L **D**

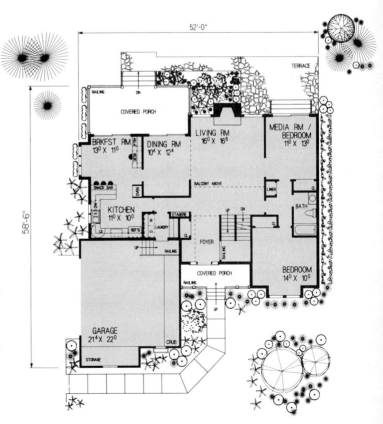

● This two-story farmhouse will be a delight for those who spend much time working at home. The second floor offers the utmost in privacy, with a secluded master bedroom full of comforting features and a studio for more industrious pursuits. Downstairs is a very livable floor plan. A U-shaped kitchen with snack bar and breakfast area with bay window and desk are only the first of the eating areas, which extend to a formal dining room and a covered rear porch for dining al fresco. The two-story living room features a cozy fireplace. A versatile room to the back could serve as a media room or a third bedroom, sharing a full bath with the large front bedroom with bay window.

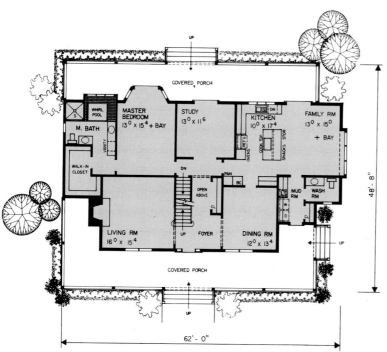

Design BB3396

First Floor: 1,829 square feet
Second Floor: 947 square feet
Total: 2,776 square feet

L **D**

● Rustic charm abounds in this pleasant farm-house rendition. Covered porches to the front and rear enclose living potential for the whole family. Flanking the entrance foyer are the living and dining rooms. To the rear is the L-shaped kitchen with island cook top and snack bar. A small family room/breakfast nook is attached. A private study is tucked away on this floor next to the master suite. On the second floor are three bedrooms and a full bath. Two of the bedrooms have charming dormer windows.

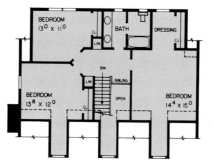

LUXURY HOMES
Over 3,000 Square Feet

For the homes in this section, luxury is not just a state of mind, it's a reality. Each is imbued with an attention to amenities and stylish flair that sets it apart from the average home. However, all maintain the same uncomplicated livability that empty-nest couples are looking for. In mostly two- and three-bedroom models, these luxury homes satisfy contemporary and traditional tastes. The floor plans include uniquely configured rooms; spacious, well-appointed master suites; specialty areas for hobbies, work or exercise; three-car garages; and hearth-warmed conversation areas. The homes include many design points—such as angled rooms, volume ceilings and elaborate entry foyers—that give them a special touch. Be sure to notice the split-bedroom personality of many of these homes. (Design BB2920 on page 139 and Design BB3557 on page 140 are good examples.)

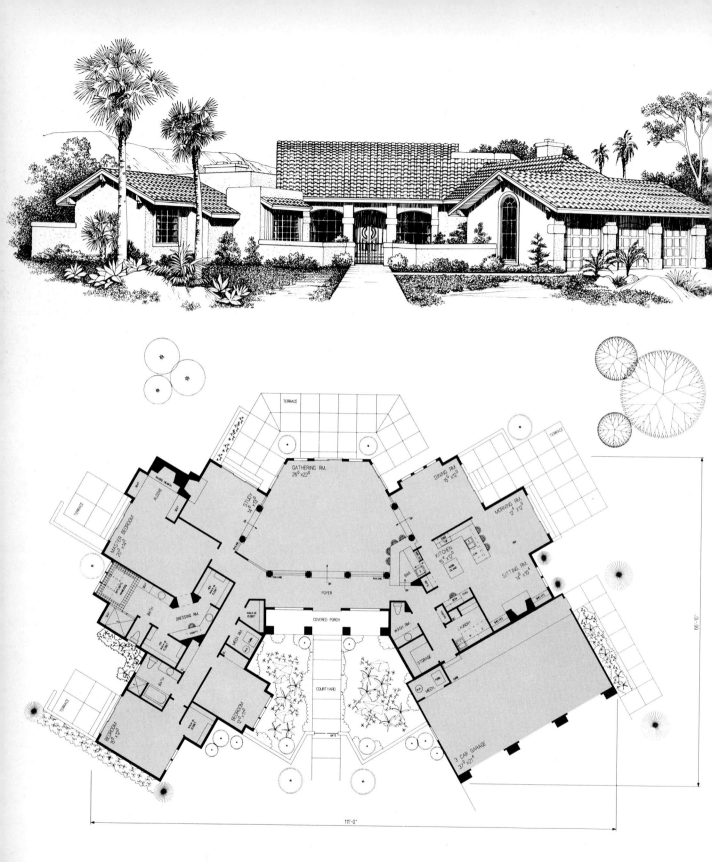

Design BB2922
Square Footage: 3,505

● Loaded with custom features, this plan seems to have everything imaginable. There's an enormous sunken gathering room and cozy study. The country-style kitchen contains an efficient work area, as well as space for relaxing in the morning and sitting rooms. Two nice-sized bedrooms and a luxurious master suite round out the plan.

Design BB3475

Square Footage: 3,286

L

● Transcend the ordinary with
this dazzling Floridian house. A
covered porch serves as a
friendly introduction to a truly
pampering design. Inside, the
foyer gives way to a sunken living room which features a corner fireplace and double doors
that lead to a covered terrace in
back. The dining room exhibits
elegance with its views overlooking a front garden. The
kitchen will delight with its
fully efficient layout that incorporates an island work station
and a round counter separating
the breakfast nook. Here you'll
also find a family room for more
casual living. Two bedrooms on
this side of the house enjoy
abundant closet space. On the
other side of the house, the master suite provides a true escape
from the hustle and bustle of the
day. A terrace offers outside
livability while, inside, the
amenities include a private bath
with a corner whirlpool tub and
a walk-in closet. Down the hall,
a den with a wet bar leads to a
privacy patio and garden area.

CUSTOMIZABLE

Custom Alterations? See page 221
for customizing this plan to your
specifications.

137

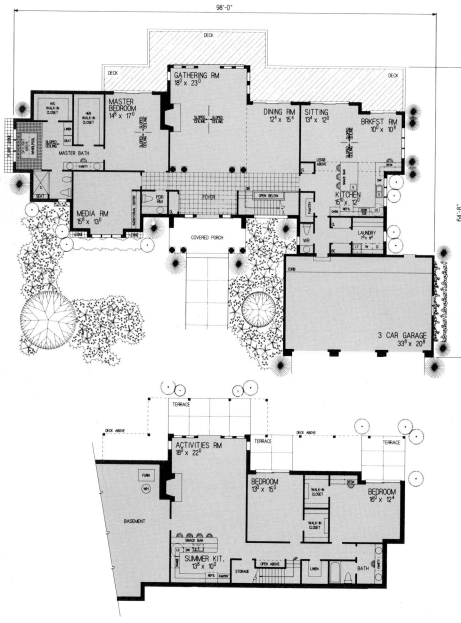

Design BB3311

Main Level: 2,662 square feet
Lower Level: 1,548 square feet
Total: 4,210 square feet

L **D**

● Here's a hillside haven for family living with plenty of room to entertain in style. Enter the main level from a dramatic columned portico that leads to a large entry hall. The gathering room is straight back and adjoins a formal dining area. A true gourmet kitchen with plenty of room for casual eating and conversation is nearby. The abundantly appointed master suite on this level is complemented by a luxurious bath. Note the media room to the front of the house. On the lower level are two more bedrooms, a full bath, a large activity area with fireplace and a convenient summer kitchen.

CUSTOMIZABLE

Custom Alterations? See page 221 for customizing this plan to your specifications.

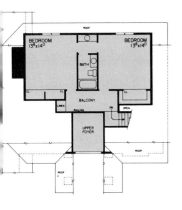

Design BB2920

First Floor: 3,067 square feet
Second Floor: 648 square feet; Total: 3,715 square feet

L **D**

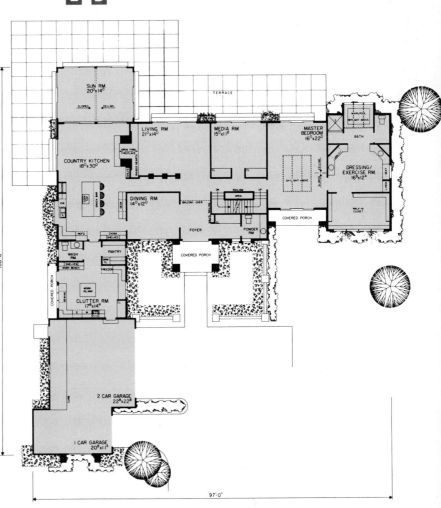

● This contemporary design also has a great deal to offer. Study the living areas. A fireplace opens up to both the living room and country kitchen. Privacy is the key word when describing the sleeping areas. the first floor master bedroom is away from the traffic of the house and features a dressing/exercise room, whirlpool tub and shower and a spacious walk-in closet. Two more bedrooms and a full bath are on the second floor. The three car garage is arranged so that the owners have use of a double-garage with an attached single on reserve for guests. The cheerful sun room adds 296 sq. ft. to the total.

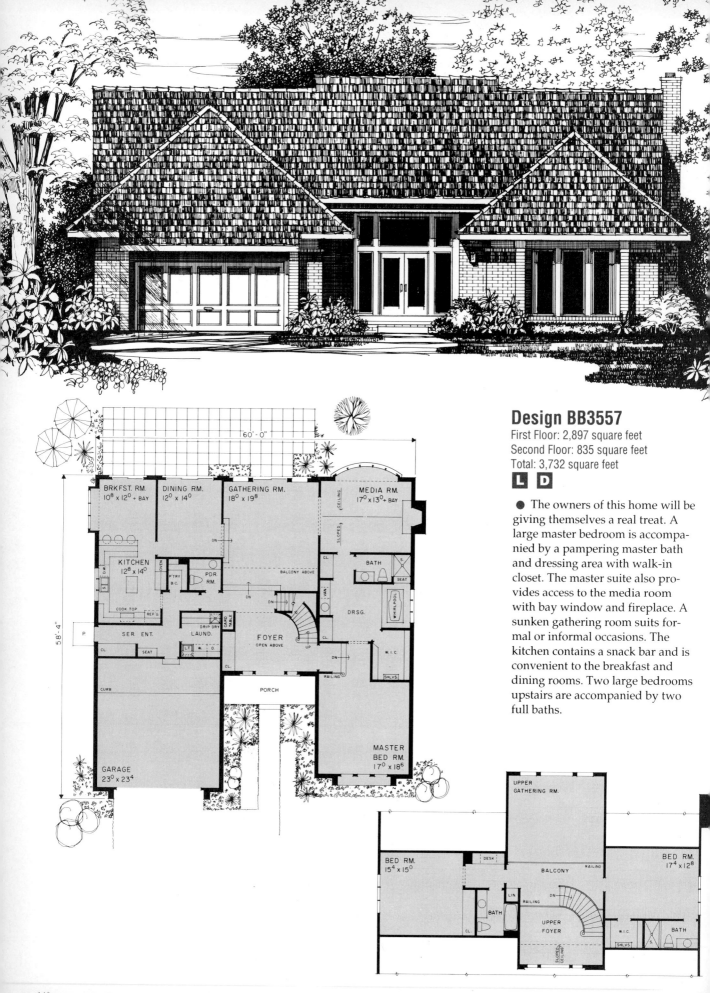

Design BB3557

First Floor: 2,897 square feet
Second Floor: 835 square feet
Total: 3,732 square feet

L D

● The owners of this home will be giving themselves a real treat. A large master bedroom is accompanied by a pampering master bath and dressing area with walk-in closet. The master suite also provides access to the media room with bay window and fireplace. A sunken gathering room suits formal or informal occasions. The kitchen contains a snack bar and is convenient to the breakfast and dining rooms. Two large bedrooms upstairs are accompanied by two full baths.

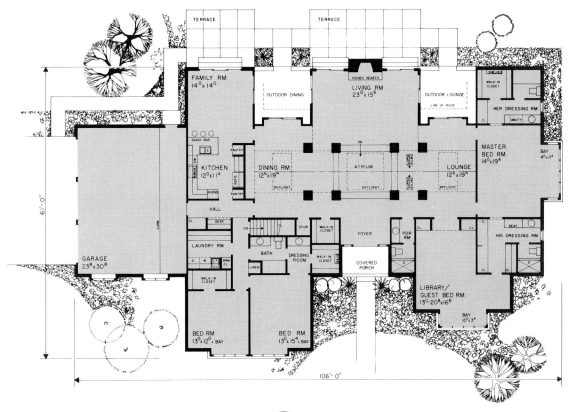

Floor plan labels:

TERRACE TERRACE

FAMILY RM. 14⁰x14⁰ OUTDOOR DINING LIVING RM. 23⁰x15⁶ OUTDOOR LOUNGE LINE OF ROOF SHELVES WALK-IN CLOSET HER DRESSING RM. CL VANITY

SNACK BAR PANTRY DN MASTER BED RM. 14⁰x19⁴ BAY 4⁰x11⁴

KITCHEN 12⁰x11⁴ DINING RM. 12⁶x19⁴ ATRIUM LOUNGE 12⁶x19⁴

RANGE D/W REF'G SKYLIGHT SKYLIGHT SKYLIGHT

OVENS PANTRY

HALL CL DESK DN STOR WALK-IN CLOSET FOYER PDR RM CL CL SEAT HIS DRESSING RM.

LAUNDRY RM. BATH DRESSING ROOM WALK-IN CLOSET COVERED PORCH CL

D W BRM CL LINEN

GARAGE 23⁸x30⁸ WALK-IN CLOSET LIBRARY/ GUEST BED RM. 13⁰-20⁸x16⁸ BAY 10⁰x3³

BED RM. 13⁰x12⁰+ BAY BED RM. 13⁰x15⁴+ BAY

61'-0" 106'-0"

SIGNATURE SERIES LUXURY HOMES

Design BB2791
Square Footage: 3,809

● The use of vertical paned windows and the hipped roof highlight the exterior of this unique design. Upon entrance one will view a charming sunken atrium with skylight above plus a skylight in the dining room and one in the lounge. Formal living will be graciously accommodated in the living room. It features a raised-hearth fireplace, two sets of sliding glass doors to the rear terrace plus two more sliding doors, one to an outdoor dining terrace and the other to an outdoor lounge. Informal living will be enjoyed in the family room with snack bar and in the large library. All will praise the fine planning of the master suite. It features a bay window, His and Hers dressing room with private baths and an abundance of closet space.

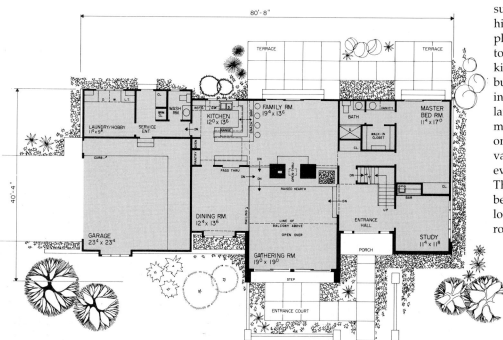

Terrace terrace

BED RM.
11⁰ x 13⁶

BED RM.
10⁰ x 10²

BATH

ATTIC

LINEN

ATTIC

CL

CEILING CLIP.

CL

ATTIC

LOUNGE
19⁰ x 9⁶

DN

UPPER ENTRANCE

BED RM.
11⁴ x 12⁰

CEILING CLIP.

RAILING

ROOF

UPPER GATHERING RM.

SLOPED CEILING

ROOF

80'-8"

TERRACE

TERRACE

40'-4"

LAUNDRY/HOBBY
19⁰ x 9⁸

WASH RM.

SERVICE ENT.

CL

REF.

FAMILY RM.
19⁴ x 13⁶

KITCHEN
12⁰ x 13⁶

RANGE

SNACK BAR

BATH

VANITY

MASTER BED RM.
11⁴ x 17⁰

WALK-IN CLOSET

CL

S

PANTRY OVEN

PASS THRU

DN

OPEN-THRU

RAISED HEARTH

DN

UP

BAR

CL

GARAGE
23⁴ x 23⁴

CURB

DINING RM.
12⁴ x 13⁶

RAILING

LINE OF BALCONY ABOVE

OPEN OVER

ENTRANCE HALL

PORCH

STUDY
11⁴ x 11⁸

GATHERING RM.
19⁰ x 19⁰

STEP

ENTRANCE COURT

Design BB2782

First Floor: 2,060 square feet
Second Floor: 897 square feet
Total: 2,957 square feet

D

● What makes this such a distinctive four-bedroom design? This plan includes great formal and informal living for the family at home or when entertaining guests. The formal gathering room and informal family room share a dramatic raised-hearth fireplace. Other features of the sunken gathering room include: high, sloped ceilings, built-in planter and sliding glass doors to the front entrance court. The kitchen has a snack bar, many built-ins, a pass-through to dining room and easy access to the large laundry/washroom. The master bedroom suite is located on the main level for added privacy and convenience. There's even a study with a built-in bar. The upper level has three more bedrooms, a bath and a lounge looking down into the gathering room.

Design BB2857

Square Footage: 2,982

L

● You'll applaud the many outstanding features of this home. Notice first the master bedroom. It has His and Hers baths, each with a large walk-in closet, sliding glass doors to a private terrace, and an adjacent study. Two family bedrooms are separate from the master for total privacy. The gathering room is designed for entertaining. It has its own balcony and a fireplace as a focal point. The U-shaped kitchen is efficient and has an attached breakfast room and snack bar pass-through to the dining room.

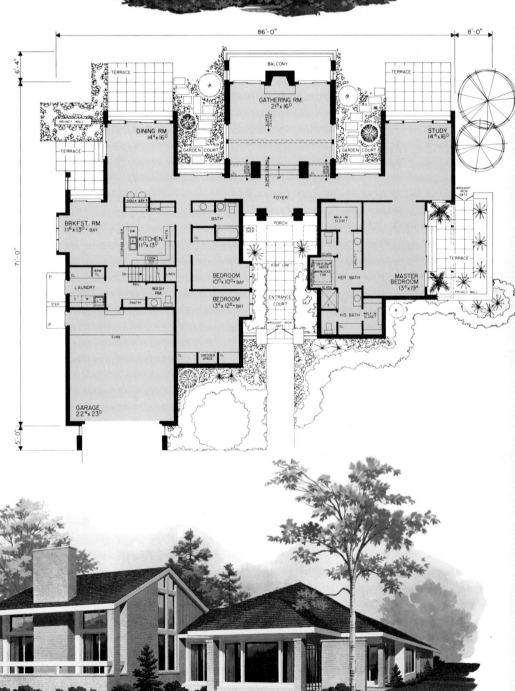

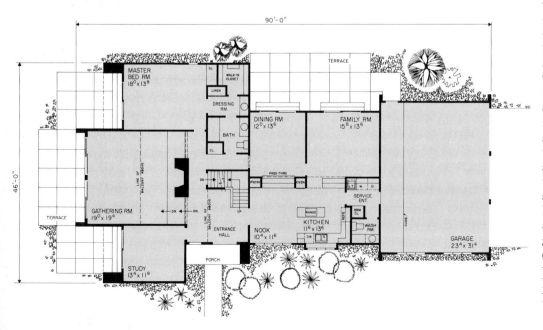

Design BB2781

First Floor: 2,132 square feet
Second Floor: 1,156 square feet
Total: 3,288 square feet

L **D**

● This beautifully designed two-story could be con-
sidered a dream house of a
lifetime. The exterior is
sure to catch the eye of
anyone who takes sight of
its unique construction.
The front kitchen features
an island range, adjacent
breakfast nook and pass-
thru to formal dining room.
The master bedroom suite
with its privacy and con-
venience on the first floor
has a spacious walk-in
closet and dressing room.
The side terrace is accessible through sliding glass
doors from the master bedroom, gathering room and
study. The second floor has
three bedrooms and storage
space galore. Also notice
the lounge which has a
sloped ceiling and a sky-
light above. This delightful
area looks down into the
gathering room. The out-
door balconies overlook the
wrap-around terrace. Surely an outstanding trend
house for decades to come.

Design BB3404

First Floor: 3,358 square feet
Second Floor: 868 square feet
Total: 4,226 square feet

L **D**

● Farmhouse design does a double take in this unusual and elegant rendition. Notice that most of the living takes place on the first floor: formal living room and dining room, gigantic family room with enormous firepit and porch access, guest bedroom or den and master bedroom suite. Upstairs there are two smaller bedrooms and a dramatic balcony overlook to the family room below.

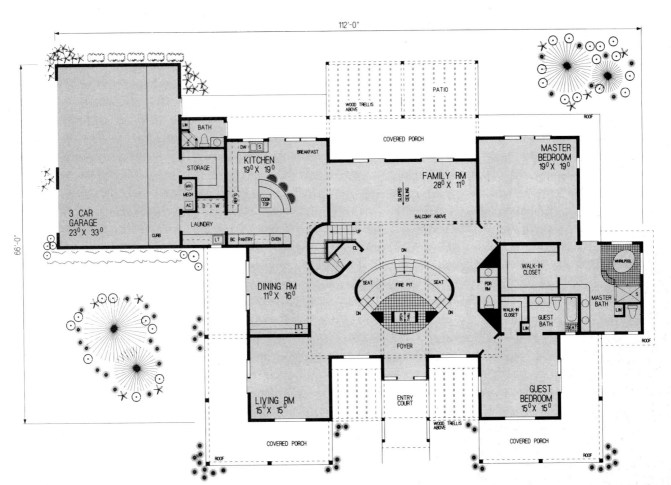

Design BB3505

First Floor: 2,899 square feet
Second Floor: 1,539 square feet
Total: 4,438 square feet

● A sweeping veranda with
tapered columns supports the low-
pitched roof and its delicately
detailed cornice work. The wood
railing effectively complements the
lattice-work below. Horizontal siding and double-hung windows
with muntins and shutters enhance
the historic appeal of this 1½-story
home. Inside, the spacious central
foyer has a high ceiling and a dramatic, curving staircase to the second floor. Two formal areas flank
the foyer and include the living
room to the left and the dining
room to the right. The U-shaped
kitchen easily services the latter
through a butler's pantry. A library
and gathering room flank the
kitchen and will delight the family.
Sleeping accommodations excel
with a spacious master suite. Here,
a private bath and two closets—
one a walk-in—guarantee satisfaction. At the top of the dramatic
staircase to the second floor is a
generous sitting area which looks
down on the foyer. Three bedrooms are directly accessible from
this area. A bonus room further
enhances this fabulous family
home.

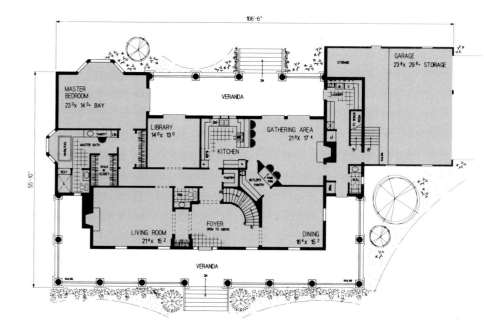

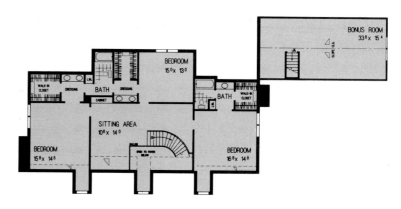

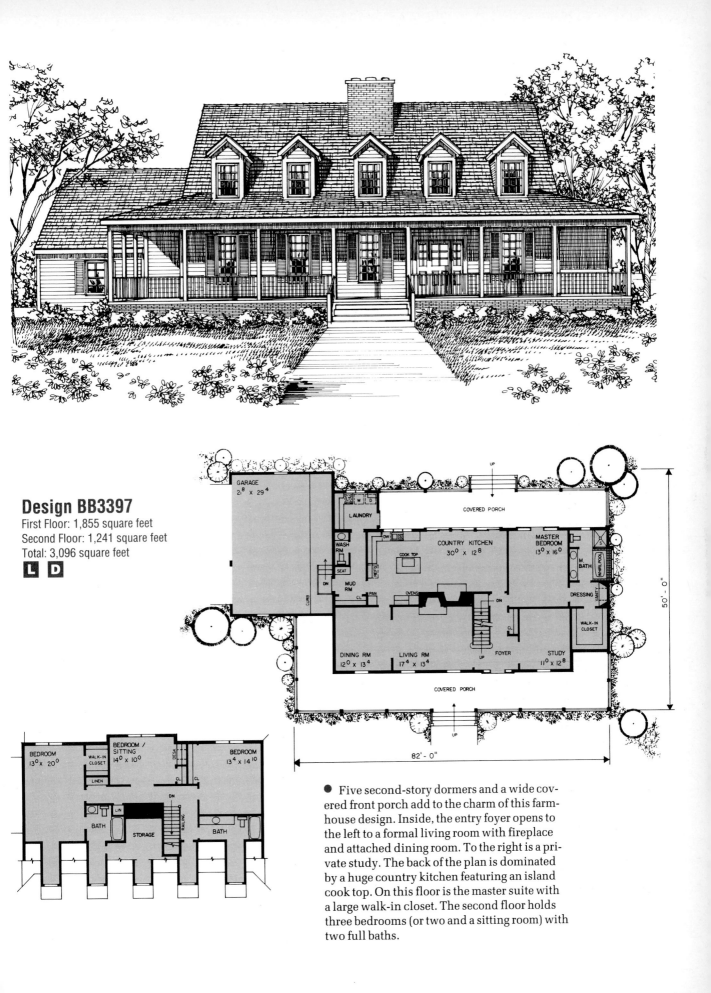

Design BB3397

First Floor: 1,855 square feet
Second Floor: 1,241 square feet
Total: 3,096 square feet

L **D**

GARAGE
2,8 x 29,4

LAUNDRY

COVERED PORCH

WASH RM

DW

COUNTRY KITCHEN
30,0 x 12,8

MASTER BEDROOM
13,0 x 16,0

SEAT

COOK TOP

REF/G

M. BATH

WHIRLPOOL

DN

MUD RM

CL

PAN

OVENS

DN

DRESSING

VANITY

CL

WALK-IN CLOSET

DINING RM
12,0 x 13,4

LIVING RM
17,4 x 13,4

UP

FOYER

STUDY
11,0 x 12,8

COVERED PORCH

82'-0"

50'-0"

UP

BEDROOM
13,0 x 20,0

WALK-IN CLOSET

LINEN

BEDROOM / SITTING
14,0 x 10,0

DESK

CL

CL

BEDROOM
13,4 x 14,10

BATH

LIN

DN

RAILING

STORAGE

BATH

● Five second-story dormers and a wide covered front porch add to the charm of this farmhouse design. Inside, the entry foyer opens to the left to a formal living room with fireplace and attached dining room. To the right is a private study. The back of the plan is dominated by a huge country kitchen featuring an island cook top. On this floor is the master suite with a large walk-in closet. The second floor holds three bedrooms (or two and a sitting room) with two full baths.

Design BB3550

First Floor: 2,328 square feet
Second Floor: 712 square feet
Total: 3,040 square feet

L **D**

● A transitional 1½-story home combines the best of contemporary and traditional elements. This one uses vertical wood siding, stone and multi-paned windows to beautiful advantage. The floor plan makes great use of space with first-floor living and dining areas and a first-floor master suite. Two secondary bedrooms, a full bath and an open lounge area are found on the second floor. The garage is accessed from the island kitchen through the laundry.

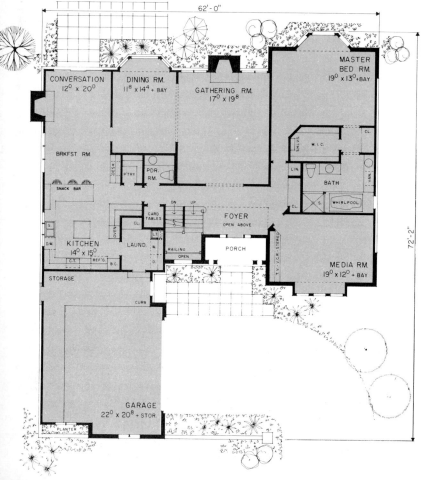

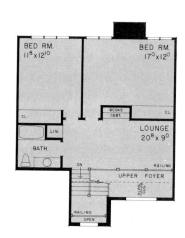

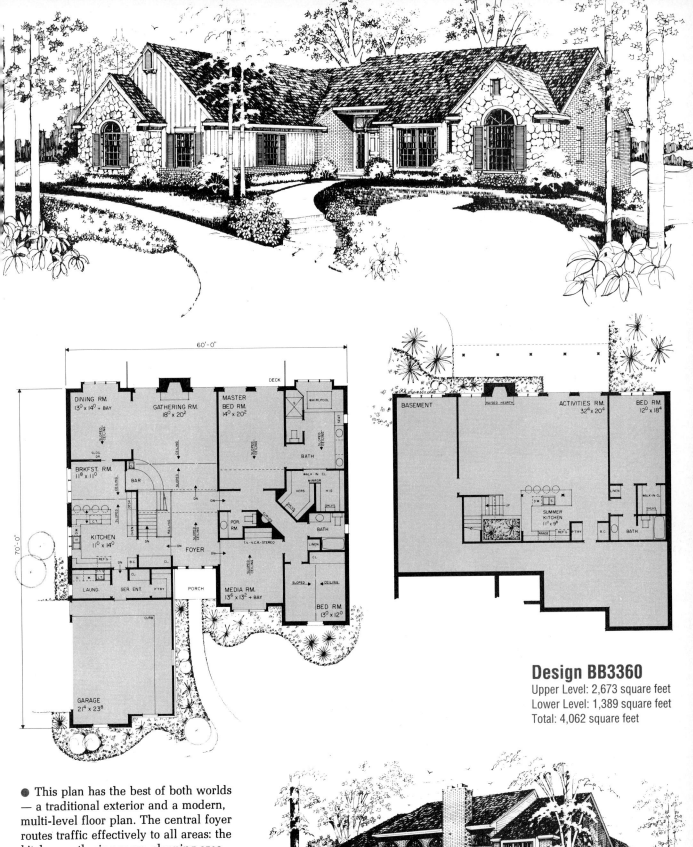

DINING RM.
13⁰ x 14⁰ + BAY

GATHERING RM.
18⁰ x 20²

MASTER BED RM.
14⁰ x 20²

DECK

WHIRLPOOL

SEAT

SLOPED CEILING

BLDG. OR

SLOPED CEILING

BATH

CEILING

SLOPED CEILING

BRKFST. RM.
11⁶ x 11⁰

BAR

DESK

SLOPED CEILING

WALK-IN CL.

HERS MIRROR HIS

OVEN

DN

DN

SHLVS

KITCHEN
11⁰ x 14⁰

SLOPED

DN

DN

SLOPED CEILING

FOYER

POR. RM.

BATH

C.T.

REF.

B.C.

CL.

DN

CL.

T.V.-V.C.R.-STEREO

LINEN

CL.

D.W.

LT.

LAUND.

SER. ENT.

P'TRY

PORCH

MEDIA RM.
13⁶ x 13² + BAY

SLOPED CEILING

SLOPED CEILING

BED RM.
13⁰ x 12⁰

GARAGE
21⁴ x 23⁸

CURB

60'-0"

70'-0"

BASEMENT

RAISED HEARTH

ACTIVITIES RM.
32⁴ x 20⁴

BED RM.
12⁰ x 18⁴

UP

D.W.

LINEN

WALK-IN CL.

SUMMER KITCHEN
11⁰ x 9⁸

RANGE REF. P'TRY

B.C.

SHLVS

BATH

Design BB3360

Upper Level: 2,673 square feet
Lower Level: 1,389 square feet
Total: 4,062 square feet

● This plan has the best of both worlds
— a traditional exterior and a modern,
multi-level floor plan. The central foyer
routes traffic effectively to all areas: the
kitchen, gathering room, sleeping area,
media room and the stairs leading to the
lower level. Highlights include a master
suite with luxurious bath and lower-
level activities room with fireplace and
kitchen. Also note the bedroom on this
level.

Design BB3575

Main Level: 1,650 square feet
Upper Level: 628 square feet
Lower Level: 977 square feet
Total: 3,255 square feet

L

● This contemporary design accommodates hillside lots well with its lower-level living areas. The guest bedroom located here accesses a full bath with an exercise room nearby. Also notable about this area is the activities room with its raised-hearth fireplace. A spacious, two-story gathering room with a large fireplace and a balcony defines the main floor. A formal dining room, also with a balcony, connects to the breakfast room with outside access and the modern kitchen. A laundry room facilitates ease in everyday living and sits on the other side of the two-car garage. The master bedroom, with its private bath with whirlpool tub, finishes off this floor. Upstairs, two family bedrooms–each with their own balcony–share a full hall bath.

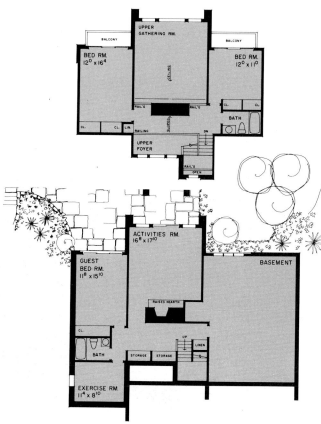

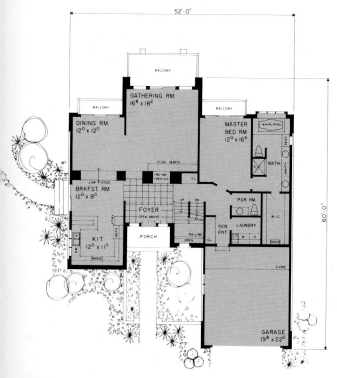

Design BB3366

Main Level: 1,638 square feet
Upper Level: 650 square feet; Lower Level: 934 square feet
Total: 3,222 square feet

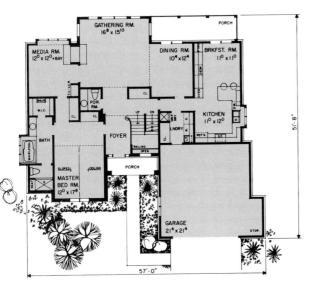

● There is much more to this design than meets the eye. While it may look like a 1½-story plan, bonus recreation and hobby space in the walk-out basement adds almost 1,000 square feet. The first floor holds living and dining areas as well as the master bedroom suite. Two family bedrooms on the second floor are connected by a balcony area that overlooks the gathering room below. Notice the covered porch beyond the breakfast and dining rooms.

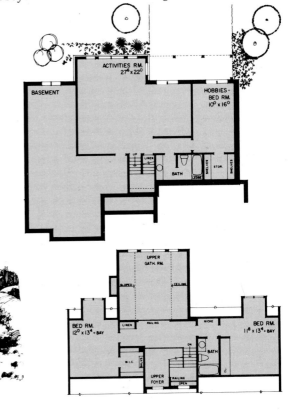

Design BB3378

First Floor: 2,959 square feet
Second Floor: 1,440 square feet
Total: 4,399 square feet

L **D**

● This large traditional home fits right in whether built in the busy city or a secluded rural area. Living areas on the first floor include a media room with bay window, gathering room with raised-hearth fireplace and a formal dining room. The kitchen area supplies room enough for a crowd with a snack bar and a 17-foot breakfast room with terrace access. A convenient first-floor master suite also includes terrace access, along with a sitting room and a dressing and bath area fit for a king. Two bedrooms and two full baths on the second floor are joined by a lounge and spacious bonus room. Note the three-car garage.

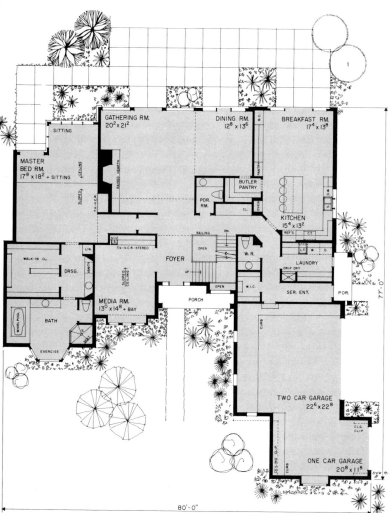

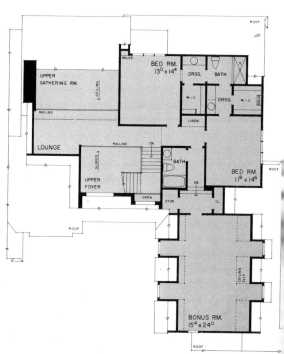

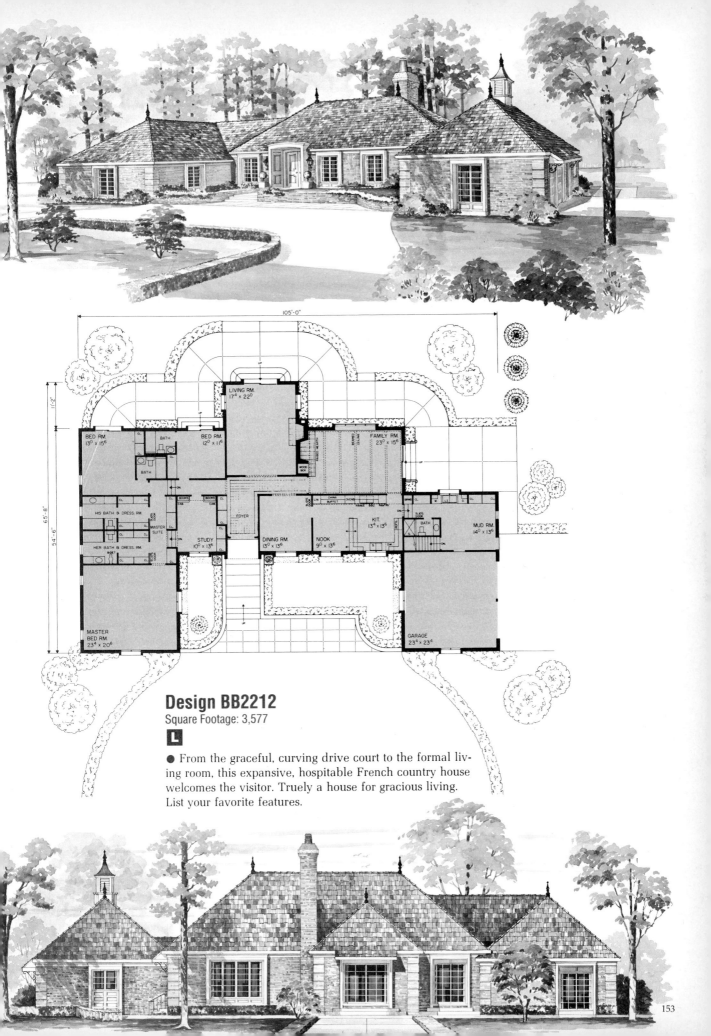

Design BB2212

Square Footage: 3,577

L

● From the graceful, curving drive court to the formal living room, this expansive, hospitable French country house welcomes the visitor. Truely a house for gracious living. List your favorite features.

Design BB3353

First Floor: 2,191 square feet
Second Floor: 874 square feet
Total: 3,065 square feet

L **D**

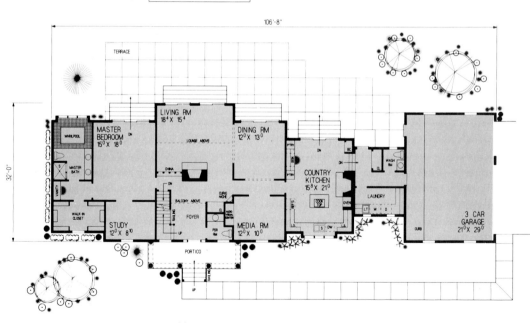

● This captivating 1½ story Southern Colonial provides the best in livability. On the first floor are the living room, dining room and private media room. A country kitchen with fireplace offers casual living space. The master suite is also located on this floor and has a lavish master bath with whirlpool spa. Upstairs are two family bedrooms, each with its own bath, and a central lounge overlooking the living room.

Design BB3334

First Floor: 2,193 square feet
Second Floor: 831 square feet
Total: 3,024 square feet

● A traditional favorite, this home combines classic style with progressive floor planning. Four bedrooms are split — master suite and one bedroom on the first floor, two more bedrooms upstairs. The second-floor lounge overlooks a large, sunken gathering room near the formal dining area. A handy butler's pantry connects the dining room and kitchen.

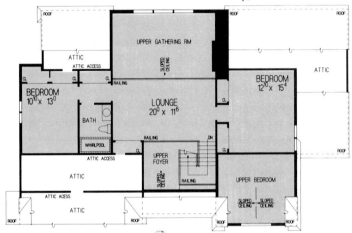

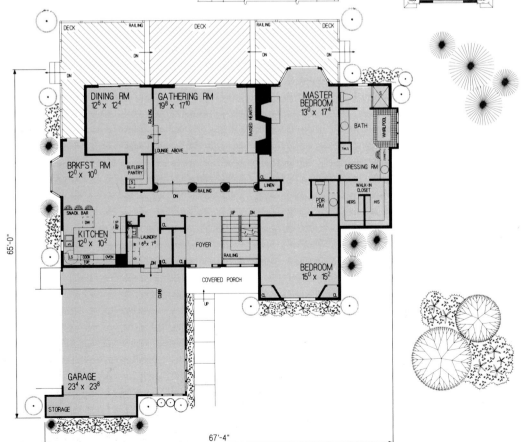

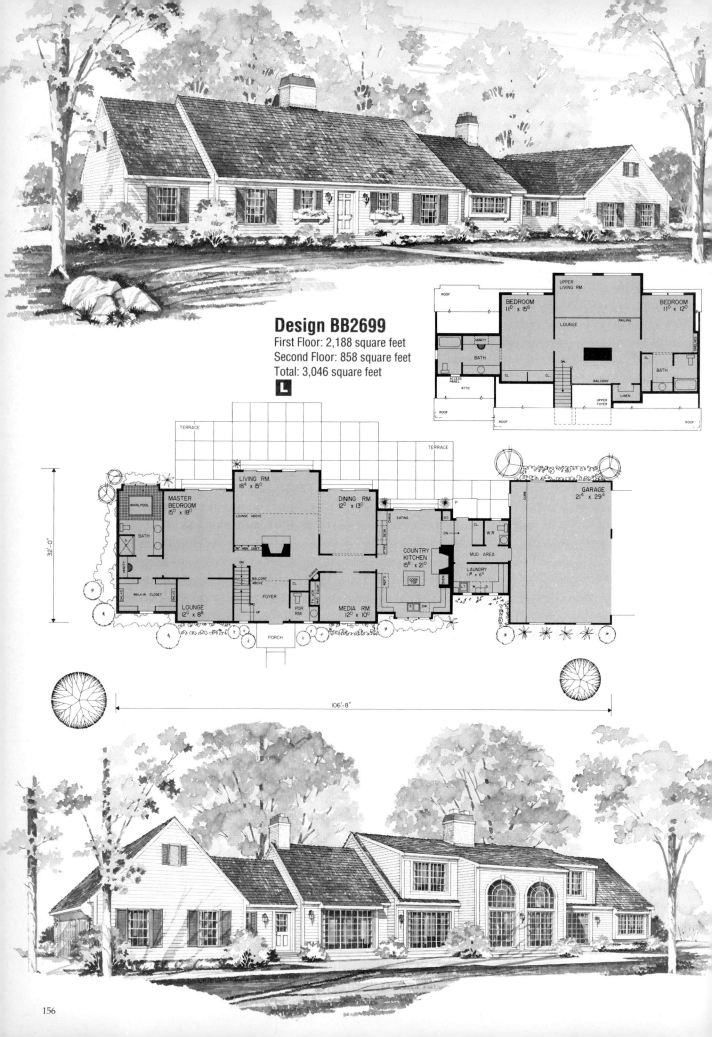

Design BB2699

First Floor: 2,188 square feet
Second Floor: 858 square feet
Total: 3,046 square feet

L

Second Floor

ROOF
BEDROOM 11⁰ x 15⁸
UPPER LIVING RM.
BEDROOM 11⁰ x 12⁰
LOUNGE
RAILING
VANITY
BATH
SHELVES
CL
CL
DN
CL
BATH
ACCESS PANEL
ATTIC
BALCONY
LINEN
ROOF
ROOF
UPPER FOYER
ROOF
ROOF

First Floor

TERRACE
TERRACE
LIVING RM. 18⁴ x 15⁰
DINING RM. 12⁰ x 13⁰
GARAGE 21⁴ x 29⁴
MASTER BEDROOM 15⁰ x 18⁰
WHIRLPOOL
LOUNGE ABOVE
EATING
P
BATH
36" HIGH CABT.
COUNTRY KITCHEN 15⁸ x 21⁰
CL
W R
VANITY
DN
MUD AREA
SHLVS
WALK-IN CLOSET
SHLVS
DN
BALCONY ABOVE
CL
COOK TOP
OVEN
LAUNDRY 11⁴ x 6⁰
LOUNGE 12⁰ x 8⁸
FOYER
PDR. RM.
MEDIA RM. 12⁰ x 10⁰
PORCH

32'-0"
106'-8"

156

Design BB2888
Square Footage: 3,018

L

● This is an outstanding Early American design for the 20th-Century. The exterior detailing with narrow clapboards, multi-paned windows and cupola are the features of yesteryear. Interior planning, though, is for today's active family. Formal living room, in-

formal family room plus a study are present. Every activity will have its place in this home. Picture yourself working in the kitchen. There's enough counter space for two or three helpers. Four bedrooms are in the private area. Stop and imagine your daily routine if

you occupied the master bedroom. Both you and your spouse would have plenty of space and privacy. The flower porch, accessible from the master bedroom, living and dining rooms, is a very delightful "plus" feature. Study this design's every detail.

Design BB2995

First Floor: 2,465 square feet
Second Floor: 617 square feet
Total: 3,082 square feet

L **D**

● This New England Colonial delivers beautiful proportions and great livability on 1½ levels. The main area of the house, the first floor, holds a living room, library, family room, dining room and gourmet kitchen. The master bedroom, also on this floor, features a whirlpool tub and sloped ceiling. A long rear terrace stretches the full width of the house. Two bedrooms on the second floor share a full bath; each has a built-in deck.

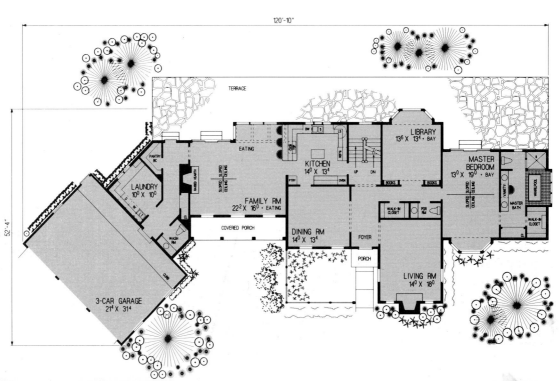

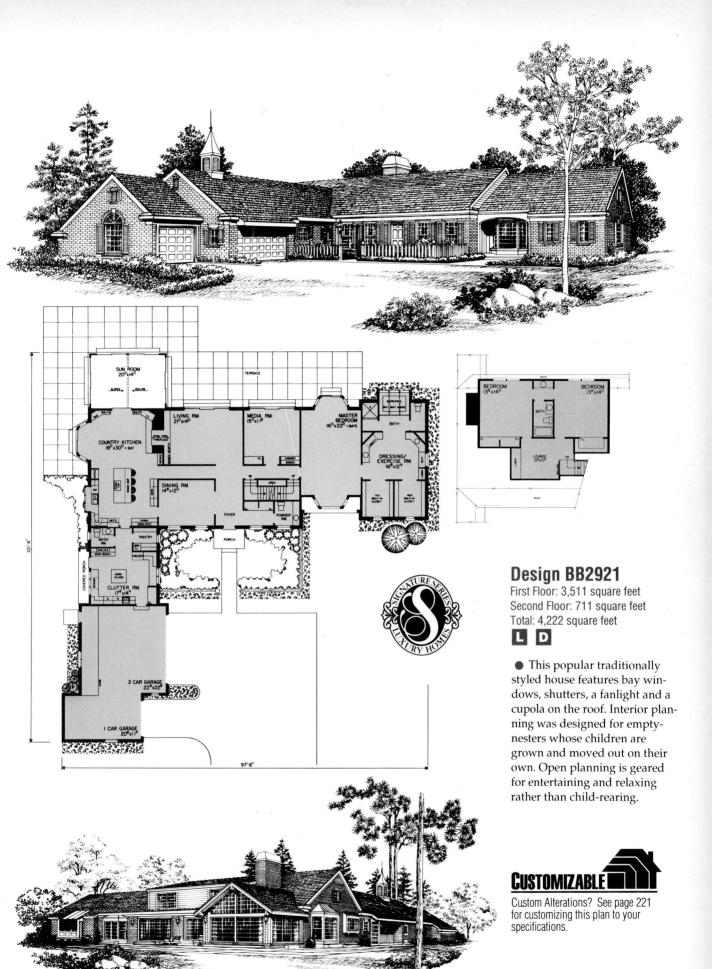

Design BB2921

First Floor: 3,511 square feet
Second Floor: 711 square feet
Total: 4,222 square feet

L **D**

● This popular traditionally styled house features bay windows, shutters, a fanlight and a cupola on the roof. Interior planning was designed for empty-nesters whose children are grown and moved out on their own. Open planning is geared for entertaining and relaxing rather than child-rearing.

CUSTOMIZABLE

Custom Alterations? See page 221 for customizing this plan to your specifications.

● Here are two more examples of the rambling Cape Cod house that illustrate just how delightful the appearance of those added dependents can be. The appealing result is houses with varying roof planes, projecting and recessed exterior walls and interesting, irregular configurations. In addition to charm, these two houses deliver exceptional country-estate livability for the growing, active family. Each one has a central entrance leading to a foyer, but from there the many features are distinct.

Design BB2615
First Floor: 2,563 square feet
Second Floor: 552 square feet
Total: 3,115 square feet

L D

SPANISH AND SOUTHWESTERN HOMES

*W*arm-weather climates have always attracted more mature homeowners and the style of homes native to these climates has long been popular. The classic Southwestern or Spanish-style home lends itself well to empty-nester living. Rooms are open, light-filled and casual with large window areas to capture grand views. Outdoor living is essential and manifests itself in all varieties of porches, patios, terraces, balconies and other fresh-air spots. Exteriors allow all the well-known features of Spanish and Southwestern design: stucco siding, tile roofs, graceful arches and curves, and simplistic ornamentation. Among the homes in this section are Floridian homes, Mission-style, Spanish Eclectic, Spanish Colonial and some unique Pueblo-style plans. Empty-nesters will appreciate some of the more outstanding features in these designs: the media room with built-ins in Design BB2949 and the angled kitchen area in Design BB2948

Design BB3428

First Floor: 2,623 square feet
Second Floor: 551 square feet; Total: 3,174 square feet

● High sloping ceilings and plenty of windows lend a light, airy feel to this Southwestern design. Flanking the two-story foyer are the sleeping areas, the regal master suite to the left and three more bedrooms (or two plus study) to the right. Overlooking the back yard are the dining room and living room with raised-hearth fireplace. The U-shaped kitchen has a pass-through to the family room which also has a fireplace. Doors here and in the dining room open onto the covered porch. Notice the pot shelves scattered throughout the plan.

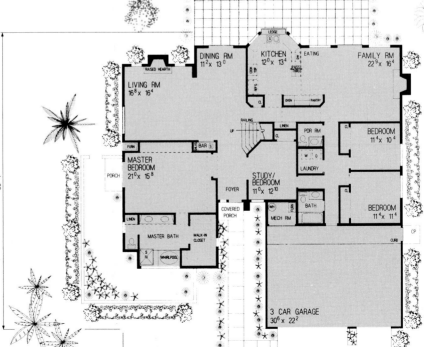

CUSTOMIZABLE

Custom Alterations? See page 221 for customizing this plan to your specifications.

162

● This design is carefully zoned for utmost livability. The entry foyer routes traffic to all areas of the house. To the rear is the living room/dining room combination with built-in china cabinet. To the left, the kitchen is open to the breakfast room and family room with fireplace. The master bedroom is on the right and features a whirlpool and a private porch. Upstairs are three more bedrooms and an outdoor balcony.

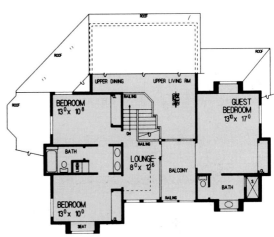

Design BB3426

First Floor: 1,859 square feet
Second Floor: 969 square feet
Total: 2,828 square feet

Custom Alterations? See page 221 for customizing this plan to your specifications.

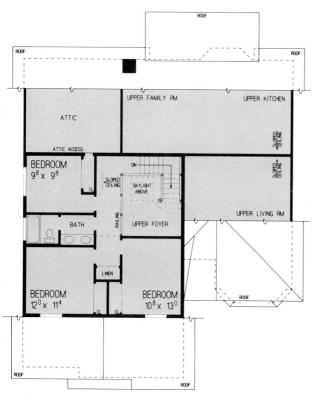

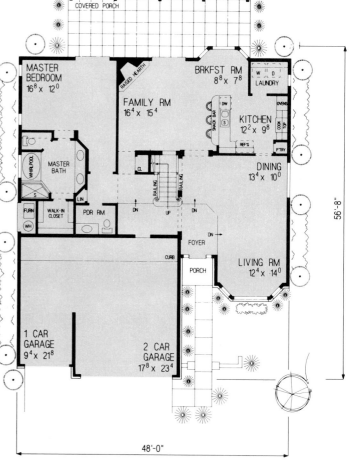

Labels on second floor plan (left): ROOF, ROOF, ROOF, ROOF, ROOF, ATTIC, ATTIC ACCESS, UPPER FAMILY RM, UPPER KITCHEN, SLOPED CEILING, SLOPED CEILING, BEDROOM 9⁸ x 9⁸, CL, DN, SLOPED CEILING, SKYLIGHT ABOVE, RAILING, UPPER FOYER, UPPER LIVING RM, BATH, BEDROOM 12⁰ x 11⁴, LINEN, BEDROOM 10⁸ x 13⁰

Labels on first floor plan (right): COVERED PORCH, MASTER BEDROOM 16⁸ x 12⁰, RAISED HEARTH, FAMILY RM 16⁴ x 15⁴, BRKFST RM 8⁸ x 7⁸, W D LAUNDRY, MASTER BATH, SNACK BAR, DW, KITCHEN 12² x 9⁸, OVENS, REFS, P'TRY, WHRLPOOL, CL, LIN, DINING 13⁴ x 10⁰, FURN, WALK-IN CLOSET, PDR RM, DN, UP, DN, WH, DN, FOYER, LIVING RM 12⁴ x 14⁰, CURB, PORCH, 1 CAR GARAGE 9⁴ x 21⁸, 2 CAR GARAGE 17⁸ x 23⁴, 56'-8", 48'-0"

Design BB3420

First Floor: 1,617 square feet
Second Floor: 658 square feet; Total: 2,275 square feet

● Here is a moderate-sized house with a wealth of amenities typical of much larger homes. Interesting window treatments include two bay windows, one in the living room and one in the breakfast room. In the kitchen there's a snack bar pass-through to the family room which boasts a corner raised-hearth fireplace. Also on this level, the master suite features a large bath with whirlpool and access to the rear covered porch. Upstairs are three more bedrooms and a shared bath. Notice the attic storage space.

CUSTOMIZABLE

Custom Alterations? See page 221 for customizing this plan to your specifications.

Design BB3418

First Floor: 1,283 square feet
Second Floor: 552 square feet
Total: 1,835 square feet

● This home is ideal for the economically minded who don't want to sacrifice livability. The entry foyer opens directly into the two-story living room with fireplace. To the right, the kitchen with peninsula cooktop and snack bar conveniently serves both the breakfast room and the formal dining room. Also on this level, the master bedroom boasts an enormous bath with a whirlpool and His and Hers walk-in-closets. Three other bedrooms are located upstairs to ensure peace and quiet. Also notice the abundant storage space in the attic.

CUSTOMIZABLE

Custom Alterations? See page 221 for customizing this plan to your specifications.

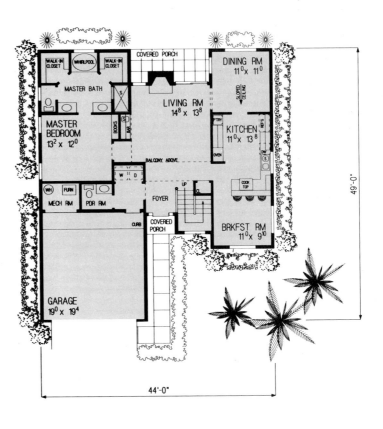

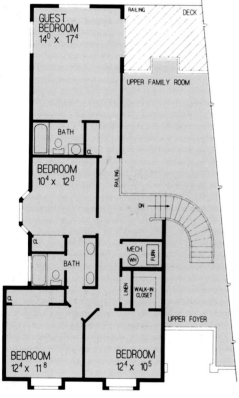

Design BB3414

First Floor: 2,024 square feet
Second Floor: 1,144 square feet
Total: 3,168 square feet

● Though seemingly compact from the exterior, this home allows for "wide-open-spaces" living. The two-story entry connects directly to a formal living/dining area, a fitting complement to the more casual family room and cozy breakfast room. Split-bedroom planning puts the master suite on the first floor for utmost privacy. Up the curved staircase are three family bedrooms, a guest room with deck and two full baths.

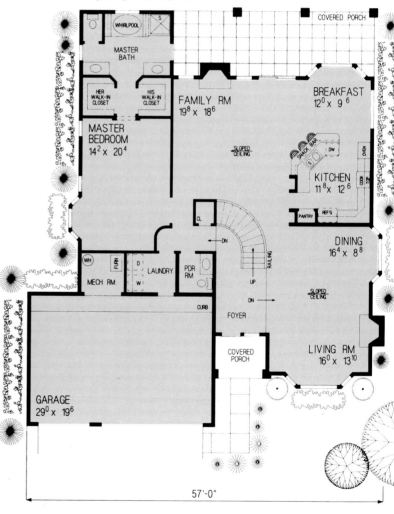

CUSTOMIZABLE

Custom Alterations? See page 221 for customizing this plan to your specifications.

Design BB3435

First Floor: 1,946 square feet
Second Floor: 986 square feet
Total: 2,932 square feet

L

● Here's a grand Spanish Mission home designed for family living. Enter at the angled foyer which contains a curved staircase to the second floor. Family bedrooms are here along with a spacious guest suite. The master bedroom is found on the first floor and has a private patio and whirlpool overlooking an enclosed garden area. Besides a living room and dining room connected by a through-fireplace, there is a family room with casual eating space. There is also a library with large closet. You'll appreciate the abundant built-ins and interesting shapes throughout this home.

CUSTOMIZABLE

Custom Alterations? See page 221 for customizing this plan to your specifications.

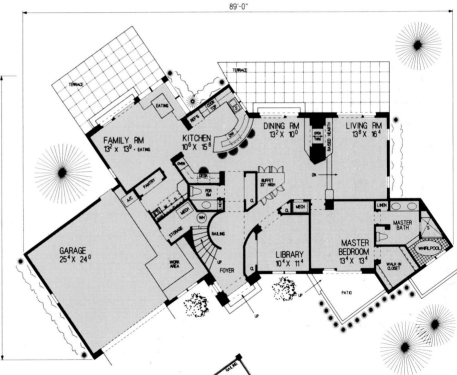

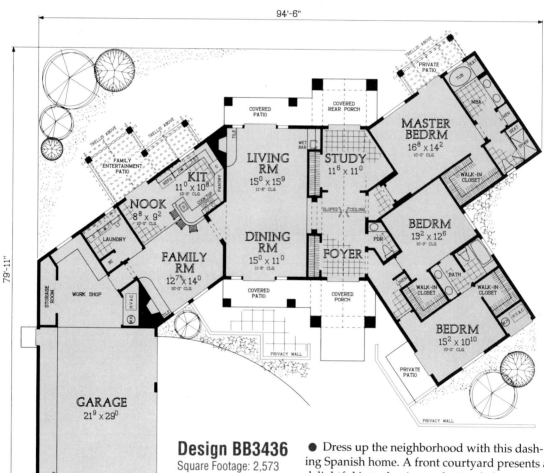

94'-6"

79'-11"

COVERED PATIO

COVERED REAR PORCH

PRIVATE PATIO

TRELLIS ABOVE

SEAT

TUB

MBA

MASTER BEDRM
16⁸ x 14²
10'-0" CLG.

LINEN

SEAT

SHWR

WALK-IN CLOSET

FAMILY ENTERTAINMENT PATIO

TRELLIS ABOVE

WET BAR

KIT
11⁰ x 10⁸
10'-0" CLG.

PANTRY

LIVING RM
15⁰ x 15⁹
11'-6" CLG.

STUDY
11⁶ x 11⁰

NOOK
8⁸ x 9²
10'-0" CLG.

COOK TOP

SLOPED CEILING

PDR

BEDRM
13² x 12⁶
10'-0" CLG.

LAUNDRY

DINING RM
15⁰ x 11⁰
11'-6" CLG.

FOYER

LINEN

BATH

FAMILY RM
12⁷ x 14⁰
10'-0" CLG.

WALK-IN CLOSET

WALK-IN CLOSET

STORAGE ROOM

WORK SHOP

HVAC

COVERED PATIO

COVERED PORCH

HVAC

BEDRM
15² x 10¹⁰
10'-0" CLG.

PRIVACY WALL

PRIVATE PATIO

GARAGE
21⁹ x 29⁰

CURB

PRIVACY WALL

Design BB3436
Square Footage: 2,573

CUSTOMIZABLE

Custom Alterations? See page 221 for customizing this plan to your specifications.

● Dress up the neighborhood with this dashing Spanish home. A front courtyard presents a delightful introduction to the inside living spaces. These excel with a central living room/dining room combination. A wet bar here makes entertaining easy. In the kitchen, a huge pantry and interesting angles are sure to please the house gourmet. A breakfast nook with a corner fireplace further enhances this area. Notice the laundry room nearby as well as the expansive work shop just off the three-car garage. The master bedroom makes room for a private bath with a whirlpool tub and dual lavatories; a walk-in closet adds to the modern amenities here. Two additional bedrooms make use of a Hollywood bath. Each bedroom is highlighted by a spacious walk-in closet.

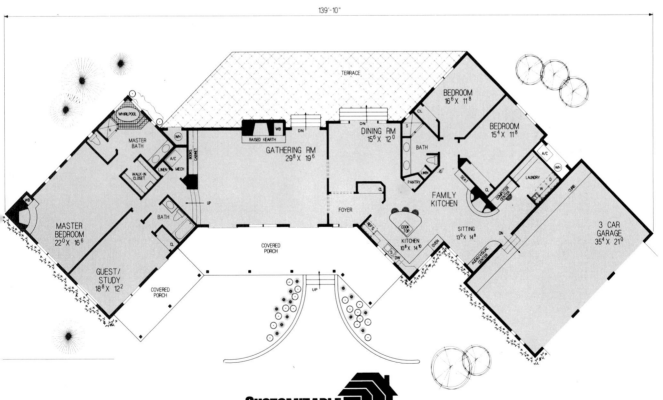

TERRACE

BEDROOM
16⁶ X 11⁸

BEDROOM
15⁴ X 11⁸

WHIRLPOOL

MASTER BATH

WALK-IN CLOSET

LINEN

MECH

DINING RM
15⁶ X 12⁰

GATHERING RM
29⁸ X 19⁶

RAISED HEARTH

BATH

PANTRY

FAMILY KITCHEN

LAUNDRY

3 CAR GARAGE
35⁴ X 21⁰

BATH

FOYER

COOK TOP

KITCHEN
10⁸ X 14¹⁰

SITTING
13⁰ X 14⁰

COMPUTER CENTER

AUDIO/VISUAL CENTER

MASTER BEDROOM
22⁰ X 16⁶

COVERED PORCH

GUEST/ STUDY
18⁸ X 12²

COVERED PORCH

139'-10"

Design BB3405
Square Footage: 3,144

L

CUSTOMIZABLE
Custom Alterations? See page 221 for customizing this plan to your specifications.

● In classic Santa Fe style, this home strikes a beautiful combination of historic exterior detailing and open floor planning on the inside. A covered porch running the width of the facade leads to an entry foyer that connects to a huge gathering room with fireplace and formal dining room. The family kitchen allows special space for casual gatherings. The right wing of the home holds two family bedrooms and full bath. The left wing is devoted to the master suite and guest room or study. Built-ins abound throughout the house.

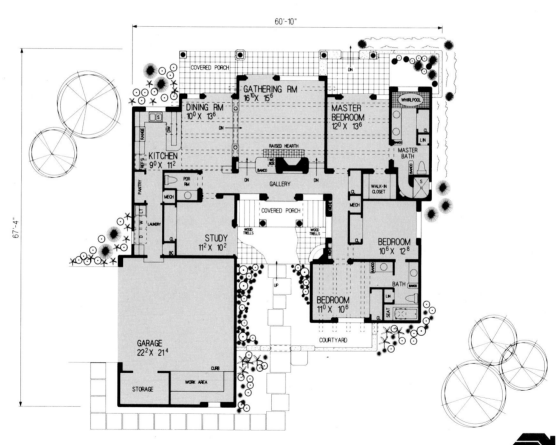

Design BB3431
Square Footage: 1,907

● Graceful curves welcome you into the courtyard of this Santa Fe home. Inside, a gallery directs traffic to the work zone on the left or the sleeping zone on the right. Straight ahead lies a sunken gathering room with beamed ceiling and raised-hearth fireplace. A large pantry offers extra storage space for kitchen items. The covered rear porch is accessible from the dining room, gathering room and secluded master bedroom. Luxury describes the feeling in the master bath with whirlpool tub, separate shower, double vanity and closet space. Two family bedrooms share a compartmented bath. The study could serve as a guest room, media room or home office.

CUSTOMIZABLE
Custom Alterations? See page 221 for customizing this plan to your specifications.

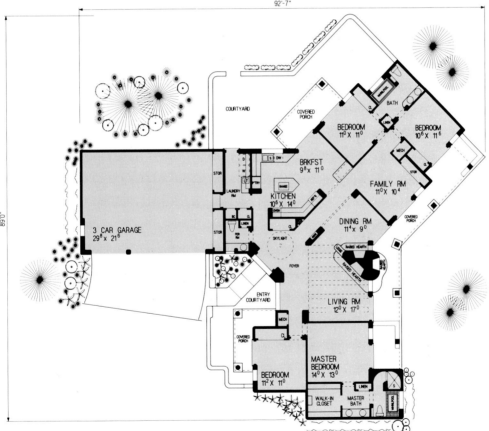

Design BB3433

Square Footage: 2,350

● Santa Fe styling creates interesting angles in this one-story home. A grand entrance leads through a courtyard into the foyer with circular skylight, closet space and niches, and convenient powder room. Turn right to the master suite with deluxe bath and a bedroom close at hand, perfect for a nursery, home office or exercise room. Two more family bedrooms are placed quietly in the far wing of the house. Fireplaces in the living room, dining room and covered porch create various shapes. Make note of the island range in the kitchen, extra storage in the garage, and covered porches on two sides.

CUSTOMIZABLE

Custom Alterations? See page 221 for customizing this plan to your specifications.

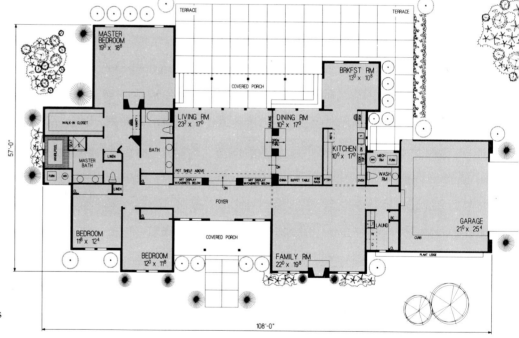

Design BB3402

Square Footage: 3,212

● This one-story pairs the customary tile and stucco of Spanish design with a livable floor plan. The sunken living room with its open-hearth fireplace promises to be a cozy gathering place. For more casual occasions, there's a family room with fireplace off the entry foyer. Also noteworthy: a sizable kitchen and a sumptuous master suite.

CUSTOMIZABLE

Custom Alterations? See page 221 for customizing this plan to your specifications.

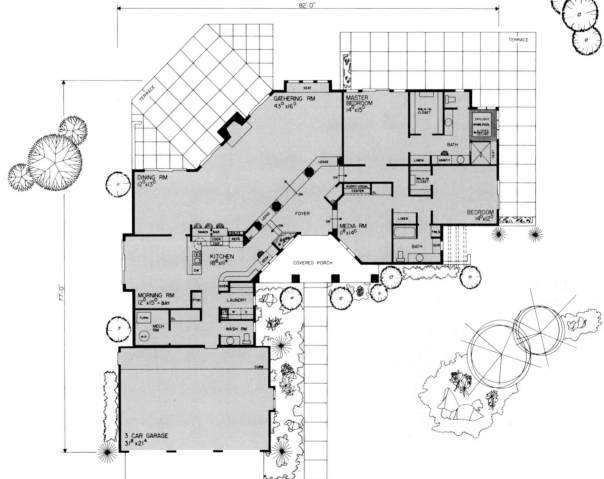

Design BB2949
Square Footage: 2,922

D

● Spanish and western influences take center stage in a long, low stucco design. You'll enjoy the Texas-sized gathering room that opens to a formal dining area and has a snack bar through to the kitchen. More casual dining is accommodated in the nook. A luxurious master suite is graced by plenty of closet space and a soothing whirlpool spa. Besides another bedroom and full bath, there is a media room that could easily double as a third bedroom or guest room.

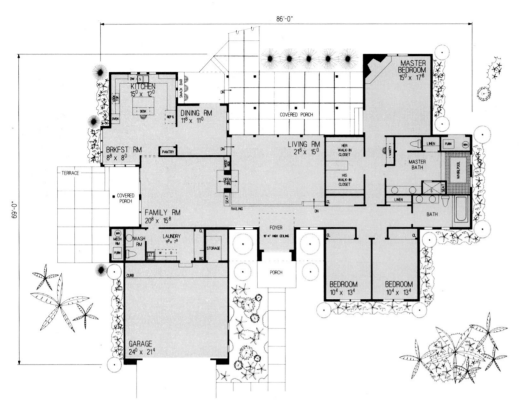

Design BB3401

Square Footage: 2,850

● This Southwestern design caters to families who enjoy outdoor living and entertaining. Doors open onto a shaded terrace from the master bedroom and living room, while a sliding glass door in the family room accesses a smaller terrace. Also notice the outdoor bar with pass-through window to the kitchen.

Custom Alterations? See page 221 for customizing this plan to your specifications.

CUSTOMIZABLE

Custom Alterations? See page 221 for customizing this plan to your specifications.

Design BB3400
Square Footage: 2,784

● Abundant terrace space favors an outdoor lifestyle in this charming one-story. Each room has access to a porch or terrace; think of the added entertainment possibilities! Interior highlights include corner fireplaces in the master suite and family room, a dining room with bay window, and a regal master bath. Note the dramatic two-story foyer.

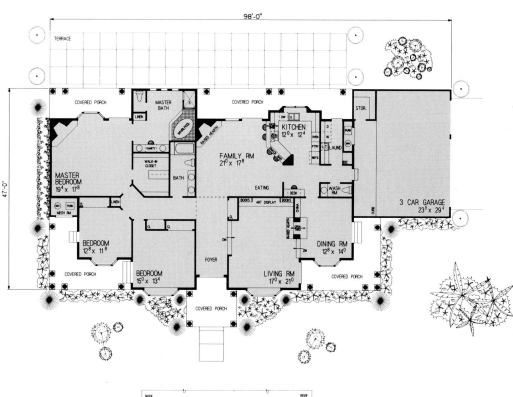

98'-0"

TERRACE

47'-0"

COVERED PORCH	MASTER BATH		COVERED PORCH		STOR.
LINEN				KITCHEN 12⁰ x 12⁴	
VANITY		RAISED HEARTH	FAMILY RM 21⁰ x 17⁸		LAUND
WALK-IN CLOSET		BATH			
MASTER BEDROOM 19⁴ x 17⁸			EATING	DESK	WASH RM
LINEN			ART DISPLAY	BOOKS	3 CAR GARAGE 23⁸ x 29⁴
MECH RM			BOOKS	RAISED HEARTH	DINING RM 12⁸ x 14⁰
BEDROOM 12⁸ x 11⁸	CL	CL	DN		
COVERED PORCH	BEDROOM 15⁰ x 13⁴	FOYER	LIVING RM 17⁰ x 21⁰	COVERED PORCH	

COVERED PORCH

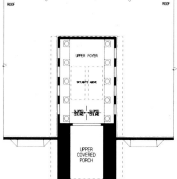

ROOF   ROOF

UPPER FOYER

SKYLIGHT ABOVE

UPPER COVERED PORCH

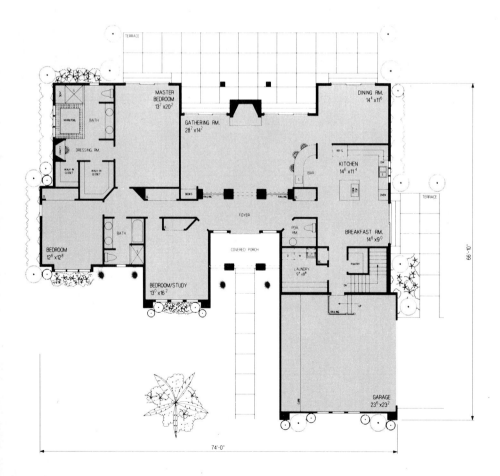

Design BB2950

Square Footage: 2,559

● A natural desert dweller, this stucco, tile-roofed beauty is equally comfortable in any clime. Inside, there's a well-planned design. Common living areas — gathering room, formal dining room, and breakfast room — are offset by a quiet study that could be used as a bedroom or guest room. A master suite features two walk-in closets, a double vanity, and whirlpool spa. The two-car garage has a service entrance; close by is an adequate laundry area and a pantry. Notice the warming hearth in the gathering room and the snack bar area for casual dining.

Design BB2948

Square Footage: 1,830

● Styled for Southwest living, this home is a good choice in any region. All on one story, look for three bedrooms, one a master suite with deluxe bath and one an optional study. The large gathering room/dining room combination contains a fireplace, sliding glass doors to the terrace, and a snack bar served by the uniquely shaped kitchen. Notice the covered porch with open skylights and the extra storage space in the garage.

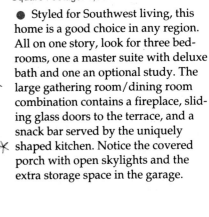

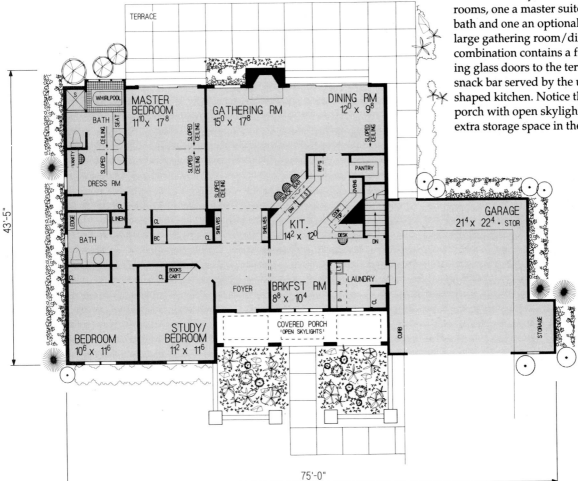

TERRACE

MASTER BEDROOM 11¹⁰ x 17⁸

GATHERING RM 15⁰ x 17⁸

DINING RM 12⁰ x 9⁸

SLOPED CEILING

BATH
SEAT
WHIRLPOOL
VANITY
DRESS RM
LEDGE
LINEN
BATH
CL

REF'S
PANTRY
OVENS
SNACK BAR
DW
SHELVES
KIT. 14² x 12⁰
DESK
DN

GARAGE 21⁴ x 22⁴ + STOR

BOOKS CAB'T
CL
FOYER
BRKFST RM 8⁸ x 10⁴
LAUNDRY
W
D
CL
STORAGE

BEDROOM 10⁶ x 11⁶

STUDY/ BEDROOM 11² x 11⁶

COVERED PORCH OPEN SKYLIGHTS

43'-5"

75'-0"

CUSTOMIZABLE

Custom Alterations? See page 221 for customizing this plan to your specifications.

Design BB3344
Square Footage: 3,054

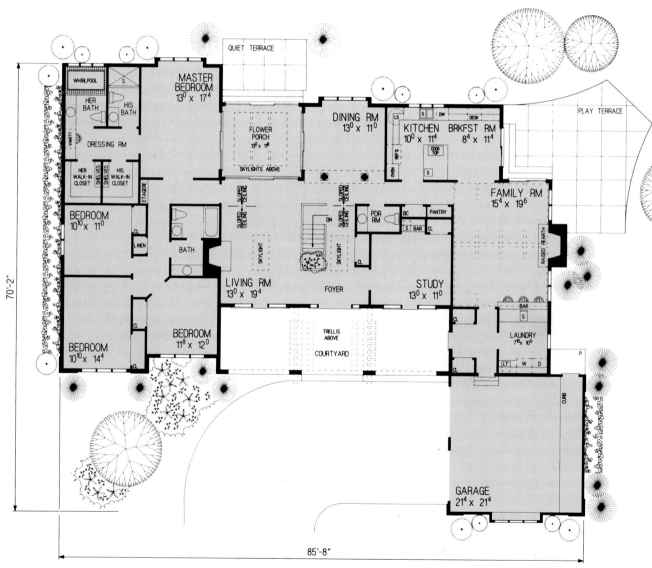

● This home features interior planning for today's active family. Living areas include a living room with fireplace, a cozy study and family room with wet bar. Convenient to the kitchen is the formal dining room with attractive bay window overlooking the back yard. The four-bedroom sleeping area contains a sumptuous master suite. Also notice the cheerful flower porch with access from the master suite, living room and dining room.

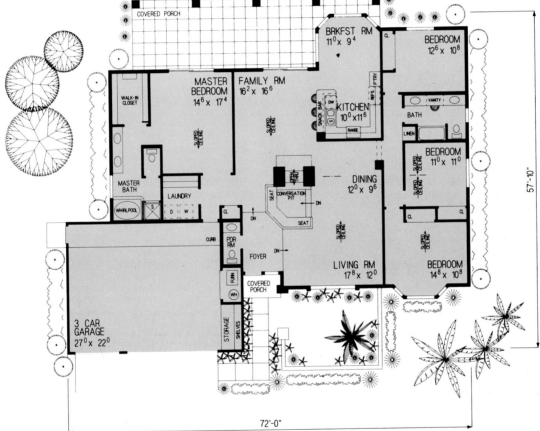

COVERED PORCH

BRKFST RM
11⁰ x 9⁴

BEDROOM
12⁶ x 10⁸

MASTER
BEDROOM
14⁶ x 17⁴

FAMILY RM
16² x 16⁶

KITCHEN
10⁰ x 11⁶

WALK-IN
CLOSET

SNACK BAR

VANITY

BATH

DW

REF'G

P'TRY

RANGE

LINEN

BEDROOM
11⁰ x 11⁰

MASTER
BATH

LAUNDRY

DINING
12⁰ x 9⁶

CONVERSATION
PIT

SEAT

WHIRLPOOL

D W

SEAT

CURB

PDR
RM

FOYER

LIVING RM
17⁸ x 12⁰

BEDROOM
14⁸ x 10⁸

FURN

WH

COVERED
PORCH

STORAGE

SHELVES

3 CAR
GARAGE
27⁰ x 22⁰

57'-10"

72'-0"

Design BB3430

Square Footage: 2,394

● This dramatic design benefits from open planning. The centerpiece of the living area is a
sunken conversation pit which shares a through-
fireplace with the family room. The living room
and dining room share space beneath a sloped
ceiling. The open kitchen features a snack bar
and breakfast room and conveniently serves all
living areas. Split zoning in the sleeping area
places the private master suite to the left of the
plan and three more bedrooms, including one
with a bay window, to the right.

CUSTOMIZABLE

Custom Alterations? See page 221
for customizing this plan to your
specifications.

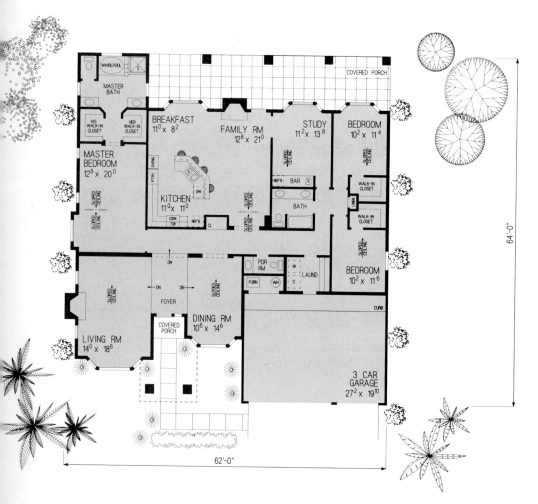

Design BB3413
Square Footage: 2,517

● Though distinctly Southwest in design, this home has some features that are universally appealing. Note, for instance, the central gallery, perpendicular to the raised entry hall, and running almost the entire width of the house. An L-shaped, angled kitchen serves the breakfast room and family room in equal fashion. Sleeping areas are found in four bedrooms including an optional study and exquisite master suite.

Custom Alterations? See page 221 for customizing this plan to your specifications.

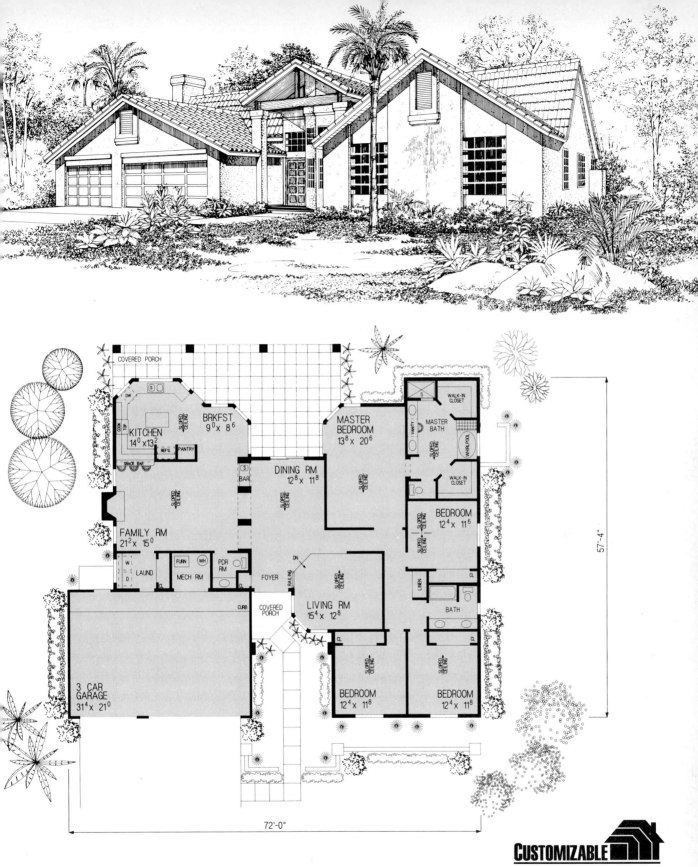

COVERED PORCH

KITCHEN
14⁰ x 13²

BRKFST
9⁰ x 8⁶

MASTER BEDROOM
13⁸ x 20⁶

WALK-IN CLOSET

MASTER BATH

WHR POOL

WALK-IN CLOSET

DINING RM
12⁸ x 11⁸

BEDROOM
12⁴ x 11⁶

FAMILY RM
21² x 15⁰

LINEN

BATH

LAUND

FURN

WH

PDR RM

MECH RM

FOYER

LIVING RM
15⁴ x 12⁸

DN

3 CAR GARAGE
31⁴ x 21⁰

COVERED PORCH

CURB

BEDROOM
12⁴ x 11⁸

BEDROOM
12⁴ x 11⁸

57'-4"

72'-0"

CUSTOMIZABLE

Custom Alterations? See page 221 for customizing this plan to your specifications.

Design BB3423
Square Footage: 2,577

● This spacious Southwestern home will be a pleasure to come home to. Immediately off the foyer are the dining room and step-down living room with bay window. The highlight of the four-bedroom sleeping area is the master suite with porch access and a whirlpool for soaking away the day's worries. The informal living area features an enormous family room with fireplace and bay-windowed kitchen and breakfast room. Notice the snack bar pass-through to the family room.

Design BB3421
Square Footage: 2,145

● Split-bedroom planning makes the most of a one-story design. In this case the master suite is on the opposite side of the house from two family bedrooms. Gourmets can rejoice at the abundant work space in the U-shaped kitchen and will appreciate the natural light afforded by the large bay window in the breakfast room. A formal living room has a sunken conversation area with a cozy fireplace as its focus. The rear covered porch can be reached through sliding glass doors in the family room.

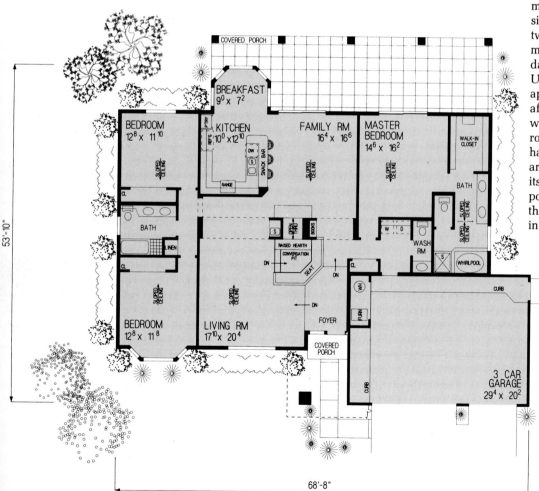

CUSTOMIZABLE
Custom Alterations? See page 221 for customizing this plan to your specifications.

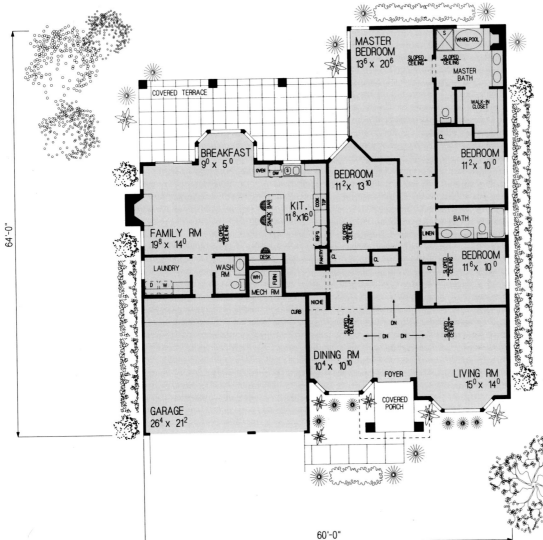

COVERED TERRACE

MASTER BEDROOM
13⁶ x 20⁶

WHIRLPOOL
SLOPED CEILING

MASTER BATH

WALK-IN CLOSET

BREAKFAST
9⁰ x 5⁰

OVEN   DW

KIT.
11⁸ x 16⁰

SNACK BAR

REF.

COOK TOP

BEDROOM
11² x 13¹⁰
SLOPED CEILING

BEDROOM
11² x 10⁰

FAMILY RM
19⁸ x 14⁰
SLOPED CEILING

DESK

PANTRY

BATH

LINEN

LAUNDRY

WASH RM

D   W

WH
MECH

FURN.
RM

BEDROOM
11⁶ x 10⁰
SLOPED CEILING

CURB

NICHE

SLOPED CEILING

DN
DN   DN

SLOPED CEILING

GARAGE
26⁴ x 21²

DINING RM
10⁴ x 10¹⁰

FOYER

COVERED PORCH

LIVING RM
15⁰ x 14⁰

64'-0"

60'-0"

Design BB3415
Square Footage: 2,406

● Relax and enjoy the open floor plan of this lovely one-story. Its family room with fireplace and space for eating are a suitable complement to the formal living and dining rooms to the front of the house. There are four bedrooms, or three if you choose to make one a den, and 2½ baths. Don't miss the large pantry and convenient laundry area.

CUSTOMIZABLE
Custom Alterations? See page 221 for customizing this plan to your specifications.

Design BB3411

Square Footage: 2,441

● You'll love the entry to
this Southwestern home — it
creates a dramatic first im-
pression and leads beautifully to the formal living and
dining rooms. Beyond, look
for an open family room and
dining area in the same
proximity as the kitchen.
Sliding glass doors here
open to a backyard patio.
Take your choice of four
bedrooms or five, depending
on how you wish to use the
optional room. The huge
master suite is not to
be missed.

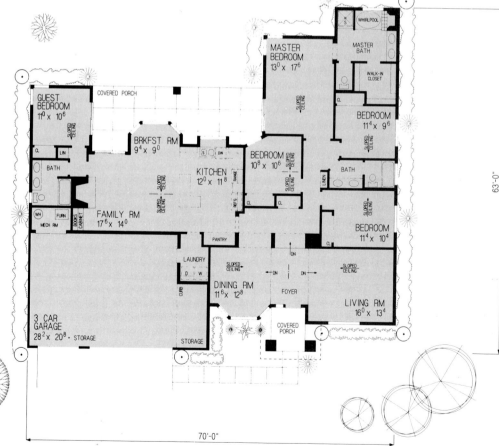

CUSTOMIZABLE

Custom Alterations? See page 221
for customizing this plan to your
specifications.

Design BB3602

quare Footage: 2,195

● This lovely one-story home fits ight into sunny regions—or any rea of the country for that matter. ts stucco exterior and easily ccessed outdoor living areas make t an all-time favorite. Inside, the loor plan accommodates empty-ester lifestyles. There is plenty of oom for both formal and informal ntertaining: living room, dining oom, family room and morning oom. A quiet study or media room rovides a getaway for more inti-nate occasions. Sleeping areas are plit with the master bedroom and ath on one side and a secondary edroom and bath on the other. A hird bedroom can be built if the xtra room is needed. Other special eatures include a warming hearth n the family room, a private porch ff the study and a grand rear deck.

185

COVERED PORCH

MASTER
BEDROOM
13⁰ x 13⁸

FAMILY RM
12⁸ x 18⁶

BREAKFAST
7⁶ x 9⁴

WHIRLPOOL

MASTER
BATH

SLOPED CEILING

SLOPED CEILING

SLOPED CEILING

S

WALK-IN
CLOSET

KIT.
9⁴ x 13⁴

OVENS

SNACK BAR

DW

COOK TOP

BEDROOM
9⁸ x 9¹⁰

CL

SLOPED CEILING

PANTRY

REFG

BATH

PDR
RM

S

BAR

DINING
13⁴ x 9⁶

LINEN

HALF WALL

BEDROOM
12⁰ x 10⁰

LT

LAUND

W

D

STUDY
9⁸ x 9⁶

DN

SLOPED CEILING

WH

FURN

CL

CURB

FOYER

HALF WALL

LIVING RM
13⁴ x 13⁴

GARAGE
21⁴ x 19⁸

COVERED PORCH

60'-0"

50'-0"

Design BB3422

Square Footage: 1,932

● An enclosed entry garden greets visitors to this charming Southwestern home. Inside, the foyer is flanked by formal and informal living areas — a living room and dining room to the right and a cozy study to the left. To the rear, a large family room, breakfast room and open kitchen have access to a covered porch and overlook the back yard. Notice the fireplace and bay window. The three-bedroom sleeping area includes a master with a spacious bath with whirlpool.

CUSTOMIZABLE

Custom Alterations? See page 221 for customizing this plan to your specifications.

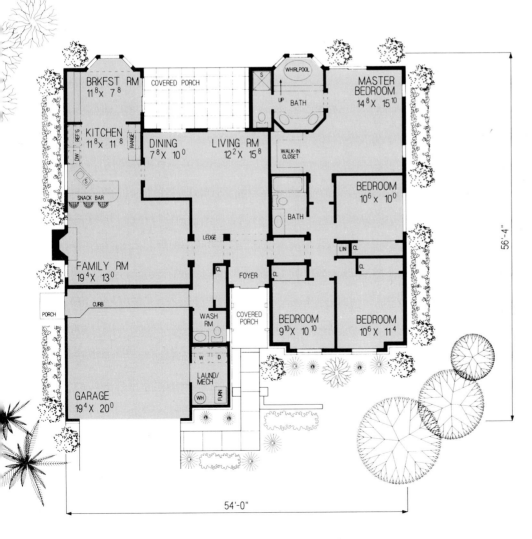

BRKFST RM
11⁸ x 7⁸

COVERED PORCH

KITCHEN
11⁸ x 11⁸

REF'G

DW

RANGE

DINING
7⁸ x 10⁰

LIVING RM
12² x 15⁸

WHIRLPOOL

S

UP BATH

MASTER BEDROOM
14⁸ x 15¹⁰

WALK-IN CLOSET

BEDROOM
10⁶ x 10⁰

SNACK BAR

BATH

LEDGE

FAMILY RM
19⁴ x 13⁰

LIN CL

CL

CL

CL

FOYER

PORCH

CURB

WASH RM

COVERED PORCH

BEDROOM
9¹⁰ x 10¹⁰

BEDROOM
10⁶ x 11⁴

W D

LAUND/ MECH

WH FURN

GARAGE
19⁴ x 20⁰

56'-4"

54'-0"

Design BB3419

Square Footage: 1,965

● This attractive, multi-gabled exterior houses a compact, livable interior. The entry foyer effectively routes traffic to all areas: left to the family room and kitchen, straight back to the dining room and living room, and right to the four-bedroom sleeping area. The spacious family room provides an informal gathering space while the living and dining rooms are perfect for formal occasions. The highlight of the sleeping area is the master bedroom with its whirlpool, walk-in closet and view of the back yard.

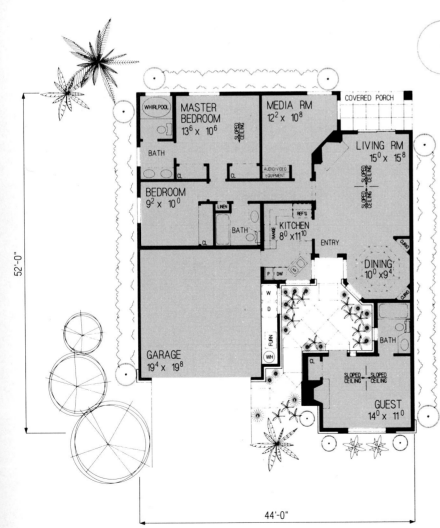

Design BB3416

Square Footage: 1,375

● Here's a Southwestern design that will be economical to build and a pleasure to occupy. The front door opens into a spacious living room with corner fireplace and dining room with coffered ceiling. The nearby kitchen serves both easily. A few steps away is the cozy media room with built-in space for audio-visual equipment. Down the hall are two bedrooms and two baths; the master features a whirlpool. A guest room is found across the entry court and includes a fireplace and sloped ceiling.

Custom Alterations? See page 221 for customizing this plan to your specifications.

VACATION AND RETIREMENT HOMES

*L*eisure and recreation are a big part of the empty-nester lifestyle. And what better way to relax than in your own cozy getaway! In this section is a splendid group of homes for vacation living, whether it be mountain retreat or seaside cottage. Casual living is the order of the day in these homes. Large living areas, most with warming fireplaces and huge windows for views, make up the gathering areas of these homes. Dining rooms and kitchens usually overlook the gathering spots so that the cook misses none of the fun. Sleeping accommodations vary from elaborate master suites with accompanying secondary bedrooms, to simple two-bedroom/one-bath plans. Many have large upstairs lofts or bunk rooms where grandchildren can pile in together for an indoor camping adventure. All plans cater to outdoor lifestyles with decks and terraces (see Designs BB4061 and BB2488), covered terraces (see Design BB1499), and second-floor balconies (see Design BB2427).

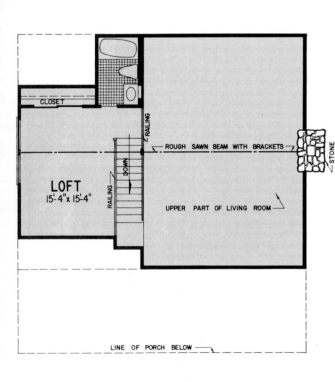

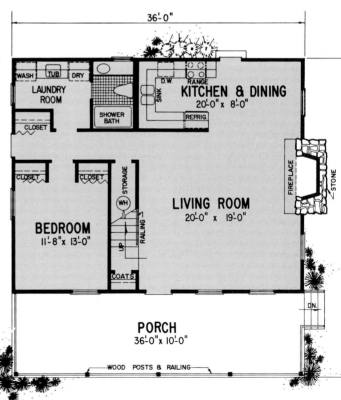

Design BB4061
First Floor: 1,008 square feet
Second Floor: 323 square feet
Total: 1,331 square feet

D

LIFESTYLE HOME PLANS

● This charming farmhouse design will be economical to build and a pleasure to occupy. Like most vacation homes, this design features an open plan. The large living area includes a living room and dining room and a massive stone fireplace. A partition separates the kitchen from the living room. Also downstairs are a bedroom, full bath, and laundry room. Upstairs is a spacious sleeping loft overlooking the living room. Don't miss the large front porch — this will be a favorite spot for relaxing.

Design BB2488

First Floor: 1,113 square feet
Second Floor: 543 square feet
Total: 1,656 square feet

D

CUSTOMIZABLE

Custom Alterations? See page 221 for customizing this plan to your specifications.

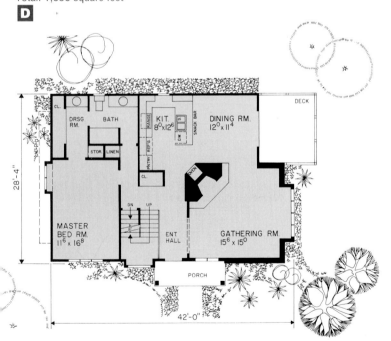

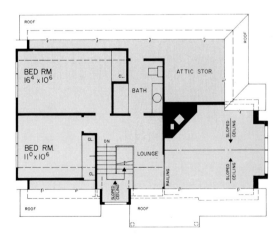

● A cozy cottage for the young at heart! Whether called upon to serve the young active family as a leisure-time retreat at the lake, or the retired couple as a quiet haven in later years, this charming design will perform well. As a year round second home, the up-stairs with its two sizable bedrooms, full bath and lounge area looking down into the gathering room below, will ideally accommodate the younger generation. When called upon to function as a retirement home, the second floor will cater to the visiting family members and friends. Also, it will be available for use as a home office, study, sewing room, music area, the pursuit of hobbies, etc. Of course, as an efficient, economical home for the young, growing family, this design will function well.

LIFESTYLE HOME PLANS

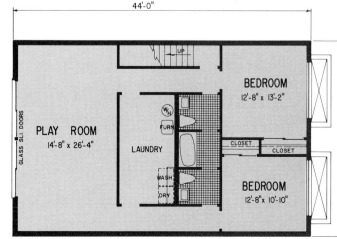

44'-0"

DN

DOWN

OPEN RAIL

CLOSET

CLOSET

B/C

GREAT ROOM
15'-0" X 27'-4"

KITCHEN
15'-8" X 8'-2"

RANGE

D/W

BEDROOM
12'-4" X 13'-6"

CLOSET

DECK

PANTRY

CLOS.

REF'G

BEDROOM
12'-4" X 13'-6"

SLOPED CLG

GLASS SLI. DOORS

SLOPED CLG

SLOPED CLG

SLOPED CLG

28'-0"

DN

Design BB4027

Square Footage: 1,232

● Good things come in small packages, too! The size and shape of this design will help hold down construction costs without sacrificing livability. The enormous great room is a multi-purpose living space with room for a dining area and several seating areas. Also notice the sloped ceilings. Sliding glass doors provide access to the wraparound deck and sweeping views of the outdoors. The well-equipped kitchen includes a pass-through and pantry. Two bedrooms, each with sloped ceilings, and compartmented bath round out the plan.

44'-0"

UP

PLAY ROOM
14'-8" x 26'-4"

W.H.

FURN.

LAUNDRY

WASH

DRY

GLASS SLI. DOORS

BEDROOM
12'-8" x 13'-2"

CLOSET

CLOSET

BEDROOM
12'-8" x 10'-10"

Optional Basement

Design BB2485

Main Level: 1,108 square feet
Lower Level: 983 square feet
Total: 2,091 square feet

● This hillside vacation home gives the appearance of being a one-story from the road. However, since it is built off the edge of a slope, the rear exterior is a full two-story structure. Notice the projecting deck and how it shelters the terrace. Each of the generous glass areas is protected from the summer sun by the overhangs and the extended walls. The clerestory windows of the front exterior provide natural light to the center of the plan.

GARAGE
21⁴ x 21⁸

CURB

PORCH

WALK-IN CLOSET

DRESSING RM.

ENTRY

CL

DN

S D.W.

KITCHEN
9⁴ x 5⁶

RANGE

BATH

B CL

REF'G

PANTRY

NOOK
9⁴ x 8⁰

CLERESTORY ABOVE

MASTER BED RM.
11⁸ x 14⁰

BALCONY

SLOPED CEILING

DINING RM.
12⁰ x 11⁶

DN

GATHERING RM.
15⁴ x 17⁴

DECK

54'-0"

40'-0"

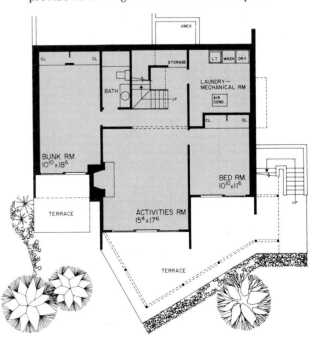

UNEX

CL

CL

STORAGE

L.T. WASH. DRY.

BATH

UP

LAUNDRY — MECHANICAL RM.

AIR COND.

CL.

CL.

BUNK RM.
10¹⁰ x 18⁶

BED RM.
10¹⁰ x 11⁶

TERRACE

ACTIVITIES RM.
15⁴ x 17⁶

UP

TERRACE

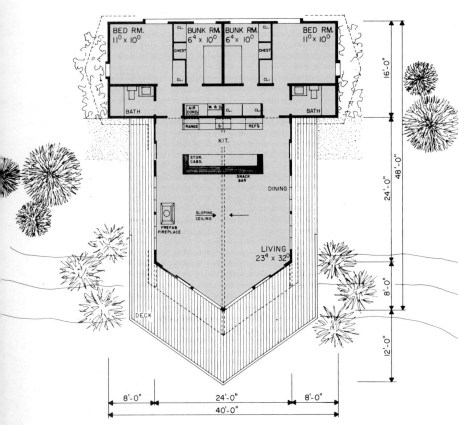

Design BB2439
Square Footage: 1,312

● Here is a wonderfully organized plan with an exterior that will command the attention of each and every passerby. Certainly the roof lines and the pointed glass gable-end wall will be noticed immediately. The delightful deck will be quickly noticed, too. Inside a visitor will be thrilled by the spaciousness of the huge living room. The ceilings slope upward to the exposed ridge beam. A free-standing fireplace will make its contribution to a cheerful atmosphere. The sleeping zone has two bedrooms, two bunk rooms, two full baths, two built-in chests and fine closet space.

Design BB4293
Square Footage: 1,873

This spacious layout has a big, big advantage-a country kitchen with all the trimmings: 300 square feet, a large island counter and breakfast bar, plenty of space for more formal dining, and a laundry room close at hand. The great room is also the center of attention, showing off clerestory windows and a large fireplace. What's more, the entrance is grand indeed, with a raised bridge leading into a large foyer. The master bedroom is long on living and storage space, and the rear deck ties everything together, connecting with the kitchen, great room, and master bedroom.

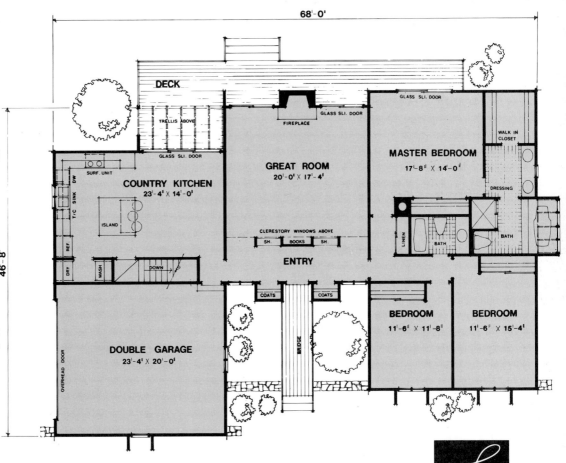

Design BB1475

First Floor: 1,120 square feet
Second Floor: 522 square feet
Lower Level: 616 square feet
Total: 2,258 square feet

● Built to accommodate the slopes, this hillside design with an exposed lower level meets winter vacation needs without a second thought. The covered lower terrace is the ideal entrance to a ski lounge with raised-hearth fireplace and walk-in ski storage area. The main floor holds sloped-ceilinged dining and living areas (with another raised hearth here), a kitchen with a patio, two bedrooms and a full bath. Enjoy the view from the balcony lounge on the second floor where there are two more bedrooms and another full bath.

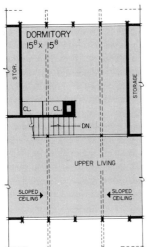

DORMITORY
15⁸ x 15⁸

STOR.

STORAGE

CL.   CL.

— DN.

UPPER LIVING

SLOPED CEILING →   ← SLOPED CEILING

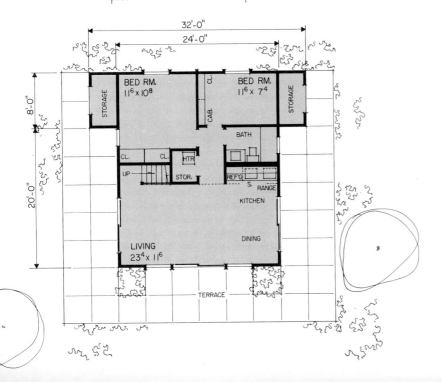

32'-0"

24'-0"

STORAGE

BED RM.
11⁶ x 10⁸

CL.

CAB.

BED RM.
11⁶ x 7⁴

STORAGE

8'-0"

BATH

CL.   CL.

HTR

UP

STOR.

REF'G

S.

RANGE

20'-0"

KITCHEN

LIVING
23⁴ x 11⁶

DINING

TERRACE

Design BB1424

First Floor: 672 square feet
Second Floor: 256 square feet
Total: 928 square feet

● This chalet-type vacation home with its steep, overhanging roof, will catch the eye of even the most casual onlooker. It is designed to be completely livable whether the season be for swimming or skiing. The dormitory on the upper level will sleep many vacationers, while the two bedrooms of the first floor provide the more convenient and conventional sleeping facilities. The upper level overlooks the living and dining area with its beamed ceiling. The lower level provides everything that one would want for vacation living.

Design BB1499

Main Level: 896 square feet; Upper Level: 298 square feet
Lower Level: 896 square feet; Total: 2,090 square feet

● Three level living results in family living patterns which will foster a delightful feeling of informality. Upon arrival at this charming second home, each family member will enthusiastically welcome the change in environment – both indoors and out. Whether looking down into the living room from the dormitory balcony, or walking through the sliding doors onto the huge deck, or participating in some family activity in the game room, everyone will count the hours spent here as relaxing ones. Study the plan carefully. Note the sleeping facilities on each of the three levels. Two bedrooms and a dormitory in all to sleep the family and friends comfortably. There are two full baths, a separate laundry room and plenty of storage. Don't miss the efficient U-shaped kitchen.

Design BB2431

First Floor: 1,057 square feet
Second Floor: 406 square feet
Total: 1,463 square feet

● Dramatic use of glass and sweeping lines characterize a classic favorite—the A-frame. The sloped ceiling and exposed beams in the living room are gorgeous touches complemented by a wide deck for enjoying fresh air. The convenience of the central bath with attached powder room is accentuated by space here for a washer and dryer. The truly outstanding feature of this plan, however, is its magnificent master suite. There's a private balcony outside and a balcony lounge inside—the scenery is splendid from every angle.

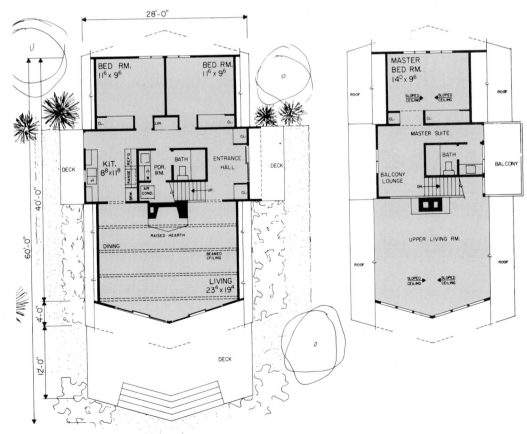

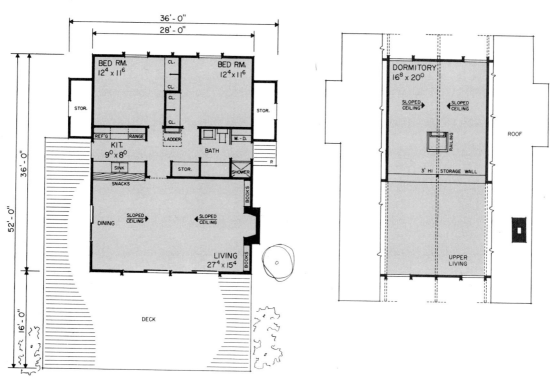

Design BB1472

First Floor: 1,008 square feet; Second Floor: 546 square feet; Total: 1,554 square feet

● Wherever perched, this smart leisure-time home will surely make your visits memorable ones. The large living area with its sloped ceiling, dramatic expanses of glass and attractive fireplace will certainly offer the proper atmosphere for quiet relaxation. Keeping house will be no chore for the weekend homemaker. The kitchen is compact and efficient. There is plenty of storage space for all the necessary recreational equipment. There is a full bath and even a stall shower accessible from the outside for use by the swimmers. A ladder leads to the second floor sloped ceiling dormitory which overlooks the living/dining area. Ideal for the younger generation.

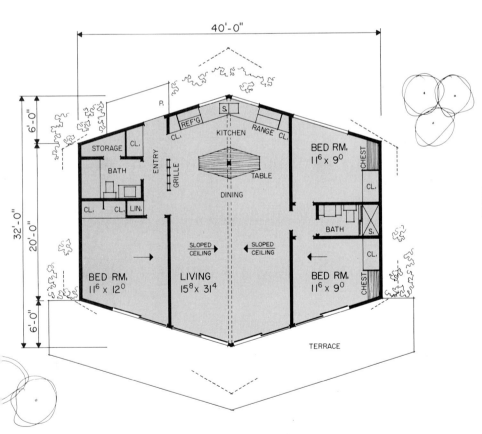

40'-0"

6'-0"

32'-0" / **20'-0"**

6'-0"

STORAGE   CL.

BATH

CL.   CL.   LIN.

ENTRY   GRILLE

CL.

KITCHEN

REF'G   S   RANGE   CL.

TABLE

DINING

BED RM. 11⁶ x 9⁰   CHEST

CL.

BATH   S

CHEST   CL.

BED RM. 11⁶ x 12⁰

LIVING 15⁸ x 31⁴

SLOPED CEILING   SLOPED CEILING

BED RM. 11⁶ x 9⁰

TERRACE

Design BB1438
Square Footage: 1,040

● Vacations begin with this
unique house. The angled terrace is
echoed throughout the floor plan—
with this orientation, no view is
missed. The living room features a
sloped ceiling and large dimensions. In the kitchen, a built-in table
accommodates a feast. Three bedrooms sleep all. Two of these
include built-in chests and well-
balanced proportions. Another
bedroom located on the other side
of the house will make a nice master retreat. Two full baths and storage space round out the amenities.

Design BB1482

First Floor: 1,008 square feet
Second Floor: 637 square feet
Total: 1,645 square feet

● Five bedrooms and a 27-foot living area! This darling chalet will take on the whole gang. A fireplace provides a warm glow and a snack bar in the kitchen means carefree dining. This plan also offers two full baths (one with access from outside and with a laundry area) and a second-floor master bedroom with a balcony overlooking the wood deck below.

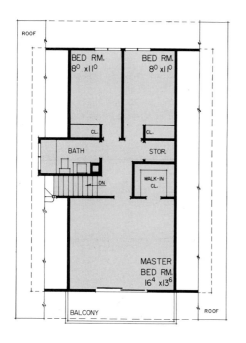

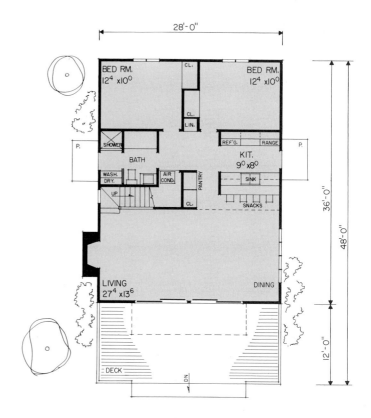

Design BB2427

First Floor: 784 square feet
Second Floor: 504 square feet
Total: 1,288 square feet

● Make your vacation dreams a reality with this fabulous chalet. A wood deck stretches the width of the house and finds the living room nearby. The kitchen utilizes a dining area and an efficient layout. A first-floor bedroom enjoys the use of a full hall bath. Upstairs, focus your attention on the master bedroom with its wall of closets and balcony. A dormitory sits across the hall from the master bedroom and leaves room for all the kids. Storage space abounds in this design—perfect for all of your seasonal storage needs.

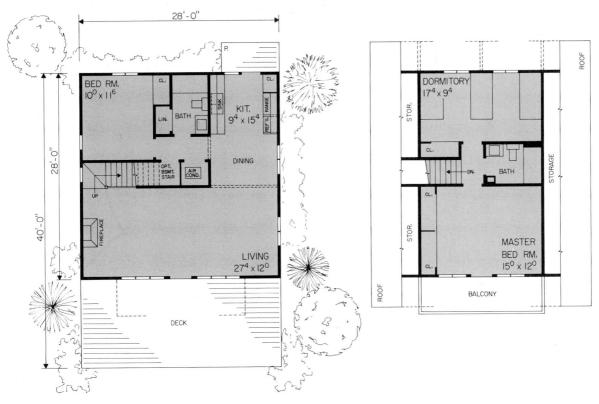

Design BB1440
Square Footage: 1,248

● Take time off and escape to this accommodating house. Livability centers around a large living room with a fireplace in its center. A kitchen stretches along one wall, thus economizing space. With two decks to enjoy—be sure to orient one with maximum sun exposure in mind—a range of activities is possible. This plan incorporates four bedrooms cleverly designed with two on either side of the house. Identical dimensions create pleasing symmetry.

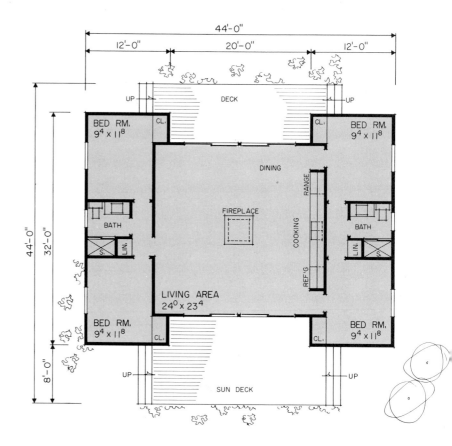

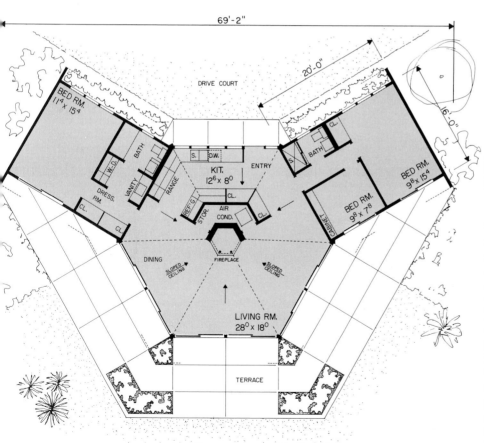

69'-2"

20'-0"

16'-0"

DRIVE COURT

BED RM.
11⁹ x 15⁴

W.D.

BATH

VANITY

DRESS.
RM.

RANGE

CL.

CL.

S.

D.W.

KIT.
12⁶ x 8⁰

REF'G.

STOR.

AIR
COND.

CL.

ENTRY

CL.

S.

BATH

CABINET

BED RM.
9⁸ x 7⁸

BED RM.
9⁸ x 15⁴

DINING

SLOPED
CEILING

FIREPLACE

SLOPED
CEILING

LIVING RM.
28⁰ x 18⁰

TERRACE

Design BB1404
Square Footage: 1,336

● Here is an exciting design,
unusual in character, yet fun to live
in. This design, with its frame exterior and large glass areas, has
as its dramatic focal point a hexagonal living area which gives way
to interesting angles. The spacious
living area features sliding glass
doors through which traffic may
pass to the terrace stretching across
the entire length of the house. The
wide overhanging roofs project
over the terraces, thus providing
partial protection from the weather. The sloping ceilings converge
above the unique, open fireplace.
The sleeping areas are located in
each wing from the hexagonal
center.

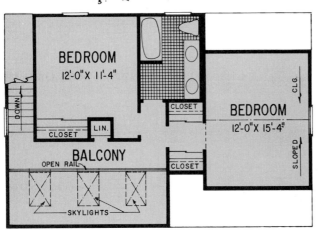

BEDROOM
12'-0" X 11'-4"

CLOSET

LIN.

CLOSET

DOWN

BEDROOM
12'-0" X 15'-4"

CLG.

SLOPED

CLOSET

BALCONY

OPEN RAIL

SKYLIGHTS

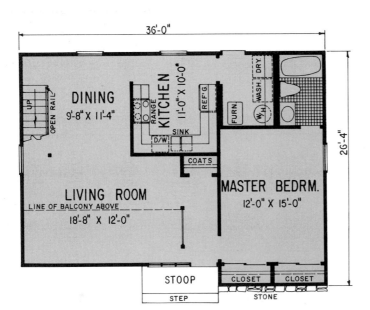

36'-0"

26'-4"

UP

OPEN RAIL

DINING
9'-8" X 11'-4"

KITCHEN
11'-0" X 10'-0"

RANGE

REF'G

FURN

WASH

DRY.

W.H.

SINK

D/W

COATS

LIVING ROOM
LINE OF BALCONY ABOVE
18'-8" X 12'-0"

MASTER BEDRM.
12'-0" X 15'-0"

STOOP

STEP

CLOSET

CLOSET

STONE

Design BB4153

First Floor: 893 square feet
Second Floor: 549 square feet
Total: 1,442 square feet

L **D**

● The rectangular shape of this design will make it an economical and easy-to-build choice for those wary of high construction costs. The first floor benefits from the informality of open planning; the living room and dining room combine to make one large living space. The partitioned kitchen is conveniently adjacent yet keeps the cooking process out of the living area. Also downstairs is the master bedroom and bath. The second floor houses two large bedrooms, a full bath and a balcony over the living room. Notice the skylights.

Design BB2464

First Floor: 960 square feet
Second Floor: 448 square feet
Total: 1,408 square feet

● This economical-to-build leisure home boasts a wealth of features to satisfy the most discerning tastes. The list begins with a wood deck just outside the sliding glass doors of the 31' living area. The list continues with the U-shaped kitchen, the snack bar, the pantry and closet storage wall, the two full baths (one with stall shower), three bedrooms and the raised-hearth fireplace. Perhaps the favorite highlight will be the manner in which the second floor overlooks the first floor. The second-floor balcony adds an even greater dimension of spaciousness and interior appeal.

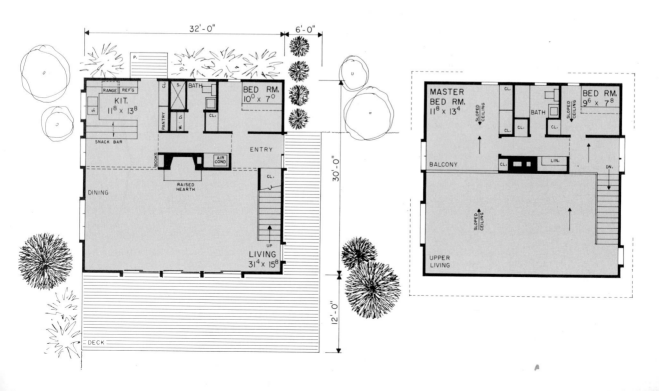

Design BB4114

Main Level: 852 square feet
Upper Level: 146 square feet
Total: 998 square feet

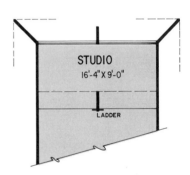

STUDIO
16'-4" X 9'-0"

LADDER

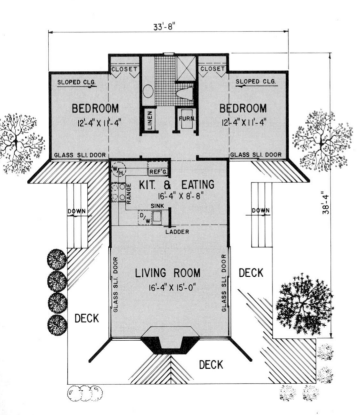

33'-8"

CLOSET   CLOSET

SLOPED CLG.   SLOPED CLG.

BEDROOM
12'-4" X 11'-4"

LINEN   FURN.

BEDROOM
12'-4" X 11'-4"

GLASS SLI. DOOR   GLASS SLI. DOOR

REF'G

KIT. & EATING
16'-4" X 8'-8"

RANGE   SINK   D/W

LADDER

DOWN   DOWN

38'-4"

GLASS SLI. DOOR

LIVING ROOM
16'-4" X 15'-0"

GLASS SLI. DOOR

DECK

DECK

DECK

● This home was designed with the outdoors in mind. A large, wraparound deck provides ample space for sunning and relaxing. Huge windows and sliding glass doors open up the interior with lots of sunlight and great views — a must in a vacation home. Open planning makes for relaxed living patterns; the kitchen, living, and eating area flow together into one large working and living space. An upstairs loft provides added space for a lounge or an extra sleeping area.

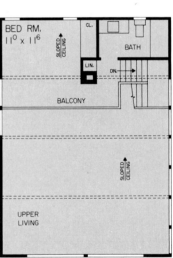

Design BB1496

First Floor: 768 square feet
Second Floor: 288 square feet
Total: 1,056 square feet

● Make your mountain getaway—or any getaway at all—a reality with this delightfully planned vacation home. A wooden walkway opens to a deck just outside the living and dining areas of this home—entry is also gained via a side door to the kitchen area. Dual storage closets off the kitchen will hold all of your necessities as well as your recreational items. The kitchen utilizes an island work space that doubles as a snack bar. Two bedrooms and full bathrooms grace this fine home. One of the bedrooms, on the second floor, enjoys a balcony overlook to the living room below.

Design BB1486

Square Footage: 480

● For that prime piece of property, this little house will delight all vacationers. Two sets of sliding glass doors open to the living and dining area. A kitchen with a double sink, closet and porch door is just a step away. Two bedrooms share the same dimensions while utilizing a full hall bath. Whether you decide to build this house on your own or with the aid of professional help, you will not have long to wait for its completion.

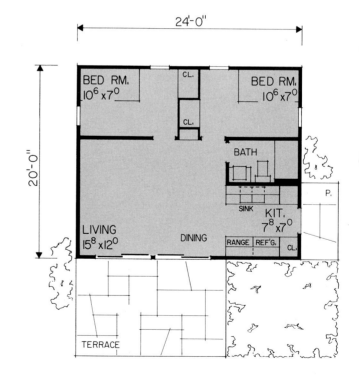

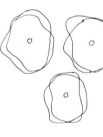

24'-0"

20'-0"

BED RM.
10^6x7^0

CL.

BED RM.
10^6x7^0

CL.

BATH

P.

LIVING
15^8x12^0

DINING

SINK

KIT.
7^8x7^0

RANGE   REF'G.   CL.

TERRACE

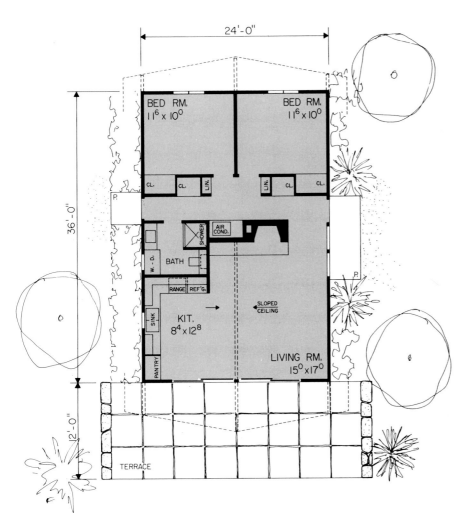

BED RM.
11⁶ x 10⁰

BED RM.
11⁶ x 10⁰

CL.　CL.　LIN.　　LIN.　CL.　CL.

P.

SHOWER

AIR COND.

W. D.

BATH

RANGE　REF'G.

SINK

KIT.
8⁴ x 12⁸

SLOPED CEILING →
← SLOPED CEILING

P.

PANTRY

LIVING RM.
15⁰ x 17⁰

24'-0"

36'-0"

12'-0"

TERRACE

Design BB2423

Square Footage: 864

● A true vacationer's delight, this two-bedroom home extends the finest modern livability. Two sets of sliding glass doors open off the kitchen and living room where a sloped ceiling lends added dimension. In the kitchen, full counter space and cabinetry assure ease in meal preparation. A pantry stores all of your canned and boxed goods. In the living room, a fireplace serves as a nice design as well as a practical feature. The rear of the plan is comprised of two bedrooms of identical size. A nearby full bath holds a washer/dryer unit. Two additional closets, as well as two linen closets, add to storage capabilities.

When You're Ready To Order . . .

Let Us Show You Our Home Blueprint Package.

Building a home? Planning a home? Our Blueprint Package contains nearly everything you need to get the job done right, whether you're working on your own or with help from an architect, designer, builder or subcontractors. Each Blueprint Package is the result of many hours of work by licensed architects or professional designers.

QUALITY

Hundreds of hours of painstaking effort have gone into the development of your blueprint set. Each home has been quality-checked by professionals to insure accuracy and buildability.

VALUE

Because we sell in volume, you can buy professional-quality blueprints at a fraction of their development cost. With our plans, your dream home design costs only a few hundred dollars, not the thousands of dollars that custom architects charge.

SERVICE

Once you've chosen your favorite home plan, you'll receive fast efficient service whether you choose to mail your order to us or call us toll free at 1-800-521-6797.

SATISFACTION

Our years of service to satisfied home plan buyers provide us the experience and knowledge that guarantee your satisfaction with our product and performance.

ORDER TOLL FREE 1-800-521-6797

After you've studied our Blueprint Package and Important Extras on the following pages, simply mail the accompanying order form on page 221 or call toll free on our Blueprint Hotline: 1-800-521-6797. We're ready and eager to serve you.

Each set of blueprints is an interrelated collection of floor plans, interior and exterior elevations, dimensions, cross-sections, diagrams and notations showing precisely how your house is to be constructed.

Here's what you get:

Frontal Sheet
This artist's sketch of the exterior of the house, done in realistic perspective, gives you an idea of how the house will look when built and landscaped. Large ink-line floor plans show all levels of the house and provide a quick overview of your new home's livability, as well as a handy reference for studying furniture placement.

Foundation Plan
Drawn to 1/4-inch scale, this sheet shows the complete foundation layout including support

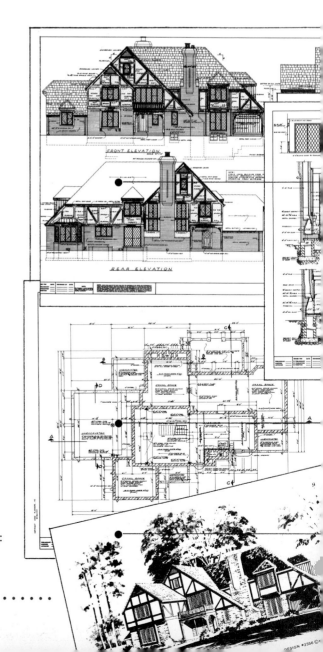

walls, excavated and unexcavated areas, if any, and foundation notes. If slab construction rather than basement, the plan shows footings and details for a monolithic slab. This page, or another in the set, also includes a sample plot plan for locating your house on a building site.

Detailed Floor Plans

Complete in 1/4-inch scale, these plans show the layout of each floor of the house. All rooms and interior spaces are carefully dimensioned and keys are provided for cross-section details given later in the plans. The positions of all electrical outlets and switches are clearly shown.

House Cross-Sections

Large-scale views, normally drawn at 3/8-inch equals 1 foot, show sections or cut-aways of the foundation, interior walls, exterior walls,

floors, stairways and roof details. Additional cross-sections are given to show important changes in floor, ceiling or roof heights or the relationship of one level to another. Extremely valuable for construction, these sections show exactly how the various parts of the house fit together.

Interior Elevations

These large-scale drawings show the design and placement of kitchen and bathroom cabinets, laundry areas, fireplaces, bookcases and other built-ins. Little "extras," such as mantelpiece and wainscoting drawings, plus moulding sections, provide details that give your home that custom touch.

Exterior Elevations

Drawings in 1/4-inch scale show the front, rear and sides of your house and give necessary notes on exterior materials and finishes. Particular attention is given to cornice detail, brick and stone accents or other finish items that make your home distinctive.

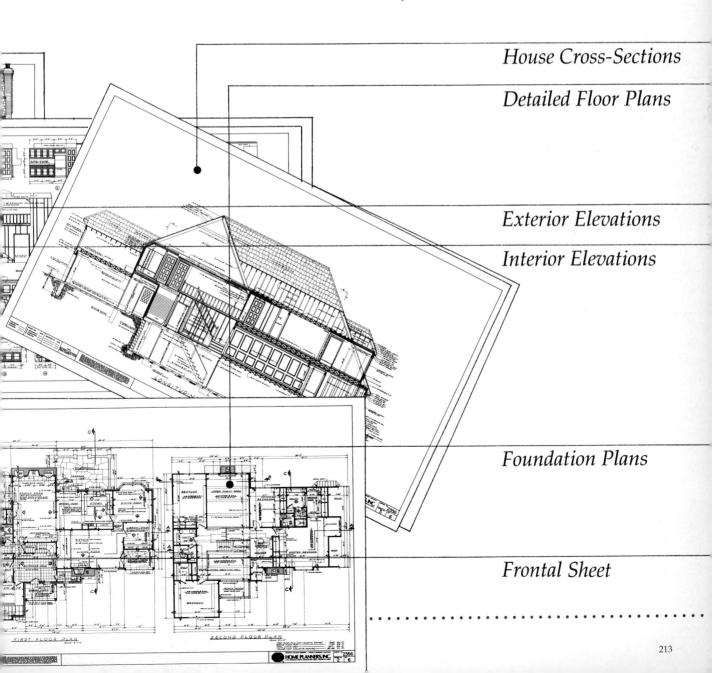

House Cross-Sections

Detailed Floor Plans

Exterior Elevations

Interior Elevations

Foundation Plans

Frontal Sheet

Important Extras To Do The Job Right!

Introducing seven important planning and construction aids developed by our professionals to help you succeed in your home-building project.

To Order, Call Toll Free 1-800-521-6797

To add these important extras to your Blueprint Package, simply indicate your choices on the order form on page 221 or call us Toll Free 1-800-521-6797 and we'll tell you more about these exciting products.

. . . .

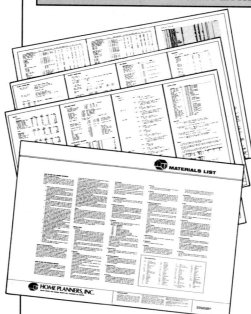

MATERIALS LIST

For many of the designs in our portfolio we offer a customized materials take-off that is invaluable in planning and estimating the cost of your new home. This comprehensive list outlines the quantity, type and size of material needed to build your house (with the exception of mechanical system items). Included are:

- framing lumber
- roofing and sheet metal
- windows and doors
- exterior sheathing material and trim
- masonry, veneer and fireplace materials
- tile and flooring materials
- kitchen and bath cabinetry
- interior drywall and trim
- rough and finish hardware
- many more items

(Note: Because of differing local codes, building methods, and availability of materials, our Materials Lists do not include mechanical materials. To obtain necessary take-offs and recommendations, consult heating, plumbing and electrical contractors. Materials Lists are not sold separately from the Blueprint Package.)

This handy list helps you or your builder cost out materials and serves as a ready reference sheet when you're compiling bids. It also provides a cross-check against the materials specified by your builder and helps coordinate the substitution of items you may need to meet local codes.

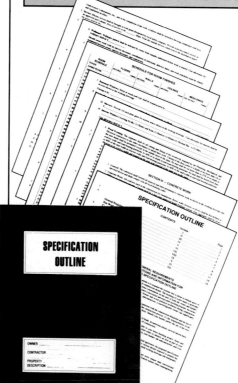

SPECIFICATION OUTLINE

This valuable 16-page document is critical to building your house correctly. Designed to be filled in by you or your builder, this booklet lists 166 stages or items crucial to the building process.

For the layman, it provides a comprehensive review of the construction process and helps in making the specific choices of materials, models and processes. For the builder, it serves as a guide to preparing a building quotation and forms the basis for the construction program.

Designed primarily as a reference for the homeowner, this Specification Outline can become a legally binding document. Once it is filled out and agreed upon by owner and builder, it becomes a complete Project Specification.

When combined with the blueprints, a signed contract and schedule, the Specification Outline becomes a legal document and record for the building of your home. Many home builders find it useful to order two of these outlines—one as a worksheet in formulating the specifications and another to be carefully completed as a legal document.

Plan-A-Home®

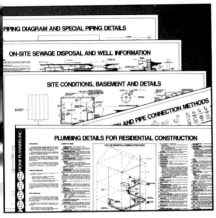

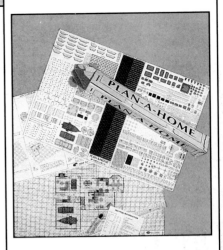

PLUMBING

The Blueprint Package includes locations for all the plumbing fixtures in your new house, including sinks, lavatories, tubs, showers, toilets, laundry trays and water heaters. However, if you want to know more about the complete plumbing system, these 24x36-inch detail sheets will prove very useful. Prepared to meet requirements of the National Plumbing Code, these six fact-filled sheets give general information on pipe schedules, fittings, sump-pump details, water-softener hookups, septic system details and much more. Color-coded sheets include a glossary of terms.

ELECTRICAL

The locations for every electrical switch, plug and outlet are shown in your Blueprint Package. However, these Electrical Details go further to take the mystery out of household electrical systems. Prepared to meet requirements of the National Electrical Code, these comprehensive 24x36-inch drawings come packed with helpful information, including wire sizing, switch-installation schematics, cable-routing details, appliance wattage, door-bell hookups, typical service panel circuitry and much more. Six sheets are bound together and color-coded for easy reference. A glossary of terms is also included.

Plan-A-Home® is an easy-to-use tool that helps you design a new home, arrange furniture in a new or existing home, or plan a remodeling project. Each package contains:

- More than *700 peel-off planning symbols* on a self-stick vinyl sheet, including walls, windows, doors, all types of furniture, kitchen components, bath fixtures and many more. All are made of durable, peel-and-stick vinyl you can use over and over.

- A reusable, transparent, *1/4-inch scale planning grid* made of tough mylar that matches the scale of actual working drawings (1/4-inch equals 1 foot). This grid provides the basis for house layouts of up to 140x92 feet.

- *Tracing paper* and a protective sheet for copying or transferring your completed plan.

- A *felt-tip pen*, with water-soluble ink that wipes away quickly.

With Plan-A-Home®, you can make basic planning decisions for a new house or make modifications to an existing house. Use with your Blueprint Package to test modifications to rooms or to plan furniture arrangements before you build. Plan-A-Home® lets you lay out areas as large as a 7,500 square foot, six-bedroom, seven-bath house.

CONSTRUCTION

The Blueprint Package contains everything an experienced builder needs to construct a particular house. However, it doesn't show all the ways that houses can be built, nor does it explain alternate construction methods. To help you understand how your house will be built—and offer additional techniques—this set of drawings depicts the materials and methods used to build foundations, fireplaces, walls, floors and roofs. Where appropriate, the drawings show acceptable alternatives. These six sheets will answer questions for the advanced do-it-yourselfer or home planner.

MECHANICAL

This package contains fundamental principles and useful data that will help you make informed decisions and communicate with subcontractors about heating and cooling systems. The 24 x 36-inch drawings contain instructions and samples that allow you to make simple load calculations and preliminary sizing and costing analysis. Covered are today's most commonly used systems from heat pumps to solar fuel systems. The package is packed full of illustrations and diagrams to help you visualize components and how they relate to one another.

. . .

◘ *The Deck Blueprint Package*

Many of the homes in this book can be enhanced with a professionally designed Home Planners' Deck Plan. Those home plans highlighted with a ◘ have a matching or corresponding deck plan available which includes a Deck Plan Frontal Sheet, Deck Framing and Floor Plans, Deck Elevations and a Deck Materials List. A Standard Deck Details Package, also available, provides all the how-to information necessary for building *any* deck. Our Complete Deck Building Package contains 1 set of Custom Deck Plans of your choice, plus 1 set of Standard Deck Building Details all for one low price. Our plans and details are carefully prepared in an easy-to-understand format that will guide you through every stage of your deck-building project. This page contains a sampling of 12 of the 25 different Deck layouts to match your favorite house. See page 218 for prices and ordering information.

SPLIT–LEVEL SUN DECK
Deck Plan D100

BI-LEVEL DECK WITH COVERED DINING
Deck Plan D101

WRAP–AROUND FAMILY DECK
Deck Plan D104

DECK FOR DINING AND VIEWS
Deck Plan D107

TREND–SETTER DECK
Deck Plan D110

TURN–OF–THE–CENTURY DECK
Deck Plan D111

WEEKEND ENTERTAINER DECK
Deck Plan D112

CENTER–VIEW DECK
Deck Plan D114

KITCHEN–EXTENDER DECK
Deck Plan D115

SPLIT–LEVEL ACTIVITY DECK
Deck Plan D117

TRI–LEVEL DECK WITH GRILL
Deck Plan D119

CONTEMPORARY LEISURE DECK
Deck Plan D120

L The Landscape Blueprint Package

For the homes marked with an **L** in this book, Home Planners has created a front-yard landscape plan that matches or is complementary in design to the house plan. These comprehensive blueprint packages include a Frontal Sheet, Plan View, Regionalized Plant & Materials List, a sheet on Planting and Maintaining Your Landscape, Zone Maps and Plant Size and Description Guide. These plans will help you achieve professional results, adding value and enjoyment to your property for years to come. Each set of blueprints is a full 18" x 24" in size with clear, complete instructions and easy-to-read type. Six of the forty front-yard Landscape Plans to match your favorite house are shown below.

Regional Order Map

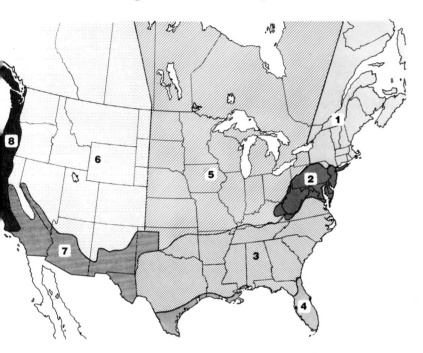

Most of the Landscape Plans shown on these pages are available with a Plant & Materials List adapted by horticultural experts to 8 different regions of the country. Please specify Geographic Region when ordering your plan. See page 218 for prices, ordering information and regional availability.

Region	**1**	Northeast
Region	**2**	Mid-Atlantic
Region	**3**	Deep South
Region	**4**	Florida & Gulf Coast
Region	**5**	Midwest
Region	**6**	Rocky Mountains
Region	**7**	Southern California & Desert Southwest
Region	**8**	Northern California & Pacific Northwest

CAPE COD COTTAGE
Landscape Plan L202

GAMBREL–ROOF COLONIAL
Landscape Plan L203

CENTER–HALL COLONIAL
Landscape Plan L204

CLASSIC NEW ENGLAND COLONIAL
Landscape Plan L205

COUNTRY–STYLE FARMHOUSE
Landscape Plan L207

TRADITIONAL SPLIT–LEVEL
Landscape Plan L228

Price Schedule & Plans Index

House Blueprint Price Schedule
(Prices guaranteed through December 31, 1994)

	1-set Study Package	4-set Building Package	8-set Building Package	1-set Reproducible Sepias
Schedule A	$210	$270	$330	$420
Schedule B	$240	$300	$360	$480
Schedule C	$270	$330	$390	$540
Schedule D	$300	$360	$420	$600
Schedule E	$390	$450	$510	$660

Additional Identical Blueprints in same order...............$50 per set
Reverse Blueprints (mirror image)..................................$50 per set
Specification Outlines ....$7 each
Materials Lists:
    Schedule A-D $40
    Schedule E $50
Exchanges ....$40 exchange fee for the first set; $10 for each
    additional set
    $60 total exchange fee for 4 sets
    $90 total exchange fee for 8 sets

Deck Plans Price Schedule

CUSTOM DECK PLANS

Price Group	Q	R	S
1 Set Custom Plans	$25	$30	$35

Additional identical sets:...$10 each
Reverse sets (mirror image):..$10 each

STANDARD DECK DETAILS
1 Set Generic Construction Details................................$14.95 each

COMPLETE DECK BUILDING PACKAGE

Price Group	Q	R	S
1 Set Custom Plans 1 Set Standard Deck Details	$35	$40	$45

Landscape Plans Price Schedule

Price Group	X	Y	Z
1 set	$35	$45	$55
3 sets	$50	$60	$70
6 sets	$65	$75	$85

Additional Identical Sets ....$10 each
Reverse Sets (mirror image) ....$10 each

These pages contain all the information you need to price your blueprints. In general the larger and more complicated the house, the more it costs to design and thus the higher the price we must charge for the blueprints. Remember, however, that these prices are far less than you would normally pay for the services of a licensed architect or professional designer.

Custom home designs and related architectural services often cost thousands of dollars, ranging from 5% to 15% of the cost of construction. By ordering our blueprints you are potentially saving enough money to afford a larger house, or to add those "extra" amenities such as a patio, deck, swimming pool or even an upgraded kitchen or luxurious master suite.

Index

To use the Index below, refer to the design number listed in numerical order (a helpful page reference is also given). Note the price index letter and refer to the House Blueprint Price Schedule above for the cost of one, four or eight sets of blueprints or the cost of a reproducible sepia. Additional prices are shown for identical and reverse blueprint sets, as well as a very useful Materials List for some of the plans. Also note in the Index below those plans that have matching or complementary Deck Plans or Landscape Plans. Refer to the schedules above for prices of these plans. Some of our plans can be customized through Home Planners' Home Customizer® Service. These plans are indicated below with this symbol: 🏠. See page 221 for more information.

To Order: Fill in and send the order form on page 221—or call toll free 1-800-521-6797.

DESIGN	PRICE	PAGE	CUSTOMIZABLE	DECK	DECK PRICE	LANDSCAPE	LANDSCAPE PRICE	REGIONS
BB1404	A	205						
BB1424	A	197						
BB1438	A	201						
BB1440	A	204						
BB1472	A	200						
BB1475	B	196						
BB1482	A	202						
BB1486	A	210						
BB1496	A	209						
BB1499	B	198						
BB1754	B	105						
BB2170	B	61				L221	X	1-3,5,6,8
BB2182	B	78						
BB2212	D	153				L217	Y	1-8
BB2423	A	211						
BB2427	A	203						
BB2431	A	199						
BB2439	A	194						
BB2464	A	207						
BB2485	B	193						
BB2488	A	191	🏠	D102	Q			

DESIGN	PRICE	PAGE	CUSTOMIZABLE	DECK	DECK PRICE	LANDSCAPE	LANDSCAPE PRICE	REGIONS
BB2490	A	35	🏠					
BB2493	C	131	🏠					
BB2500	B	20		D100	Q	L204	Y	1-3,5,6,8
BB2505	A	70	🏠	D113	R	L226	X	1-8
BB2510	A	10		D105	R	L200	X	1-3,5,6,8
BB2528	B	83		D100	Q			
BB2563	B	11	🏠	D114	R	L201	Y	1-3,5,6,8
BB2565	B	56		D101	R	L225	X	1-3,5,6,8
BB2573	C	116		D114	R	L220	Y	1-3,5,6,8
BB2581	C	32						
BB2594	C	109		D120	R			
BB2597	B	51		D114	R	L226	X	1-8
BB2606	A	65	🏠	D112	R	L221	X	1-3,5,6,8
BB2607	B	64		D101	R	L220	Y	1-3,5,6,8
BB2615	D	160		D106	S	L211	Y	1-8
BB2671	B	85		D114	R	L234	Y	1-8
BB2672	B	44		D112	R	L226	X	1-8
BB2699	C	156				L211	Y	1-8
BB2707	A	74	🏠	D117	S	L226	X	1-8
BB2708	C	29		D112	R			
BB2718	C	18		D105	R			

DESIGN	PRICE	PAGE	CUSTOMIZABLE	DECK	DECK PRICE	LANDSCAPE	LANDSCAPE PRICE	REGIONS
BB2721	C	110						
BB2729	B	30				L234	Y	1-8
BB2753	B	82		D112	R			
BB2754	B	79						
BB2771	C	33						
BB2778	C	107		D120	R			
BB2781	C	144		D121	S	L230	Z	1-8
BB2782	C	142		D101	R			
BB2784	C	108						
BB2789	C	106		D117	S	L228	Y	1-8
BB2791	D	141						
BB2795	B	81						
BB2802	B	60	🏠	D118	R	L220	Y	1-3,5,6,8
BB2803	B	58	🏠	D118	R	L225	X	1-3,5,6,8
BB2804	B	59	🏠	D118	R	L232	Y	4,7
BB2805	B	75		D113	R	L220	Y	1-3,5,6,8
BB2806	B	76		D113	R	L220	Y	1-3,5,6,8
BB2807	B	77		D113	R	L220	Y	1-3,5,6,8
BB2809	B	89						
BB2818	B	84	🏠	D101	R	L234	Y	1-8
BB2822	A	126				L229	Y	1-8
BB2827	C	125				L229	Y	1-8
BB2828	B	124						
BB2853	A	25						
BB2857	D	143				L239	Z	1-8
BB2858	C	101						
BB2864	A	88	🏠	D100	Q	L225	X	1-3,5,6,8
BB2869	B	53						
BB2871	B	80		D117	S			
BB2873	C	100						
BB2877	C	117		D114	R			
BB2878	B	50	🏠	D112	R	L200	X	1-3,5,6,8
BB2880	C	120	🏠	D114	R	L212	Z	1-8
BB2883	C	13						
BB2884	B	27						
BB2887	A	127						
BB2888	D	157				L211	Y	1-8
BB2892	B	26						
BB2902	B	86				L234	Y	1-8
BB2905	B	28		D121	S	L229	Y	1-8
BB2913	B	87		D124	S			
BB2915	C	103		D114	R	L212	Z	1-8
BB2920	D	139	🏠	D104	S	L212	Z	1-8
BB2921	D	159	🏠	D104	S	L212	Z	1-8
BB2922	D	136						
BB2930	B	98	🏠					
BB2931	B	54	🏠					
BB2947	B	52	🏠	D112	R	L200	X	1-3,5,6,8
BB2948	B	177	🏠					
BB2949	C	173		D123	S			
BB2950	C	176						
BB2962	B	114	🏠					
BB2964	B	17						
BB2967	B	16						
BB2995	D	158		D106	S	L217	Y	1-8
BB3302	A	14	🏠					
BB3310	C	40		D111	S	L227	Z	1-8
BB3311	D	138		D109	S	L220	Y	1-3,5,6,8
BB3314	B	46						
BB3315	D	22						
BB3319	C	96	🏠	D112	R	L217	Y	1-8
BB3321	C	23	🏠	D116	R	L209	Y	1-6,8
BB3322	C	37	🏠	D118	R	L234	Y	1-8
BB3323	C	129	🏠			L223	Z	1-3,5,6,8
BB3330	A	24						
BB3331	A	15						
BB3332	B	119						
BB3334	C	155						
BB3336	B	113						
BB3340	B	55						
BB3343	C	12						
BB3344	D	178						
BB3345	B	68	🏠					
BB3346	B	112	🏠					
BB3347	D	34						
BB3348	C	118						
BB3350	B	72		D115	Q	L205	Y	1-3,5,6,8
BB3351	C	21		D115	Q	L209	Y	1-6,8
BB3353	C	154		D113	R	L206	Z	1-6,8

DESIGN	PRICE	PAGE	CUSTOMIZABLE	DECK	DECK PRICE	LANDSCAPE	LANDSCAPE PRICE	REGIONS
BB3355	A	66	🏠	D117	S	L220	Y	1-3,5,6,8
BB3357	D	111		D115	Q	L211	Y	1-8
BB3360	D	149						
BB3366	D	151				L220	Y	1-3,5,6,8
BB3368	C	102		D104	S	L220	Y	1-3,5,6,8
BB3373	A	62		D110	R	L202	X	1-3,5,6,8
BB3374	A	62		D110	R	L202	X	1-3,5,6,8
BB3375	A	63		D110	R	L202	X	1-3,5,6,8
BB3376	B	73		D114	R	L205	Y	1-3,5,6,8
BB3377	C	115		D110	R	L203	Y	1-3,5,6,8
BB3378	E	152		D115	Q	L211	Y	1-8
BB3390	C	133		D106	S	L207	Z	1-6,8
BB3393	C	132		D115	Q	L207	Z	1-6,8
BB3396	C	134		D111	S	L207	Z	1-6,8
BB3397	D	147		D110	R	L209	Y	1-6,8
BB3400	C	175	🏠					
BB3401	C	174	🏠					
BB3402	C	172	🏠					
BB3403	C	42		D115	Q	L237	Y	7
BB3404	D	145		D106	S	L230	Z	1-8
BB3405	D	169	🏠			L236	Z	3,4,7
BB3408	C	95				L230	Z	1-8
BB3411	C	184	🏠					
BB3413	C	180	🏠					
BB3414	C	166	🏠					
BB3415	C	183	🏠					
BB3416	A	188	🏠					
BB3418	A	165	🏠					
BB3419	B	187	🏠					
BB3420	B	164	🏠					
BB3421	B	182	🏠					
BB3422	B	186	🏠					
BB3423	C	181	🏠					
BB3426	C	163	🏠					
BB3428	C	162	🏠					
BB3430	C	179	🏠					
BB3431	B	170	🏠					
BB3433	C	171	🏠			L213	Z	1-8
BB3435	D	167	🏠			L227	Z	1-8
BB3436	C	168	🏠			L227	Z	1-8
BB3438	C	5				L209	Y	1-6,8
BB3440	C	94	🏠	D120	R	L233	Y	3,4,7
BB3441	C	41	🏠			L239	Z	1-8
BB3442	A	67	🏠					
BB3444	B	7	🏠					
BB3450	C	128	🏠	D106	S	L229	Y	1-8
BB3453	A	90				L238	Y	3,4,7,8
BB3454	B	91		D110	R	L220	Y	1-3,5,6,8
BB3455	B	36		D105	R	L238	Y	3,4,7,8
BB3458	C	39						
BB3460	A	48	🏠			L200	X	1-3,5,6,8
BB3461	B	8						
BB3462	B	6				L207	Z	1-6,8
BB3465	A	47				L205	Y	1-3,5,6,8
BB3466	B	45	🏠	D110	R	L207	Z	1-6,8
BB3467	B	19	🏠			L203	Y	1-3,5,6,8
BB3468	B	4				L209	Y	1-6,8
BB3475	D	137	🏠			L236	Z	3,4,7
BB3481	B	69	🏠			L200	X	1-3,5,6,8
BB3505	E	146						
BB3550	D	148		D112	R	L220	Y	1-3,5,6,8
BB3557	D	140		D105	R	L228	Y	1-8
BB3558	C	38		D105	R	L203	Y	1-3,5,6,8
BB3559	C	97	🏠	D111	S	L217	Y	1-8
BB3560	C	99				L234	Y	1-8
BB3566	C	9		D111	S	L207	Z	1-6,8
BB3569	B	92		D105	R	L238	Y	3,4,7,8
BB3573	D	130		D111	S	L233	Y	3,4,7
BB3575	D	150				L205	Y	1-3,5,6,8
BB3600	C	104						
BB3602	C	185						
BB4027	A	192						
BB4061	A	190		D115	Q			
BB4114	A	208						
BB4115	B	122						
BB4153	A	206		D115	Q	L202	X	1-3,5,6,8
BB4293	B	195		D120	R			
BB4308	C	123				L231	Z	1-8
BB4334	B	31				L231	Z	1-8

Before You Order . . .

Before completing the coupon at right or calling us on our Toll-Free Blueprint Hotline, you may be interested to learn more about our service and products. Here's some information you will find helpful.

Quick Turnaround
We process and ship every blueprint order from our office within 48 hours. On most orders, we do even better. Normally, if we receive your order by 5 p.m. Eastern Time, we'll process it the same day and ship it the following day. Because of this quick turnaround, we won't send a formal notice acknowledging receipt of your order.

Our Exchange Policy
Since blueprints are printed in response to your order, we cannot honor requests for refunds. However, we will exchange your entire first order for an equal number of blueprints plus the following exchange fees: $40 for the first set, $10 for each additional set; $60 total exchange fee for 4 sets; $90 total exchange fee for 8 sets.... *plus* the difference in cost if exchanging for a design in a higher price bracket, or *less* the difference in cost if exchanging for a design in a lower price bracket. (Sepias are not exchangeable.) All sets from the first order must be returned before the exchange can take place. Please add $8 for postage and handling via ground service; $20 via 2nd Day Air.

About Reverse Blueprints
If you want to build in reverse of the plan as shown, we will include an extra set of reversed blueprints (mirror image) for an additional fee of $50. Although lettering and dimensions appear backward, reverses will be a useful visual aid if you decide to flop the plan. Right-reading reverses of Customizable Plans are available through our Customization Service. Call for more details.

Modifying or Customizing Our Plans
With such a great selection of homes, you are bound to find the one that suits you. However, if you need to make alterations to a design that is customizable, you need only order our Customizer® kit or call our Customization representative at 1-800-322-6797, ext. 800, to get you started (see additional information on next page). It is possible to customize many of our plans that are not part of our Home Customizer® Service.

If you decide to revise plans significantly that are not customizable through our service, we strongly suggest that you order reproducible sepias and consult a licensed architect or professional designer to help you redraw the plans.

Architectural and Engineering Seals
Some cities and states are now requiring that a licensed architect or engineer review and "seal" your blueprints prior to construction. This is often due to local or regional concerns over energy consumption, safety codes, seismic ratings, etc. For this reason, you may find it necessary to consult with a local professional to have your plans reviewed. This can normally be accomplished with minimum delays, for a nominal fee. In some cases, Home Planners can seal your plans through our Customization Service. Call for more details.

Compliance with Local Codes and Regulations
At the time of creation, our plans are drawn to specifications published by Building Officials Code Administrators (BOCA), the Southern Standard Building Code, or the Uniform Building Code and are designed to meet or exceed national building standards. Some states, counties and municipalities have their own codes, zoning requirements and building regulations. Before starting construction, consult with local building authorities and make sure you comply with local ordinances and codes, including obtaining any necessary permits or inspections as building progresses. In some cases, minor modifications to your plans by your builder, local architect or designer may be required to meet local conditions and requirements. Home Planners may be able to make these changes to Customizable Plans providing you supply all pertinent information from your local building authorities.

Foundation and Exterior Wall Changes
Most of our plans are drawn with either a full or partial basement foundation. Depending upon your specific climate or regional building practices, you may wish to convert this basement to a slab or crawlspace. Most professional contractors and builders can easily adapt your plans to alternate foundation types. Likewise, most can easily convert 2x4 wall construction to 2x6, or vice versa. If you need more guidance on these conversions, our handy Construction Detail Sheets, shown on page 215, describe how such conversions can be made. For Customizable Plans, Home Planners can easily provide the necessary changes for you.

How Many Blueprints Do You Need?
A single set of blueprints is sufficient to study a home in greater detail. However, if you are planning to obtain cost estimates from a contractor or subcontractors—or if you are planning to build immediately—you will need more sets. Because additional sets are cheaper when ordered in quantity with the original order, make sure you order enough blueprints to satisfy all requirements. The following checklist will help you determine how many you need:

_____Owner

_____Builder (generally requires at least three sets; one as a legal document, one to use during inspections, and at least one to give to subcontractors)

_____Local Building Department (often requires two sets)

_____Mortgage Lender (usually one set for a conventional loan; three sets for FHA or VA loans)

_____TOTAL NUMBER OF SETS

Toll Free 1-800-521-6797

Normal Office Hours:
8:00 a.m. to 8:00 p.m. Eastern Time
Monday through Friday
Our staff will gladly answer any questions during normal office hours. Our answering service can place orders after hours or on weekends.

If we receive your order by 5:00 p.m. Eastern Time, Monday through Friday, we'll process it the same day and ship it the following business day. When ordering by phone, please have your charge card ready. We'll also ask you for the Order Form Key Number at the bottom of the coupon. Please use our Toll-Free number for blueprint and book orders only.
For Customization orders call 1-800-322-6797, ext. 800.

By FAX: Copy the Order Form on the next page and send it on our International FAX line: 1-602-297-6219.

Canadian Customers
Order Toll-Free 1-800-848-2550
For faster, more economical service, Canadian customers may now call in orders on our Toll-Free line. Or, complete the order form at right, adding 30% to all prices, and mail in Canadian funds to:

Home Planners, Inc.
3275 W. Ina Road, Suite 110
Tucson, AZ 85741

By FAX: Copy the Order Form on the next page and send it on our International FAX line: 1-602-297-6219.

The Home Customizer®

Many of the plans in this book are customizable through our Home Customizer® service. Look for this symbol 🏠 on the pages of home designs. It indicates that the plan on that page is part of The Home Customizer® service.

Some changes to customizable plans that can be made include:

- exterior elevation changes
- kitchen and bath modifications
- roof, wall and foundation changes
- room additions
- and much more!

If the plan you have chosen to build is one of our customizable homes, you can easily order the Home Customizer® kit to start on the path to making your alterations. The kit, priced at only $19.95, may be ordered at the same time you order your blueprint package by calling on our toll-free number or using the order blank at right. Or you can wait until you receive your blueprints, spend some time studying them and then order the kit by phone, FAX or mail. If you then decide to proceed with the customizing service, the $19.95 price of the kit will be refunded to you after your customization order is received. The Home Customizer® kit includes:

- instruction book with examples
- architectural scale
- clear acetate work film
- erasable red marker
- removable correction tape
- ¼" scale furniture cutouts
- 1 set of Customizable Drawings with floor plans and elevations

The service is easy, fast and *affordable*. Because we know and work with our plans and have them available on state-of-the-art computer systems, we can make the changes efficiently at prices much lower than those charged by normal architectural or drafting services. In addition, you'll be getting custom changes directly from Home Planners—the company whose dedication to excellence and long-standing professional experience are well recognized in the industry.

Call now to learn more about how simple it can be to have the *custom home* you've always wanted.

☎ Toll Free
1-800-322-6797, Ext. 800

ORDER FORM

 HOME PLANNERS, INC., 3275 WEST INA ROAD
SUITE 110, TUCSON, ARIZONA 85741

THE BASIC BLUEPRINT PACKAGE
Rush me the following (please refer to the Plans Index and Price Schedule in this section):

_____ Set(s) of blueprints for plan number(s) _____.	$_____
_____ Set(s) of sepias for plan number(s) _____.	$_____
_____ Additional identical blueprints in same order @ $50 per set.	$_____
_____ Reverse blueprints @ $50 per set.	$_____
_____ Home Customizer® Kit(s) for Plan(s)_____ @ $19.95 per kit.	$_____

IMPORTANT EXTRAS
Rush me the following:

_____ Materials List: @ $40 Schedule A-D; $50 Schedule E $_____
_____ Specification Outlines @ $7 each. $_____
_____ Detail Sets @ $14.95 each; any two for $22.95; any three for $29.95; all four for $39.95 (save $19.85). $_____
❑ Plumbing ❑ Electrical ❑ Construction ❑ Mechanical (These helpful details provide general construction advice and are not specific to any single plan.)
_____ Plan-A-Home® @ $29.95 each. $_____

DECK BLUEPRINTS
_____ Set(s) of Deck Plan _____. $_____
_____ Additional identical blueprints in same order @ $10 per set. $_____
_____ Reverse blueprints @ $10 per set. $_____
_____ Set of Standard Deck Details @ $14.95 per set. $_____
_____ Set of Complete Building Package (Best Buy!) Includes Custom Deck Plan _____. (See Index and Price Schedule) Plus Standard Deck Details $_____

LANDSCAPE BLUEPRINTS
_____ Set(s) of Landscape Plan _____. $_____
_____ Additional identical blueprints in same order @ $10 per set. $_____
_____ Reverse blueprints @ $10 per set. $_____

Please indicate the appropriate region of the country for Plant & Material List. (See Map on page 217): Region _____

SUB-TOTAL $_____
SALES TAX (Arizona residents add 5% sales tax; Michigan residents add 4% sales tax.) $_____

POSTAGE AND HANDLING	1-3 sets	4 or more sets	
DELIVERY (Requires street address - No P.O. Boxes)			
•Regular Service Allow 4-6 days delivery	❑ $6.00	❑ $8.00	$_____
•2nd Day Air Allow 2-3 days delivery	❑ $12.00	❑ $20.00	$_____
•Next Day Air Allow 1 day delivery	❑ $22.00	❑ $30.00	$_____
POST OFFICE DELIVERY If no street address available. Allow 4-6 days delivery	❑ $8.00	❑ $12.00	$_____
OVERSEAS AIR MAIL DELIVERY Note: All delivery times are from date Blueprint Package is shipped.	❑ $30.00	❑ $50.00	$_____
	❑ Send COD		

TOTAL (Sub-total, tax, and postage) $_____

YOUR ADDRESS (please print)

Name _____

Street _____

City _____State_____Zip _____

Daytime telephone number (_____) _____

FOR CREDIT CARD ORDERS ONLY
Please fill in the information below:

Credit card number _____

Exp. Date: Month/Year _____

Check one ❑ Visa ❑ MasterCard ❑ Discover Card

Signature _____

Please check appropriate box:
❑ Licensed Builder-Contractor
❑ Home Owner

☎ **ORDER TOLL FREE**
1-800-521-6797

Order Form Key

Additional Plans Books

THE DESIGN CATEGORY SERIES

1.

ONE-STORY HOMES
A collection of 470 homes to suit a range of budgets in one-story living. All popular styles, including Cape Cod, Southwestern, Tudor and French. **384 pages. $8.95 ($11.95 Canada)**

2.

TWO-STORY HOMES
478 plans for all budgets in a wealth of styles: Tudors, Saltboxes, Farmhouses, Victorians, Georgians, Contemporaries and more. **416 pages. $8.95 ($11.95 Canada)**

3.

MULTI-LEVEL AND HILL-SIDE HOMES 312 distinctive styles for both flat and sloping sites. Includes exposed lower levels, open staircases, balconies, decks and terraces. **320 pages. $6.95 ($9.95 Canada)**

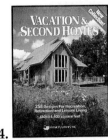

4.

VACATION AND SECON[?] HOMES 258 ideal plans for [?] favorite vacation spot or perfect retirement or starter home. Includes cottages, chalets, and 1-, 1½-, 2-, and multi-levels. **256 pages. $5.9[?] ($7.95 Canada)**

THE EXTERIOR STYLE SERIES

9.

THE ESSENTIAL GUIDE TO TRADITIONAL HOMES
Over 400 traditional homes in one special volume. American and European styles from Farmhouses to Norman French. "Readers' Choice" highlights best sellers in four-color photographs and renderings. **304 pages. $9.95 ($12.95 Canada)**

10.

THE ESSENTIAL GUIDE TO CONTEMPORARY HOMES More than 340 contemporary designs from Northwest Contemporary to Post-Modern Victorian. Four-color section of best sellers; two-color illustrations and line drawings throughout the remainder. **304 pages. $9.95 ($12.95 Canada)**

11.

VICTORIAN DREAM HOMES 160 Victorian and Farmhouse designs by three master designers. Victorian style from Second Empire homes through the Queen Anne and Folk Victorian era. Beautifully drawn renderings accompany the modern floor plans. **192 pages. $12.95 ($16.95 Canada)**

12.

WESTERN HOME PLANS[?]
Over 215 home plans from Spanish Mission and Mont[?] to Northwest Chateau and Francisco Victorian. Histor[?] notes trace the background and geographical incidence[?] each style. **208 pages. $8.95[?] ($11.95 Canada)**

OUR BEST PLAN PORTFOLIOS

LUXURY DREAM HOMES At last, th[?] home you've waite[?] A collection of 150 [?] best luxury home p[?] from seven of the m[?] highly regarded de[?] ers and architects i[?] United States. A dr[?] come true for anyo[?] interested in design[?] building or remod[?] luxury home.

NEW ENCYCLOPEDIA OF HOME DESIGNS
Our best collection of plans is now bigger and better than ever! Over 500 plans organized by architectural category including all types and styles and 269 brand-new plans. The most comprehensive plan book ever.

AFFORDABLE HOME PLANS For the prospective home builder with a modest or medium budget. Features 430 one-, 1½-, two-story and multi-level homes in a wealth of styles. Included are cost saving ideas for the budget-conscious.

15. 352 pages. $9.95 ($12.95 Canada)

16. 320 pages. $8.95 ($11.95 Canada)

17. 192 pages. $14.95 ($17.95 Canada)